S0-AYD-281

the Way

LIVING OUT GOD'S PLAN FOR YOUR LIFE AS A DISCIPLE OF CHRIST

COURSE VI
Life in **Jesus Christ**

Our Sunday Visitor

Curriculum Division

hs.osvcurriculum.com

ADVANCE REVIEW COPY

This first printing was manufactured prior to final ecclesiastical approval.

The final printing of this text will include wording of all the direct quotations from the *Catechism of the Catholic Church*.

© 2013 by Our Sunday Visitor Curriculum Division, Our Sunday Visitor.

All rights reserved. No part of this publication may be reproduced or transmitted in any form or by any means, electronic or mechanical, including photocopy, recording, or any information storage and retrieval system, without permission in writing from the publisher.

Write:
Our Sunday Visitor Curriculum Division
Our Sunday Visitor, Inc.
200 Noll Plaza
Huntington, Indiana 46750

Our Sunday Visitor High School Series is a registered trademark of Our Sunday Visitor Curriculum Division, Our Sunday Visitor, 200 Noll Plaza, Huntington, Indiana 46750.

For permission to reprint copyrighted material, grateful acknowledgement is made to the following sources:

The Scripture quotations contained herein are from the *New Revised Standard Version Bible: Catholic Edition* copyright© 1993 and 1989 by the Division of Christian Education of the National Council of the Churches of Christ in the U.S.A. Used by permission. All rights reserved.

Excerpts from Vatican Council II documents are from "Vatican Council II: Constitutions, Decrees, Declarations" edited by Austin Flannery, O.P., copyright© 1996, Costello Publishing Company Inc., Northport, NY, and are used by permission of the publisher. All rights reserved.

Catechism excerpts are taken from the *Catechism of the Catholic Church*, second edition, for use in the United States of America, copyright© 1994 and 1997, United States Catholic Conference – Libreria Editrice Vaticana.

Excerpts from the English translation of *The Liturgy of the Hours* copyright© 1974, International Committee on English in the Liturgy, Inc. All rights reserved.

Excerpts from the English translation of *The Roman Missal* © 2010, International Commission on English in the Liturgy Corporation (ICEL). All rights reserved.

Unless otherwise noted, all quotations from Papal and other Vatican documents are © Libreria Editrice Vaticana. Used by permission. All rights reserved.

United States Conference of Catholic Bishops, *The Challenge of Peace: God's Promise and Our Response: A Pastoral Letter on War and Peace,* Sections Summ. 1A, 55, 80, (Washington D.C.: United States Conference of Bishops, May 3, 1983).

"Seven Themes Of Catholic Social Teaching" from Sharing Catholic Social Teaching: Challenges and Directions by United States Conference of Catholic Bishops.

Beatitudes homily published in *Life of Christ book,* collection of homilies by Archbishop Fulton Sheen.

On the Holy Eucharist, Chapter 1 from the *Canons and Decrees of the Council of Trent,* translated by Theodore Alois Buckley.

John Paull II, *Christifideles Laici* ("On the Vocation and the Mission of the Lay Faithful in the Church and in the World").

The quotations on Page 149 are taken from the letters and *Morning Prayer* of Saint Therese of Lisieux.

The Way Student Edition
Item Number: CU5238
ISBN: 978-1-61-278046-7

1 2 3 4 5 6 7 8 015016 17 16 15 14 13
Webcrafters, Inc., Madison, Wi, USA; August 2013; Job# 106416

CONTENTS

SCRIPTURE & OTHER PRIMARY SOURCES

PRIMARY SOURCES

CHAPTER 5

My Faith

A private reflection space that allows you to track your spiritual journey, discoveries, aspirations, truths, and goals.

GO TO THE SOURCE

We send you directly to the Bible to listen to God's Word, analyze the passage, break it open, discuss it, and apply it to your life.

PRIMARY SOURCES

This feature takes you to a source that is not the Bible, such as Church documents, the Catechism, or historical writings, to help you process the core doctrines presented.

CATHOLIC LIFE

Here you will consider stories of Saints who have modeled virtues, prayer, and the life of discipleship.

A *Spiritual Practice* for the life of DISCIPLESHIP

Specific behaviors that, when done over time, help us open up to God's grace and make us instruments of his grace.

Faith & Culture

Historical, geographical, and/or cultural background may include maps, photos of architecture, or scenes from history or other cultures to give you a better appreciation for a time, place, or culture that you have read about.

GLOBAL PERSPECTIVES

This feature includes statistics, connections, and other information to step outside your own world. The information will usually bring global awareness to a subject such as the environment and the use of resources.

EXPRESSIONS OF FAITH

This feature focuses on symbols, rites, seasons, and devotions of the Catholic faith. It introduces or reacquaints you with the rich fabric, layers, and expressions of Catholicism and may answer, why do Catholics do the things that they do.

CHAPTER 1

- What gives you life?
- How is morality connected to what's happening in this picture?

A Life In Christ

 Go to the student site at
hs.osvcurriculum.com

ADVANCE REVIEW COPY

YOU WILL

- Examine why God created us.

- Explore what it means to be made in the image and likeness of God.

- Study the meaning of the Beatitudes.

- Recognize what it means to be a follower of Christ.

- Make the connection between living a moral life and happiness.

God's Plan for Us

KEY TERMS IN THIS SECTION

morality "the goodness or evil of human acts. . . . [that] depends on the . . . object (or nature), . . . of the action, the intention . . . and the circumstances of the action" (CCC, Glossary, p. 888)

sin an offense against God and an action contrary to his eternal law; purposely doing wrong

natural law the law inscribed in our hearts by God as a moral sense that allows us to discern by reason what is good and what is evil

conscience "the interior voice of a human being, within whose heart the inner law of God is inscribed" (CCC, Glossary, p. 872)

dignity worthy of honor or respect; our dignity comes from being created in the image and likeness of God

free will the power or ability to act on our own discretion and thereby shape our own life (see CCC, 1731)

Incarnation "the fact that the Son of God assumed human nature and became man in order to accomplish our salvation in that same human nature. Jesus Christ, the Son of God, the second Person of the Trinity, is both true God and true man, not part God and part man" (CCC, Glossary, p. 883)

covenant "a solemn agreement between human beings or between God and a human being involving mutual commitments or guarantees" (CCC, Glossary, p. 873)

The Gospel according to Matthew tells the account of a rich young man who approached Jesus to ask what he needed to do to get to Heaven. "'Teacher, what good deed must I do to have eternal life?'" (Matthew 19:16). This is a great universal question for each of us. The young man knew that there was a connection between doing good and getting to Heaven. He knew that doing good, what we call morality, is an expectation for anyone seeking eternal life.

The *Catechism of the Catholic Church* describes **morality** as "the ways, the rules of conduct that lead to the promised beatitude; it proscribes the ways of evil which turn [mankind] away from God and his love" (CCC, 1950). This definition connects the themes of holiness and happiness. Living a moral life leads us to God, who is the ultimate source of our happiness. In contrast, immorality, or sinning, leads us away from God and does not allow us to become the kind of people God wants us to be.

God has equipped us with a natural moral law that is engraved in the heart of every person. It allows us to tell the difference between a good act and an evil act. The natural law is "human reason ordaining him to do good and forbidding him to **sin**"[1] (CCC, 1954). Moral law is "a fatherly instruction by God" (CCC, 1975). It leads to happiness and condemns those actions that lead to evil. Our morality starts from the intimacy of love—the love of the Trinity and the love of the Father for his children.

The rich young man is not named in the Gospel according to Matthew. He asks a timeless question that everyone is called to answer with their lives. It is about the moral good and eternal life. The man senses a connection between morality and eternal life. Blessed Pope John Paul II in his encyclical *Veritatis Splendor* ("The Splendor of Truth") answers why the young man posed the question to Jesus of Nazareth. Like us, the young man likely was drawn to Jesus and that led to new questions within him about moral good.

GO TO THE SOURCE

Jesus answers the question posed by the wealthy young man.

Read Matthew 19:16.

- Why do you think Jesus gave the response that he did?
- How do most people today view wealth?

ADVANCE REVIEW COPY

> " He feels the need to draw near to the One who had begun his preaching with this new and decisive proclamation: 'The time is fulfilled, and the Kingdom of God is at hand; repent, and believe in the Gospel' (*Mk* 1:15).

—Pope John Paul II, *Veritatis Splendor*

In this course, we will address not only what the moral life is, but why it is important to live a moral life today. We will discuss commandments, rules, and characteristics we need to live a moral life, but also how to live the moral life and make connections between the moral life and the life of young people today.

Throughout this course, we will consider various expressions of the law: natural, divine, Church, and civil. One of the distinguishing characteristics of the Catholic faith is that we believe God has written on the souls of all human beings a moral sense that enables us to discern the difference between good acts and evil acts, between truth and lies. This original moral sense is called **natural law**. God has engraved in our hearts a sense of right and wrong that, when we follow it, prompts us to make good moral decisions and forbids us to sin. This natural law cannot be destroyed or removed from us, even when we reject it. It has served as a foundation for morality in all cultures throughout history, but it can be difficult to understand clearly. That's why we also need God's grace and his revealed law (see CCC, 1960).

We can tell the difference between a good act and a bad act by means of our **conscience**, which is, "the interior voice of a human being, within whose heart the inner law of God is inscribed" (CCC, Glossary, p. 872). Our consciences have to be formed, so that we learn what God has written in our hearts. This education of our

The rich young man was drawn to Jesus, prompting questions about moral goodness.

conscience takes place throughout our lives. It begins when we are children figuring out what is right and wrong. Our loved ones, Church teaching, Scripture, and prayer help us form a correct conscience. As we grow, our conscience urges us to live a virtuous life. We learn to steer away from or overcome fear, selfishness, and pride. When formed properly, our conscience protects us from resentment caused by guilt, complacency, and other human faults (see CCC, 1784). At the appropriate time, our conscience indicates those acts that are good and warns of those acts that are evil.

REFLECT

Morality connects holiness and happiness.

- What things in your life make you happy and at the same time are connected to happiness with God?

- Describe a happiness you have in life that is not connected to spending money.

EXPLAIN

Those who administer lie detector tests have commented that the reason the tests are generally accurate is because the human body is not designed to lie.

- What theological insights does this statement contain?

Our deepest desire is to be close to God.

God's Plan for Salvation

The natural law helps us discern good from evil and truth from lies. Pope Leo XIII explained that the natural law has the force of law because it comes from God and helps us interpret his higher reason (see CCC, 1954). It is one way God communicates with us. This is why Saint Paul tells us that the law is not meant for the innocent person (see 1 Timothy 1:9). Faithful people naturally follow the law that God has written on their hearts.

Our deepest desire is to be close to God because he possesses all that is good and what we truly desire—love, peace, and joy. We know that sin separates us from the Lord. "Only in God will he find the truth and happiness he never stops searching for" (CCC, 27). We cannot live fully without acknowledging God's love and giving ourselves to him. God is the source and end to all that it means to be alive. We receive our **dignity** because God has created us in his image and likeness and united us to himself through his divine grace. As a result, every human being

has dignity because we are created in God's image and likeness. He created us to share his eternal love and happiness in Heaven. The natural law expresses our human dignity and sets the standard for our basic rights and responsibilities (see CCC, 1956).

> By his providence God protects and governs all things he has made, 'reaching mightily from one end of the earth to the other, and ordering all things well.' For 'all are open and laid bare to his eyes,' even those things which are yet to come into existence through the free action of creatures.[2]
>
> —CCC, 302

The Holy Spirit, through divine inspiration, is the primary author of Sacred Scripture. He attributes actions to God letting us know that God has absolute sovereignty over all of history and the world. Through Scripture we learn to trust the Lord. "Good things and bad, life and death, poverty and wealth, come from the Lord" (Sirach 11:14).

As sons and daughters of God, we are called to trust. Jesus asks us to trust in God the Father because he takes care of even our smallest needs: "But strive first for the kingdom of God and his righteousness, and all these things will be given to you as well" (Matthew 6:33). As our needs are met, however, we must remember that they are given by God (see CCC, 304-305).

Catholic morality refers to the way that we lead our lives in response to God's law written in our souls. We call it a response because God always reaches out to us first. A Christian "no longer stands before God as a slave, in servile fear, or as a mercenary looking for wages, but as a son responding to the love of him who 'first loved us'"[3] (CCC, 1828). No matter how much we may forget or reject God, he never stops calling us to eternal life and happiness. We know that on our journey of discipleship within the Body of Christ we can say, "I will praise you with an upright heart, when I learn of your righteous ordinances" (Psalm 119:7).

Define What is natural law?

Explain Why do all human beings have dignity?

ADVANCE REVIEW COPY

The Book of Proverbs includes a verse that summarizes the Kingdom of God.

Read Proverbs 19:21.

- How does this verse give you hope?

Providence and Evil

While God is master of his plan, he makes use of us to cooperate and to carry it out. This is not a sign of weakness on our part. "For God grants his creatures not only their existence, but also the dignity of acting on their own" (CCC, 306). He has given us the responsibility to care for his creation on Earth.

We participate in God's divine plan through our good behavior, through our unceasing prayer, and through our sufferings. Sometimes, however, we don't know or see how we are collaborating with God's will. When we do enter into God's plan, we become "co-workers for his kingdom"[4] (CCC, 307).

We can be sure that God is acting through us when we do good. Our faith tells us that God is at work in the actions of those he created. Saint Paul affirms this when he writes: "There are varieties of activities, but it is the same God who activates all of them in everyone" (1 Corinthians 12:6). Jesus gave us an image for that when he said:

> 'I am the vine, you are the branches. Those who abide in me and I in them bear much fruit, because apart from me you can do nothing.'
>
> —John 15:5

So why then does evil exist? There is no easy answer to this question. Evil exists because, while we are given the free will to do good, we often have a tendency to choose to do evil instead. Evil is a consequence of **free will** given to humans. However, without free will, we would not be capable of true goodness. God gives us free will because he wants us to choose the good.

While no one part of our faith can fully explain the mystery of evil, collectively our faith as a whole can show what happens to overcome evil in the world. These gifts from God include:

- the goodness of creation
- the drama of sin and the patient love of God
- the redemptive **Incarnation** of God the Son through the Paschal Mystery
- the gift of the Holy Spirit
- Jesus' gathering of the Church
- the power of the Church's Sacraments
- Jesus' call to a blessed life (see CCC, 309)

We are invited to enter into the faith of the Church, but some people turn away from it. God could have created any kind of world he wanted. He could always make something better, as Saint Thomas Aquinas put it, but he chose to create a world that includes free will. This began with Adam and Eve. Through their Original Sin, sin and death entered the world. We add to this sinful condition through our own personal sins.

God's promise of a Redeemer gave us another chance and through Jesus' Death and Resurrection, we have been saved. "The Son of God assumed human nature and became man in order to accomplish our salvation in that same human nature" (CCC, Glossary, p. 883). However, to be saved through our own free will, we have to follow the path of salvation that Jesus won for us. On the journey, we experience pain and love, good and evil, as we prepare for the Second Coming of Jesus and our eventual return to God. We are all in a process of becoming. Until the end of the world, evil will exist alongside good (see CCC, 310).

DESCRIBE

- Give an example of an evil action you have seen or read about.
- How was that act the opposite of goodness and love?
- When have you taken a stand against evil? What was the outcome?

Saint Damien of Molokai

(1840–1889)

In 1840, Johannes and Anne-Catherine De Veuster named their newest son Joseph. As the youngest De Veuster grew up in Tremelo, Belgium, everyone noticed that he had an "all or nothing" attitude about everything he did.

Joseph was most passionate about his love for God and a determination to become an "all or nothing" priest and missionary. In religious life, Joseph took the name of Damien to honor a third-century martyr. Right before ordination, he was sent to missions in the Kingdom of Hawaii. As a young priest, he was pastor for several parishes on the main island, Oahu.

At the time, Hawaii was a busy destination for European and American trading ships, but those visitors brought diseases. Epidemics broke out, and thousands died. The spread of leprosy was especially virulent. In 1865, the king approved a quarantine for lepers who were transported to the island of Molokai. They were given food and basic supplies, but that was it. Everyone knew that leprosy, a disfiguring and hideous disease, imposed a death sentence.

In 1873, 33-year-old Father Damien volunteered for Molokai. He wanted these abandoned people to know that God loved them deeply. He arrived several years after the

ADVANCE REVIEW COPY

Aerial view of the Hawaiian island of Molokai where Saint Damien served a colony of people with Hansen's Disease, known as leprosy.

leper colony had been established. Bitter, suspicious people were fighting each other for survival. As a priest and friend, Damien began to calm them, establishing peace and order.

Molokai's new pastor then got to work. He started building houses for his parishioners. Good, clean places to live restored their spirits. He also built a church, developed farms, gardens, an orphanage, chapels, and roads. He organized a band, choir, and horseback riding programs. He also offered Catholic religious education. As the years went by, Father Damien restored pride, dignity, and hope among the people. His congregation loved him deeply. He tended to their wounds when they were dying. He built coffins and dug their graves when God called them home.

Inevitably, Father Damien also contracted leprosy, known as Hansen's disease. He died on April 15, 1889, after suffering with the disease for five years. His face and arms were covered with open sores. The flesh on his fingers was rotting and falling away. Only forty-nine years old, he had given his life for his people. Father Damien was canonized in October 11, 2009.

Think About It Why do you think Saint Damien of Molokai is an ideal patron saint for outcasts? What personality traits, spiritual gifts, and practical skills did Saint Damien have as he cared for his people on Molokai? Describe three ways that the life and ministry of Saint Damien remind us of Jesus. What lessons can we learn from Saint Damien's story about the spiritual need for hope?

Go to the student site at
hs.osvcurriculum.com

> **In the Old Testament, Joseph** reveals himself to his brothers and turns their evil actions around.

Read Genesis 45:1-15.

- How did Joseph explain who had really sent him to Egypt?
- What good came out of the evil actions of Joseph's brothers?
- What hope do you take from this reading?
- Recall a time when something good came from something that was bad. What did you learn from the situation?

Saint Thomas Aquinas reasoned that evil can exist under God, but that evil actions do not come from God. Evil comes from the voluntary actions of a person's free will, he said. "In the act of the will then is to be sought the root and origin of what in the moral order is sin," the saint wrote. While some ask if there is a God, why does evil exist? Aquinas turned that argument around: "'If there is evil, there is a God. For there would be no evil, if the order of goodness were taken away'" (*Summa Contra Gentiles, III, 71*).

Saint Thomas Aquinas makes an interesting argument that we know more about good in the world when we contrast it with evil. He said there is much good that would not exist in the world without evil—things such as justice and courage. Evil may result from actions, but we desire and strive for good results. As an analogy, he offered that sick people know best what a blessing good health is.

> "Evil things have their origin in the breaking down of good things, and still from them good things again take their rise by the providence of the ruler, as an interval of silence makes music sweet.
>
> —Saint Thomas Aquinas, *Summa Contra Gentiles*, 71

We can think about it this way: we are aware of light because of darkness and darkness because of light. As intelligent and free beings, we move toward our ultimate destinies through our choices and where we place our affections. Therefore, we can miss the mark, and as we know, we sin. The *Catechism* makes the point that God permits moral evil because he respects our freedom as his created beings, and he knows how to achieve goodness from evil.

> "For almighty God . . ., because he is supremely good, would never allow any evil whatsoever to exist in his works if he were not so all-powerful and good as to cause good to emerge from evil itself.'
>
> —Saint Augustine

Evil does not ever become a good thing, even though good may result from it. Saint Catherine of Siena wrote in *Dialogue on Providence* that, "'Everything comes from love, all is ordained for the salvation of man, God does nothing without this goal in mind.'" It would be great if all the ways of God were known to us, but we can never know all the mysteries of God.

Recall How did Saint Thomas Aquinas explain the kind of world God created?

Explain How is free will connected to the idea of evil?

Christ's Example For Us

Jesus never strayed from his Father's will. He lived in perfect communion with God. It is Christ's example that we are called to follow. We have been invited to live in God's sight, he "'who sees in secret'"[5] (CCC, 1693).

Saint Leo the Great urged Christians to recognize our dignity because we share in God's nature, which is loving, forgiving, and reasoning. "Never forget that you have been rescued from the power of darkness and brought into the light of the Kingdom of God," he wrote. One way we take part in God's Divine Nature is through the Sacraments. The grace of Christ and the Gifts of the Holy Spirit that we receive from the Seven Sacraments help us to live a life "'worthy of the gospel of Christ'"[6] (CCC, 1692). Prayer also helps us live this life.

The Sacraments and our conversations with God are signs that he did not abandon us after sin entered the world. In fact, God continues to call us and to announce the coming victory over evil that resulted from the Fall of Adam and Eve. After the Fall and the disruption of the Original Harmony of creation, we read what is called the Protoevangelium, or first Gospel (see CCC, 410). It is the first announcement of the Messiah and Redeemer. It describes the struggle between the serpent and the woman, and the final vic-

ADVANCE REVIEW COPY

Jesus never strayed from his Father's will even accepting death on the Cross.

tory of her descendant. When God spoke to the serpent, he said:

> 'I will put enmity between you and the woman, and between your offspring and hers; he will strike your head, and you will strike his heel.'
>
> —Genesis 3:15

We have studied how God revealed himself to our first parents, and, after they sinned against him, gave them the promise of redemption by offering them a **covenant**. From the creation of our first parents, we see that the world can be a place of darkness and light and the human race can do both good and evil. In the Old Testament, we see that God repeatedly reaffirmed his covenant with his Chosen People. In exchange for loving and serving him, he pledged to be our one true God, our caring and protective Father, who would send his people a messiah and savior. In time, God sent his only Son.

Recall How does Saint Leo describe God's nature?

Describe What is the Protoevangelium?

SECTION 1 REVIEW

QUICK REVIEW

1. **Define** In your own words, define morality.

2a. **Recall** What gives humans dignity?
 b. **Link** What is the relationship between morality and trust in God?

3a. **Summarize** Explain Saint Thomas Aquinas' arguments about the relationship between good and evil.
 b. **Connect** How did Saint Leo the Great encourage us to be moral people?
 c. **Explain** How is the Old Testament covenant related to morality?

4a. **Summarize** Briefly describe the life of Saint Damien of Molokai.
 b. **Link** What means did Saint Damien of Molokai use to restore the dignity of lepers?

Listen and Discuss With a group of classmates, discuss how moral living brings happiness.
- Give examples of how specific moral actions lead to happiness.
- Give examples of how immoral actions ultimately lead to unhappiness.
- Report back to the class about your discussion.

Pray Compose a short prayer asking the Holy Spirit to aid you in your efforts to live the moral life.

SELF-ASSESS

Which statement best reflects where you are now?

☐ I'm confident enough about the material in this section to be able to explain it to someone else.

☐ I have a good grasp of the material in this section, but I could use more review.

☐ I'm lost. I need help catching up before moving on.

The Word Becomes Flesh

KEY TERMS IN THIS SECTION

divine filiation through our union with Christ, we become the adopted children of God the Father

freedom "the power, rooted in reason and will, to act or not to act, to do this or that, and so to perform deliberate actions on one's own responsibility" (CCC, 1731)

Original Sin disobedience against God by our first parents, Adam and Eve. This sin marks all human beings as needing the salvation brought about through Christ.

God our Creator made everything that exists by calling it forth. The Book of Genesis says that God began creating by ordering light and dark into existence. "Then God said, 'Let there be light'; and there was light. . . . God called the light Day, and the darkness he called Night" (Genesis 1:3, 5).

Whatever God spoke came into existence to fulfill his will. After light and dark, came the waters, the dry land, plants, sun, moon and stars, living creatures, and finally human beings.

In the Gospel according to John, Jesus is called *the Word*.

> And the Word became flesh and lived among us, and we have seen his glory, the glory as of a father's only son, full of grace and truth.
>
> —John 1:14

He is the perfect expression of God the Father's love and power. Because of that love, the Word became flesh. Jesus came as one of us. He was born as a baby and grew into an adult. He experienced joy, sadness, hunger, thirst, and every other human emotion.

Everything God spoke came into existence at the creation of the world.

ADVANCE REVIEW COPY

To describe Jesus as *the Word* means that God desires a relationship with each of us because words are a means of communications with us. As Catholics, it is this relationship that lays the foundation of our morality.

- How has *the Word* spoken to you in your life?
- To what degree has *the Word* made a difference in your life?
- How has *the Word* affected the way you live and act in life?

The saints tell us that by uniting with *the Word*, we will also be sons and daughters of God through **divine filiation**. "'For this is why the Word became man, and the Son of God became the Son of man: so that man, by entering into communion with the Word and thus receiving divine sonship, might become a son of God'"[7] (CCC, 460).

Thereby, we share in Jesus' life and mission. In its most proper sense, divine filiation refers to the relationship of the Second Person of the Trinity to the Father. "In his Son and through him, he invites men to become, in the Holy Spirit, his adopted children and thus heirs of his blessed life" (CCC, 1).

Fulfilling the covenant established with his fallen children, God sent his only Son, for our salvation. As the Nicene Creed reminds us, Jesus came down from Heaven, and "by the power of the Holy Spirit became Incarnate of the Virgin Mary, and was made man" *(Roman Missal)*.

Why did the Word become flesh? The *Catechism* lists four reasons:

- *In order to save us by reconciling us with God.* Christ reconciled us with God, who, because he loved us so much, sent his Son to pay for our sins (see CCC, 457).

- *So that we might know God's love.* God sends his Son, so that we can live through him (see CCC, 458).

- *To be a model of holiness.* Jesus told us that no one comes to the Father, except through him. God directly tells the Apostles to listen to Jesus, and Jesus gives us the Beatitudes and a new law, "'This is my commandment, that you love one another as I have loved you'" (John 15:12).

- *To make us partakers of the divine nature.* Jesus, "wanting to make us sharers in his divinity, assumed our nature, so that he, made man, might make men gods"[8] (CCC, 460). Saint Peter put it this way:

> Thus he has given us, through these things, his precious and very great promises, so that through them you may escape from the corruption that is in the world . . . and may become participants of the divine nature.
>
> —2 Peter 1:4

The *Catechism* says, "We had lost the possession of the good" (CCC, 457). We needed Jesus to reconcile our sinful nature with God.

> Closed in the darkness, it was necessary to bring us the light; captives, we awaited a Savior; prisoners, help; slaves, a liberator. Are these things minor or insignificant? Did they not move God to descend to human nature and visit it, since humanity was in so miserable and unhappy a state?[9]
>
> —CCC, 457

God's love came to live among us in the form of Jesus, the Second Person of the Trinity, so that we could live through him. John tells us, "'For God so loved the world that he gave his only Son, so that everyone who believes in him may not perish but may have eternal life'" (John 3:16).

GO TO THE SOURCE

Jesus also came so that we would have a perfect model of holiness.

Read Matthew 11:28-30; John 14:1-6; Mark 9:2-8; John 15:9-17; and Mark 8:34-37.

- What does each of these teach you about holiness?
- What can you do to become more like Christ after reading these passages?
- What do these passages reveal about God the Father?

Through Jesus, we come to know the beauty, the glory, and the dignity of who we are called to be, no matter what we do.

Pope Benedict XVI has written that being Christian does not happen from a simple choice. Instead it results from an encounter with an event—the person of Jesus Christ. This gives our lives a new, decisive direction. The new direction teaches us to love God with all our heart, with all our soul, and with all our might as well as love our neighbor as we love ourselves. "'Since God has first loved us, love is now no longer a mere "command"; it is the response to the gift of love with which God draws near to us,'" Pope Benedict XVI wrote.

Compare In what ways was Jesus just like us?

Explain How does divine filiation bring us even closer to God?

Dignity of the Human Person

The starting point of Christian morality is who we are, which is sons and daughters of God. We are people with inherent dignity, that is, each one of us is beloved of God, gifted with his grace, and made in his image and likeness (see CCC, 1700). We are naturally religious beings, whose vocation is to know, love, and serve God. As children of God, we are called to live in communion with him and find our happiness through him.

Without losing his divine nature, Jesus took on our human nature so he could reveal the full extent of his Father's love for us. Jesus, who is both true God and true man, is our principal model of holiness, our mediator with God the Father, and our Savior. Jesus is our Lord and by our calling him "Lord," we profess our belief in his divinity. In his message and, more importantly, in his very life, Jesus reveals the scope and the depth of his Father's love for us. Only when we see ourselves through the eyes of Jesus do we truly see ourselves. In Jesus, we discover the beauty, the glory, and the dignity of who we are.

We have a spiritual and immortal soul, an intelligence that can reason the order of things as God created them, and a free will that allows us to direct our lives toward the good (see CCC, 1703 and 1704). **Freedom** is something that modern society values greatly. A high price has been paid by many to protect freedom or restore it. If our greatest longing is to be with our Creator, then we will naturally want to do what God's will is for us. To do that, we must be free. This kind of freedom is "an 'outstanding manifestation of the divine image'"[10] (CCC, 1705). The Second Vatican Council document *Gaudium et Spes* speaks of freedom:

ADVANCE REVIEW COPY

My Faith

Treasures of the Heart

Jesus teaches us to store up treasure in our hearts. "'Do not store up for yourselves treasures on earth, where moth and rust consume and where thieves break in and steal; but store up for yourselves treasures in heaven, where neither moth nor rust consumes and where thieves do not break in and steal. For where your treasure is, there your heart will be also'" (Matthew 6:19-21).

Answering the accompanying questions will open your eyes to the values, virtues, attitudes, and actions that you treasure most. These are the heavenly things that can help you live the life God intended, if you uphold them. Throughout this course, you will discuss the heavenly things that the heart of Christ and the heart of the Church treasure most. See how much they will resemble or enhance the things you have listed.

What does your heart really treasure?

1. What do you sincerely hope to be: holy, noble, loving and/or true?

2. What brings your heart true sadness?

3. What brings your heart true happiness?

My Faith is a personal and confidential exercise. You can use anything from this My Faith feature as part of the report you will turn in at the end of this course.

Discipleship ... within the Body of Christ ... for the glory of God and the good of the world.

Their dignity therefore requires them to act out of conscious and free choice, as moved and drawn in a personal way from within, and not by their own blind impulses or by external constraint.

—*Gaudium et Spes*, para. 17

Our freedom is weakened through sin, and God's grace is necessary to imitate his eternal goodness. We have great hope because we were created by God to be eternally happy with him in Heaven. We know and trust that God will help and support us to do what is right and to avoid evil. Jesus taught us to ask God our Father to help us avoid temptation and deliver us from evil. To do this, we must work to form a correct conscience, listen to it as God's voice written on our hearts, and act with love for God and for our neighbor. This is living the moral life, which "bears witness to the dignity of the person" (CCC, 1706).

From the beginning of time, people have been tempted to sin. This is evidenced in the account of Adam and Eve. Their sin of disobedience, which we know as **Original Sin**, inclines us toward evil. It destroyed the original harmony of creation and has left us with a divided nature. We struggle between good and evil. We abuse our freedom when we act apart from God. "People find that they are unable of themselves to overcome the assaults of evil, . . . so that everyone feels as if in chains," (*Gaudium et Spes*, para. 13). That is why Christ lived among us, to restore our freedom by cutting the bonds that sin places on us.

By his Passion, Christ delivered us from Satan and from sin. He merited for us the new life in the Holy Spirit. His grace restores what sin had damaged in us.

—CCC, 1708

By living in Christ, we live as sons and daughters of God. In doing so, we follow Jesus' example and act in right and just ways. "In union with his Savior, the disciple attains the perfection of charity which is holiness" (CCC, 1709). When we embrace the moral life out of faith, we come to see that our true treasures are found in Heaven. In doing so, we reject the empty promises of selfish desires. Our treasures in Heaven are eternal. At best, giving in to selfish desires means we will hunger for them again and again. At worst, selfishness creates more pain or even death.

Recall What is the starting point of Christian morality?

Explain What does it mean to say that humans have a divided nature?

SECTION 2 REVIEW

QUICK REVIEW

1a. **List** What are the reasons for the Incarnation?
b. **Explain** According to Pope Benedict XVI, what does encountering Jesus do to us?
c. **Trace** How do we share in divine filiation?

2a. **Describe** How are freedom and morality linked?
b. **Apply** How does sin weaken freedom?
c. **Explain** How does Jesus' example further our moral life?

ACT

Think of times in your life when you had a choice to affirm someone's dignity.

- Write a paragraph describing the situation.

- If you are proud of your action, say a prayer of thanks for God's guidance. If you feel you should have done something differently, then say a prayer for help with future decisions.

SELF-ASSESS

Which statement best reflects where you are now?

☐ I'm confident enough about the material in this section to be able to explain it to someone else.

☐ I have a good grasp of the material in this section, but I could use more review.

☐ I'm lost. I need help catching up before moving on.

ADVANCE REVIEW COPY

Responding to God's Plan

KEY TERMS IN THIS SECTION

Beatitudes eight teachings from Jesus that guide our moral attitudes and actions, and which lead to "happiness or blessedness, especially the eternal happiness of heaven" (CCC, Glossary, p. 868)

Sermon on the Mount a part of the Gospel according to Matthew in which Jesus preaches important moral teachings, including the Beatitudes

virtues habitual and firm dispositions to do what is good and right. Through repeated practice, they make it easier to practice the good

faith a gift from God and a human act by which we believe in him and all that he has revealed; the theological virtue of seeking to know and to do God's will

The moral life is not easy. We have to resist temptations and comfortable solutions to difficult problems. Our responses, however, should be governed by charity. Our deeds and words should be rooted in love for God—not in self-interest. In today's world, a world hungry for truth, we often label that hunger for truth a need for "transparency." We want to be able to see through what's being done to the underlying motives.

Saint Basil the Great, a third-century bishop, talked about the right reasons for what we do. After so many centuries, his words still get straight to the heart of the matter. "If we turn away from evil out of fear of punishment, we are in the position of slaves," he said. But, if "we obey for the sake of the good itself and out of love for him who commands . . . we are in the position of children"[11] (CCC, 1828).

Moral Motivations				
Look at the following motivations and circle the level that each one has had in your moral decision-making.				
Fear of punishment	Not much	A little	Quite A Bit	A lot
Truly desire to do the right thing	Not much	A little	Quite A Bit	A lot
Go along with what others are doing	Not much	A little	Quite A Bit	A lot
Hope that someone recognizes my good acts	Not much	A little	Quite A Bit	A lot
Because of my love of God	Not much	A little	Quite A Bit	A lot
Want to obey the law	Not much	A little	Quite A Bit	A lot
Makes me happy to do the right thing	Not much	A little	Quite A Bit	A lot
Important to my parents	Not much	A little	Quite A Bit	A lot
Want a good reputation	Not much	A little	Quite A Bit	A lot
Don't want to hurt my future	Not much	A little	Quite A Bit	A lot
Moral life brings me a clear conscience	Not much	A little	Quite A Bit	A lot

• What does this show you about the way you approach moral living?

Blessed are they who mourn, for they will be comforted.

Leading a moral life transforms our relationship with God. No longer do we stand before God as a servant motivated by fear or as an employee trying to get in the boss' good graces. Leading a moral life means we become more and more a child of God responding to him out of love, and the reason is because God loved us into being.

Describe Give one example of doing the right thing for the right reason—even when it was challenging.

Explain How does leading a moral life transform our relationship with God?

The Call to Joy

Jesus preached the **Beatitudes**—teachings meant to guide the moral attitudes and actions of those who wanted to follow him—during his **Sermon on the Mount**. The Beatitudes are at the heart of Jesus' teaching. They fulfill the promises made to Abraham and the Chosen People (see CCC, 1716).

Jesus said these statements were keys to true happiness. They free us from the false values placed on things in the world. They open us to what is truly good.

> Indeed, when God comforts, he satisfied the hunger for righteousness, he wipes away the tears of those who mourn, which means that, as well as compensating each one in a practical way, he opens the Kingdom of Heaven.
>
> —Pope Benedict XVI, *Angelus*, January 2011

The Beatitudes contradicted the idea that wealth, success, and an easy life are the sources of happiness. Jesus told his audience that those who are truly blessed and happy are those who are poor in spirit, or those who mourn, or those who are hungering and thirsting for righteousness for their neighbors. The Beatitudes bring joy to those who embrace them.

> But God chose what is foolish in the world to shame the wise; . . . God chose what is low and despised in the world, things that are not, to reduce to nothing things that are, so that no one might boast in the presence of God.
>
> —1 Corinthians 1:27, 28-29

Jesus said we should rejoice when we experience suffering in his name.

> 'Blessed are you when people revile you and persecute you and utter all kinds of evil against you falsely on my account. Rejoice and be glad, for your reward is great in heaven.'
>
> —Matthew 5:11-12a

The Eight Beatitudes

1. Blessed are the poor in spirit, for theirs is the Kingdom of Heaven.

2. Blessed are those who mourn, for they will be comforted.

3. Blessed are the meek, for they will inherit the Earth.

4. Blessed are those who hunger and thirst for righteousness, for they will be filled.

5. Blessed are the merciful, for they will receive mercy.

6. Blessed are the pure in heart, for they will see God.

7. Blessed are the peacemakers, for they will be called children of God.

8. Blessed are those who are persecuted for righteousness' sake, for theirs is the Kingdom of Heaven.

ADVANCE REVIEW COPY

The Beatitudes, like the Ten Commandments, both describe what it means to live as a member of God's People. The Beatitudes teach us the **virtues**, or attributes, that help us achieve our goals in life as Christians: building up God's Kingdom, participating in the life of the Trinity, attaining happiness on Earth and in Heaven, and living as sons and daughters of God.

The Beatitudes offer hope as they describe the types of blessings and rewards waiting for those who choose to live them. The Beatitudes challenge us to think conscientiously about our attitude toward others so that our attitude reflects love of God above everything else.

Each of the Beatitudes presents us with life goals, as well as actions that flow from those goals. Use the following questions to determine how close you are to living in the spirit of the Beatitudes. After reading the list, choose one set of questions, and reflect on how you might make these characteristics your own. How might you better follow in the footsteps of the saints who lived by the Beatitudes?

The Poor in Spirit. How much do I trust in God? How much do I think I have to control everything in order to be successful and happy? How much do I accept help when I need it? How much room in my life do I make for my relationship with God? How often do I bring my needs to God? How often do I help those who are poor in spirit or finances?

Those Who Mourn. Life involves suffering. Do I accept times of sadness, pain, loss, and failure? Or do I complain and try to assign blame? How easy it for me to feel the pain of others, and stand with them in difficult times?

The Meek. How humble am I? How often do I express my gratitude for what others do for me, or for what I have? What kind of friend am I to those who are not in the most popular crowds? How much respect do I show to those who are never in the limelight?

Those Who Hunger and Thirst for Righteousness. How important is fairness, justice, equality, and righteousness to me? How willing am I to stand up for these things even if it comes with a cost?

Blessed are the pure in heart, for they shall see God.

The Merciful. Would people who know me say that I am truly a kind person? How often have I demonstrated mercy when I didn't have to or didn't want to? Am I someone who forgives easily or do I tend to hold grudges?

The Pure in Heart. To what extent am I a person of integrity and honesty? How often do I try to manipulate or use people? Do I mean what I say? How much would people say that I am good hearted?

Peacemakers. How often do I search for peaceful means to resolve conflicts? Am I known as a peacemaker in my family, among my friends? Do I try to understand the points of view of those with whom I have disagreements?

LIST

- For each Beatitude make a list of people, living or dead, whose lives and actions exemplify that Beatitude's values.

PRIMARY SOURCES

Speaking in Toronto, on the shores of Lake Ontario, Blessed Pope John Paul II described the Beatitudes as the *Magna Carta* of Christianity. Like those who listened anxiously to Jesus at the Sermon on the Mount, the young people gathered in Toronto for World Youth Day in 2002 listened attentively to the Lord. "I have heard your festive voices, your cries, your songs, and I have felt the deep longing that beats within your hearts: *you want to be happy*!" the Pope told the crowd. The Pope ended his speech with a resounding prayer for the young people to help with God's plan of salvation:

"Only Jesus is the true Master, only Jesus speaks the unchanging message that responds to the deepest longings of the human heart, because he alone knows 'what is in each person' (cf. Jn 2:25). Today he calls you to be the salt *and* light *of the world, to choose goodness, to live in justice, to become instruments of love and peace. His call has always demanded a choice between good and evil, between light and darkness, between life and death. He makes the same invitation today to you who are gathered here on the shores of Lake Ontario.*

"To believe in Jesus is to accept what he says, even when it runs contrary to what others are saying. It means rejecting the lure of sin, however attractive it may be, in order to set out on the difficult path of the Gospel virtues.

"Young people listening to me, answer the Lord with strong and generous hearts! He is counting on you. Never forget: Christ needs you to carry out his plan of salvation! Christ needs your youth and your generous enthusiasm to make his proclamation of joy resound. . . . Answer his call by placing your lives at his service in your brothers and sisters! Trust Christ, because he trusts you.

8. *Lord Jesus Christ, proclaim once more*
    your Beatitudes in the presence of these young
    people,
    gathered in Toronto for the World Youth Day.

    Look upon them with love and listen to their young
    hearts,
    ready to put their future on the line for you.

    You have called them to be
    the 'salt of the earth and light of the world.'

    Continue to teach them the truth and beauty
    of the vision that you proclaimed on the Mountain.

    Make them men and women of the Beatitudes!
    Let the light of your wisdom shine upon them,
    so that in word and deed they may spread
    in the world the light and salt of the Gospel.

    Make their whole life a bright reflection of you,
    who are the true light that came into this world
    so that whoever believes in you will not die,
    but will have eternal life (cf. Jn 3:16)!"

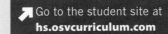
Go to the student site at
hs.osvcurriculum.com

How does Christ need you?

How can you be a man or woman of the Beatitudes?

ADVANCE REVIEW COPY

Those Who Are Persecuted in the Cause of Righteousness. How willing am I to stand up for my beliefs, even when they are unpopular or lead to personal hardships? What am I willing to stand up for?

Explain How do the Beatitudes contradict the common idea that wealth, success, and the easy life are sources of happiness?

Describe Which of the Beatitudes do you most identify with? Which do you find most challenging?

Heart of Jesus' Preaching

God has placed a desire for happiness in our hearts, and the Beatitudes help us respond to that natural longing (see CCC, 1718). We have this desire so that we will seek out God, who is the only one who can fulfill our happiness. Saint Augustine pointed out that every member of the human race wants to live happily.

> Since in seeking you, my God, I seek a happy life, let me seek you so that my soul may live, for my body draws life from my soul and my soul draws life from you.
>
> —Saint Augustine

In fact, God calls us all, as individuals and as the Body of Christ as a whole, to his own beatitude or happiness. One way to describe beatitude is extreme blessedness. The New Testament gives us four ways to characterize this kind of happiness to which God calls us:

- the coming of the Kingdom of God: "From that time Jesus began to proclaim, 'Repent, for the kingdom of heaven has come near'" (Matthew 4:17).

- the vision of God: "'Blessed are the pure in heart, for they will see God'" (Matthew 5:8).

- entering into the joy of the Lord: "'You have been trustworthy in a few things, I will put you in charge of many things; enter into the joy of your master'" (Matthew 25:21b).

- entering into God's rest: "'Today if you hear his voice, do not harden your hearts'" (Hebrews 4:7) (see CCC, 1720).

GO TO THE SOURCE

In the Parable of the Sower, Jesus explains what can happen to those who hear the Word of God.

Read Matthew 13:1-23.

- Summarize the Parable of the Sower.

- What are the four types of seeds that the sower spreads on the ground?

- How can you keep from being one of the first three kinds of seeds?

- In what ways can you "nurture the soil" so that you can make holy choices in your life?

- How does the "good soil" help us find true happiness in God?

For our part, we must grow in **faith** and moral life. Father Alfred McBride, O Praem., notes that while faith begins at our Baptism, it also demands that we increase our faith as we move through stages of development. "Unless this happens, faith remains stunted, even childish, and therefore easy to lose when adult complexity is not matched with faith advancement," he writes. This is what we are called to right now.

The Beatitudes encourage us to live lives grounded in Christian morality. "It invites us to purify our hearts of bad instincts and to seek the love of God above all else" (CCC, 1723). True happiness is found in God alone and is beyond our understanding or power. Saint Irenaeus talked about how God the "Father cannot be grasped, but because of God's love and goodness toward us, and because he can do all things, he goes so far as to grant those who love him the privilege of seeing him. . . . For 'what is impossible for men is possible for God'"[12] (CCC, 1722).

There is no amount of wealth, fame, or technology that can bring us more happiness than God. We can't find true happiness in those things, although they can be used in morally right ways to bring us closer to God. They can also be used in the wrong ways.

Wealth is something that humans have always given some instinctive honor. For centuries, many people have measured happiness by the amount of wealth a person can acquire. "Wealth is one idol of the day and notoriety is a second"[13] (CCC, 1723). The Ten Commandments, the Beatitudes, and the teachings of the Apostles, however, give us paths that lead to the Kingdom of God. Step by step, in our daily behavior and decisions, we lead ourselves on those paths, sustained by the Holy Spirit. "By the working of the Word of Christ, we slowly bear fruit in the Church to the glory of God"[14] (CCC, 1724).

The Beatitudes then help discern our choices about earthly things and shape our lives. "They purify our hearts in order to teach us to love God above all things" (CCC, 1728).

Recall What did Saint Augustine say that all members of the human race have in common?

List What are the four ways that characterize the kind of happiness to which God calls us.

SECTION 3 REVIEW

QUICK REVIEW

1a. Explain Why is the motivation for our actions important?

b. Describe Explain Saint Basil's reasons for leading a moral life.

2a. Apply Why are the Beatitudes keys to true happiness?

b. Compare How are the Beatitudes similar to the Ten Commandments?

c. Connect What goals do the Beatitudes present to us?

3a. List What are the four ways that the New Testament describes happiness that comes from living the Beatitudes?

b. Describe What did Saint Irenaeus say God grants to those who love him?

4. List Name each of the eight Beatitudes.

Listen and Discuss With a group of people, come up with at least one concrete way that you will let others know about the eight Beatitudes. It should be something practical that you can do in this coming week.

SELF-ASSESS

Which statement best reflects where you are now?

☐ I'm confident enough about the material in this section to be able to explain it to someone else.

☐ I have a good grasp of the material in this section, but I could use more review.

☐ I'm lost. I need help catching up before moving on.

ADVANCE REVIEW COPY

Following Christ

Following Jesus in the form of *discipleship* takes commitment, comes with a cost, and brings out the best in us—every one of us regardless of age, personality, or history.

Following Jesus begins with the baptismal grace we receive in the Sacrament of Baptism. Our initiation into the Body of Christ starts with Baptism. That includes forgiveness of Original Sin and all personal sins. We are born into new life and become adopted sons and daughters of God the "Father, a member of Christ and a temple of the Holy Spirit. By this very fact the person baptized is incorporated into the Church, the Body of Christ, and made a sharer in the priesthood of Christ" (CCC, 1279).

Catholics are familiar with Baptism as the gateway into the Church, and a necessary step for salvation. The Sacraments of Baptism, Confirmation, and Eucharist are the process of initiation, sometimes celebrated all at once as an adult or in stages beginning in infancy. The commitment called for in each Sacrament extends beyond the celebration. The commitment is just beginning. They set us on a moral path in life.

The white garment symbolizes putting on Christ through the graces of Baptism. This ritual indicates the lifelong commitment baptized people make. The graces of Baptism give us the power to live and act on the promptings of the Holy Spirit that guide our actions. This is how we can grow in goodness and moral virtues (see CCC, 1266).

Confirmation completes and strengthens the grace of Baptism. "By a special outpouring of the gifts of the Holy Spirit, which seal or 'confirm' the baptized in union with Christ and equip them for active participation in the worship and apostolic life of the Church" (CCC, Glossary, p. 872). Often young people preparing for Confirmation perform a service to their community as a sign of their Christian commitment that continues.

Participation in the Eucharist continues our commitment as well, and it is "the heart and the summit of the Church's life" (CCC, 1407). We

Jesus tells us the gateway to life is narrow (see Matthew 7:14).

GO TO THE SOURCE

Jesus called his first disciples by simply asking them to follow him.

Read Mark 1:16-20.

- What did Jesus say to make these four men become his disciples?
- What motivates you to follow Christ?

GLOBAL PERSPECTIVES

The Church of the Beatitudes near Tabgha, Israel, overlooks the Sea of Galilee. The church memorializes the Sermon on the Mount. Built in a Byzantine style between 1936 and 1938, it was erected near ruins of a fourth-century church. The hilltop church is simple but elegant with marble walls and a golden dome. Tour guides point out that it has an octagonal base—eight sides to represent the eight Beatitudes given by Jesus.

The first-century pilgrims who heard the Beatitudes must have pondered these mysterious but compelling statements and discussed with one another how they could begin to live them. Two thousand years later, it's the same for modern pilgrims. They leave the Church of the Beatitudes, travel down the mountain and head home thinking about how they must learn to be poor in spirit,

Entrance to the Church of the Beatitudes in Tabgha, Israel.

meek, peacemakers. That journey, they realize, will be life-long.

- Why do people make pilgrimages?
- If you could make a pilgrimage, where would you want to go and why?

Go to the student site at **hs.osvcurriculum.com**

join with Catholics worldwide to worship Jesus and give thanks to God the Father. We offer perfect worship to the Father because we are united with his Son, Jesus, in offering worship. We "dishonor [the] table" of the Eucharist if we do not move from participating in this meal to sharing with people in need (CCC, 1397).

This three-step process of initiation into the Body of Christ not only begins the journey of discipleship, it sustains the journey.

> Go in peace, glorifying the Lord by your life.
>
> —*Roman Missal*, Concluding Rites

Explain When do we begin to follow Jesus?

Recall What does the white ritual baptismal garment symbolize?

His Story Is Our Story

In the midst of the Sermon on the Mount, Jesus sums up his challenge to us in these words: "'Be perfect, therefore, as your heavenly Father is perfect'" (Matthew 5:48). Perfection means to be *completely focused on* being the people God created us to be. Jesus fulfilled completely the purpose for which he was created. It took Jesus his

whole human life to complete this task; just as it will for each of us. To help us on our journey, Jesus assures us that his story is our story. We celebrate our identification with Christ in our Baptism and Confirmation, in our participation in the Eucharist and the other Sacraments, and through all our efforts to live a Christ-like life.

Our first and last point is always Jesus Christ. "It is by looking to him in faith that Christ's faithful can hope that he himself fulfills his promises in them" (CCC, 1698). By loving Christ in the same way that he loved us, we hope to act and decide in ways that live up to our dignity. Saint John Eudes put it this way:

> I ask you to consider that our Lord Jesus Christ is your true head, and that you are one of his members. He belongs to you as the head belongs to its members; all that is his is yours: his spirit, his heart, his body and soul, and all his faculties. You must make use of all these as of your own, to serve, praise, love, and glorify God. You belong to him, as members belong to their head. And so he longs for you to use all that is in you, as if it were his own, for the service and glory of the Father.[15]
> For to me, to live is Christ.[16]
>
> —CCC, 1698

ADVANCE REVIEW COPY

PARISH
Outreach

One of the best places to see the connection between the Sacraments and moral life is when parishes reach out to the community around them. People nourished by the Sacraments take the message of Jesus to the larger society through acts of service, generosity, and kindness. Here are a few stories that demonstrate this.

When people came to Indianapolis for the Super Bowl, parishioners at historic St. John the Evangelist Church attracted people to the Gospel message with a zip line ride in front of the Church. At the bottom was a sign that read: "If you thought the zip line was a thrill, come in and spend some time with Jesus."

In New York City, a local priest started an outreach to immigrants from the nation of Ghana. With the help of parishioners, the priest began celebrating Mass on Tuesday nights and the group gathered afterward to socialize. Hundreds of people started attending.

A man flies through the air on a zip line that an Indianapolis, Indiana, parish set up during the Super Bowl.

Following a mission trip to Mexico, parishioners from a Catholic church in Wisconsin chose to bring a teenage girl to their hometown so she could have surgery on a life-threatening tumor. Before the surgery, they prayed for her and the priest anointed her at Mass.

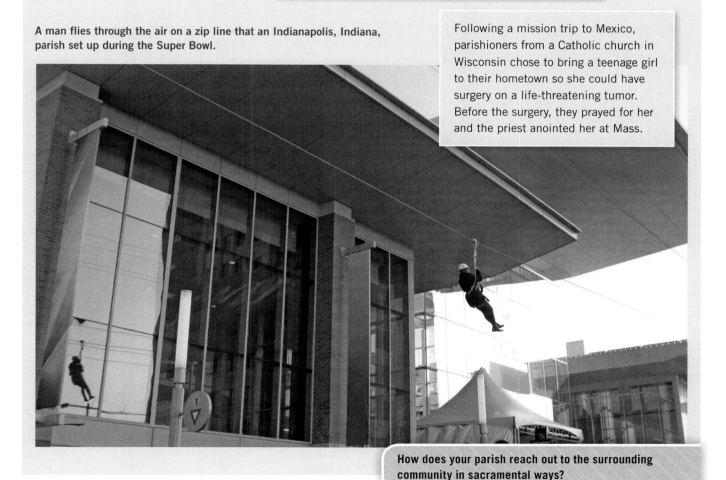

How does your parish reach out to the surrounding community in sacramental ways?

Sacraments Contain What They Signify

In **Baptism**, we die to ourselves and rise in the life Christ.

In **Confirmation**, we deepen our commitment to a life in Christ.

In the **Eucharist**, we are united into the one Body of Christ.

In the **Sacrament of Penance**, we forgive and receive forgiveness in order to reunite the broken relationships of life.

In the **Sacrament of Anointing of the Sick**, our bodies and/or souls are healed.

In **Holy Orders**, we are called to service of the local and universal Church through ordained leadership.

In **Marriage**, the two become one flesh in service of the domestic Church—the family.

SECTION 4 REVIEW

QUICK REVIEW

1a. Contrast List positive and negative connotations of the word *follower*.

b. Explain How do the Sacraments of Initiation solidify the growth of the faithful?

c. Describe How does the Eucharist extend our commitment to the moral life?

2. Link How does the Holy Spirit help us with morality and discipleship?

3. Explain How do Jesus' teachings relate to God the Father?

ACT

Review with another classmate how the Sacraments of Initiation have affected your life.

- You may want to make a chart showing each Sacrament and its effects.

- Remember that the effects of a Sacrament last much longer than the ceremony at which it is conferred.

Pray Compose a short prayer thanking the Holy Spirit for guidance in your moral life.

SELF-ASSESS

Which statement best reflects where you are now?

☐ I'm confident enough about the material in this section to be able to explain it to someone else.

☐ I have a good grasp of the material in this section, but I could use more review.

☐ I'm lost. I need help catching up before moving on.

Catholic sacramental celebrations are connected with leading a moral life. The Sacraments contain the reality of our true Catholic identity—that is, through our sacramental celebration, we become those persons and that community we are meant to be. Empowered by the Holy Spirit, we continue to live out the reality of our Catholic identity in our daily lives.

The Sacraments transform those believers who come to them with faith and sincerity. The tasks of discipleship and morality are never-ending, and the Sacraments give us the grace we need to live the moral life in Christ.

It is through those Sacraments and the power of the Holy Spirit that we participate in Jesus' Death and Resurrection. We die to sin and are reborn to new life in Christ. The Sacraments graft us as branches to the vine, which is Christ himself. We become members of the Body of Christ.

> [God] gave himself to us through his Spirit. By the participation of the Spirit, we become communicants in the divine nature. . . . For this reason, those in whom the Spirit dwells are divinized.[17]
>
> —CCC, 1988

Jesus is our great moral teacher and model. In all of his teachings, Jesus begins with the message of God's love for us. This course explores Jesus' invitation to respond to God's love by living a life of love.

If we want to thoroughly understand our purpose and our nature, we must draw near to Christ as the rich young man did. Eternal life with God awaits those who travel the path of morality and discipleship.

Explain What is Jesus' idea of perfection for us?

Analyze Why is the task of following Jesus never-ending?

ADVANCE REVIEW COPY

PRAYER

Opening Prayer

We begin in the name of the Father, and of the Son, and of the Holy Spirit. Amen.

God, our Father, we thank you for the great opportunity we have of knowing You, Creator of the world, through Jesus our Redeemer, and Savior.

Jesus, we pray that we may be faithful to spread Your Gospel to the whole world and to hold up your values of true morality, which are for our own good and for your glory.

Holy Spirit, we pray that you will be with us to give us insight and knowledge as we live our lives. Help us to see that the Commandments and Beatitudes are a blessing, not a burden.

These things we ask in Christ's name.

Amen.

Closing Prayer (based on Matthew 5:1-12)

Jesus, you said, "Blessed are the poor in spirit, for theirs is the kingdom of heaven." Keep us from being preoccupied with money, wealth, and power. Keep us prudent with all of our material goods share them with justice.

Jesus, you said, "Blessed are the gentle, for they shall inherit the earth." Help us care one another. Help us the think globally and act with justice locally.

Jesus, you said, "Blessed are those who mourn, for they shall be comforted." Let us understand that our burdens and sufferings are a participation in the Paschal Mystery.

Jesus, you said, "Blessed are those who hunger and thirst for justice, for they shall be filled." Make us thirst and hunger for you and actively spread your Gospel in our everyday lives.

Jesus, you said, "Blessed are the merciful, for they shall receive mercy." Help us to be quick to forgive and slow to condemn.

Jesus, you said, "Blessed are the clean of heart, for they shall see God." Free us from our internal struggles and help us to have an informed conscience always looking to do what is right and good.

Jesus, you said, "Blessed are the peacemakers, for they shall be called children of God." Help us make peace in our families and recognize the dignity of those we live with every day.

Jesus, you said, "Blessed are those who are persecuted for the sake of justice, for the kingdom of heaven in theirs." Make us willing to suffer for the sake of what is right rather than to seek revenge.

When Christ rose from the dead and appeared to his friends, He said: "Blessed are those who have not seen and have believed." Jesus addresses these same words to us.

O God, your only Son prayed that we might be one as you, Father, are in him, and he in you. Guide our steps, open our hearts and make us ready and able to follow him, the way and the truth and the life, who lives and reigns with you and the Holy Spirit for ever and ever.

Amen.

ADVANCE REVIEW COPY

TERMS

Use each of the following terms in a sentence that shows you know what the term means in the context of the chapter. You may include more than one term in a sentence.

morality	divine filiation
sin	freedom
natural law	Original Sin
conscience	Beatitudes
dignity	Sermon on the Mount
free will	virtues
Incarnation	faith
covenant	

PEOPLE AND IDEAS

Define each person or idea in the context of the chapter.

1. *Veritatis Splendor*

2. Pope Leo XIII

3. Saint Thomas Aquinas

4. Saint Leo the Great

5. Protoevangelium

6. The Word

7. Saint Damien of Molokai

8. Original Sin

9. Dorothy Day

10. Saint Basil the Great

11. Sermon on the Mount

UNDERSTANDING

Answer each question and complete each exercise

SECTION **1**

1. **Link** How are the Beatitudes and the Commandments related?
2. **Explain** Why does natural law have the force of law?
3. **Elaborate** Why is God's using us in his plan for salvation not a sign of human weakness?

SECTION **2**

4. **Explain** What is the connection between the Incarnation and our moral lives?
5. **Link** Why is Saint Damien of Molokai a good model for us?
6. **Describe** What does our dignity require of us?
7. **Trace** How does developing a conscience lead to greater personal freedom?

SECTION **3**

8. **Connect** How does leading a moral life transform our relationship with God?
9. **Explain** What idea do the Beatitudes contradict?
10. **Summarize** What four ways characterize the happiness of God to which we are called?

SECTION **4**

11. **Outline** How do Baptism, Confirmation, and Eucharist relate to morality?
12. **Explain** How do we show our identification with Christ?
13. **List** What does each of the Seven Sacraments signify?
14. **Connect** How do the Sacraments strengthen us to be the people God intended?

ADVANCE REVIEW COPY

CONNECTING

Visual This photo from the Easter Vigil shows a person receiving one of the Sacraments of Initiation.

Which Sacrament is this young man receiving? What happens when this Sacrament takes place? How are the Sacraments of Initiation connected to the Christian moral life?

Challenge Explain the reasons why the Catholic faith would disagree with someone who says "I don't need the Commandments, the Bible, or the Church telling me what's right and wrong. I can figure it out on my own." Use material from this chapter in your answer.

Question After completing this chapter, how would you answer someone who thinks that living a moral life restricts one's freedom?

Imagine You have been assigned to be the producer of a short video about following one of the Beatitudes today. Answer these questions as you plan the video.

- Which Beatitude would you want to portray?

- Would you use animation or live action to portray these teachings? If you prefer live action, which famous people today would you want to be in the video, or would you use faces that are unknown?

- Which popular songs would be appropriate to include?

- What would you put in the script?

SELF-ASSESS

On Your Own Make a list of the most important things you learned from this chapter. Select three things that represent your growth in understanding as you worked through this chapter. Write a paragraph explaining your choices.

With a Partner List what you found most helpful or interesting in this chapter as well as any other questions that have surfaced.

- How can this picture symbolize creation?
- How does this picture symbolize truth and/or the reality of sin?

The Reality of Sin

ADVANCE REVIEW COPY

- Explore the state of original innocence before the Fall.

- List the consequences of the disobedience of our first parents.

- Examine how all humans share in the effects of Original Sin.

- Define sin and discover its basis on disobedience against God.

- Classify sins according to their gravity.

- Learn the true meaning of freedom and how to exercise it.

- Name what is required of a morally good action.

- Recognize that human nature is inclined toward the truth.

- Study what gives humans dignity.

- Learn the keys to moral decision-making.

ADVANCE REVIEW COPY

Original Innocence and Original Sin

KEY TERMS IN THIS SECTION

original innocence the state after creation but before the Fall when mankind lived in harmony with God and participated in his interior life

Original Holiness the initial state of our first parents in which they had a share in the divine life

Original Justice the harmony between God, our first parents, and all creation

self-assertion the promotion of ourselves, our views, and our ideas contrary to the dictates of reason

The Book of Genesis opens with the words, "In the beginning, when God created the heavens and the earth. . . ." (Genesis 1:1). It then describes the Creator's work in creating day and night, separating the dry land from the waters, fashioning the stars and planets, giving life to all the creatures of the Earth. Finally, on the sixth day, God created man.

> Then God said: 'Let us make humankind in our image, according to our likeness; and let them have dominion over the fish of the sea, and over the birds of the air, and over the cattle, and over all the wild animals of the earth, and over every creeping thing that creeps upon the earth.'

—Genesis 1:26

Man and woman were created for each other. They are created to be a communion of person, or helpmates. They are equal as people and complementary as male and female. In marriage, a man and woman unite to become one, and they can bring children into the world.

QUOTATION TO BE INCLUDED IN FINAL PRINTING.

(*Catechism of the Catholic Church*, 372).

God spoke to the first humans made in his image and likeness. He told them to populate the Earth and to subdue the Earth as the planet's stewards (see CCC, 373). God gave them the plants and fruit trees for food. And then, Genesis tells

us that "God saw everything that he had made, and, indeed, it was very good" (Genesis 1:31).

In God's original plan, man and woman literally lived in a perfect world. This was a state of **original innocence**—humankind's existence before the Fall, prior to Original Sin. This mystery of living in God's grace is a gift. In the words of Blessed Pope John Paul II, it reveals that our "fullness and deepest dimension is determined by grace." It is when we participate in the interior life of God himself. This dimension is the source of our original innocence. Here is how the *Catechism* describes it:

QUOTATION TO BE INCLUDED IN FINAL PRINTING.

—CCC, 374

As we form and inform our moral conscience and commit ourselves to the Christian moral life, it helps to remind ourselves of God's original intent for humans. The Catholic Church, with her authority to interpret Scripture, teaches that our first parents, Adam and Eve, were created in a state of **Original Holiness and Justice**. The grace of Original Holiness was a sharing in the life of God (see CCC, 375). Our first parents were free of the three sources of temptation that have plagued mankind since the Fall to

ADVANCE REVIEW COPY

today, namely, the temptations coming from the world, the flesh, and the devil. So man was free from the triple concupiscence, "The desire of the flesh, the desire of the eyes, and the pride in riches" (1 John 2:16). These subjected people to the pleasures of the senses, the inordinate desire for earthly goods, and **self-assertion**, meaning the promotion of ourselves, contrary to the dictates of reason.

Jesus Christ has redeemed us, but Original Innocence does not describe the world in which we live. Today we live with the effects of Original Sin. In the Lord's Prayer, we pray for God to deliver us from the evil that exists after the Fall. Only through the saving grace of Christ can we understand the impact of Original Sin. Through God's Revelation, the reality of sin gradually became apparent. The ancient Israelites—the Chosen People of God—couldn't fully comprehend the meaning of the account of the Fall although they attempted to discern the wounded human condition.

QUOTATION TO BE
INCLUDED IN FINAL PRINTING.

—CCC, 388

Original Sin is an essential truth of the faith, and the *Catechism* describes it as

QUOTATION TO BE
INCLUDED IN FINAL PRINTING.

(CCC, 389).

Original Sin is the disobedience against God by our first parents who chose to follow their will rather than God's. In this way, they lost the state of Original Holiness and became subject to death. These impacts where inherited by all human beings.

The Fall, as recorded in the figurative language of Genesis Chapter 3, affirms

QUOTATION TO BE
INCLUDED IN FINAL PRINTING.

(CCC, 390).

The grace of Original Holiness before the Fall was a sharing in the life of God.

Sin and God's Love

From the account of creation and the Fall, we learn how sin entered into the world. It helps to understand where evil, pain, sickness, and death originate. They all have their origins in one source—the reality of Original Sin. Man chose to disobey God's command and in doing so let his trust in the Creator die. This was the first sin.

QUOTATION TO BE
INCLUDED IN FINAL PRINTING.

(CCC, 397). Man chose himself over God. The state of holiness was lost as man sought to be like God, but

(CCC, 398).

Scripture discusses the consequences of this disobedience.

- Immediately, Adam and Eve are afraid of God and have a distorted view of him, that of a jealous God (see CCC, 399).

- The harmony of Original Justice is gone.

- The control of the soul's spiritual abilities over the body is broken.

REFLECT

People are still impacted by the Original Sin of our first parents.

- Can you see the effects of Original Sin in the world today? Explain.

- What are the signs in your everyday life that "something is wrong?"

Statistical studies of Internet crime report that young people have been more involved with sinful use of this technology than other age groups. Young people have grown up with computers; the temptations can be much greater for them. Adults, however, are also participating in sinful use of the Internet. Statistics released in 2012 reported that:

- Every second, 28,258 Internet users are viewing pornography
- The largest group of Internet porn "consumers" is young people aged 12 to 17
- More than half of all American children, aged 8 to 14, have been involved in a cyber bullying incident
- More than ten million Americans a year are victims of identity theft through checking or credit card account fraud.

It is a complex world full of new potential but new temptations too. It's even more important to hear and follow Saint Paul's 2,000-year-old advice to the people of Ephesus who were battling different temptations. "Therefore take up the whole armor of God, so that you may be able to withstand on that evil day, and having done everything, to stand firm" (Ephesians 6:13).

Name and briefly describe the leading sinful uses of the Internet being reported today.

What is cyberbullying? Explain how this sin is being committed?

One click can yield positive information or sinful practice.

Faith & Culture

➚ Go to the student site at **hs.osvcurriculum.com**

- The union of man and woman is now filled with tensions, lust, and domination.

- Harmony among creation is shattered and subject to decay.

- Finally, man will return to the ground as death enters human history (see CCC, 400).

Sin and corruption follow the history of the Israelites and humans in general. We can see this in our own experience as we feel the attraction to do what is evil—things that cannot come from our good Creator (see CCC, 401). Just as we all sin through the sin of our first parents, we are universally saved through Christ.

> Therefore just as one man's trespass led to condemnation for all, so one man's act of righteousness leads to justification and life for all. For just as by the one man's disobedience the many were made sinners, so by the one man's obedience the many will be made righteous.
>
> —Romans 5:18-19

Let's look again at the theological foundations of our Catholic morality. The *Catechism* discusses how Original Sin is transmitted to all humans.

QUOTATION TO BE INCLUDED IN FINAL PRINTING.

(CCC, 404). We are all implicated through Adam's sin, just as we are all saved through Christ's justice. Still, the transmission of Original Sin is a mystery and cannot be fully explained. We know that our first parents committed the Original Sin that impacted human nature and was transmitted to all mankind.

QUOTATION TO BE INCLUDED IN FINAL PRINTING.

—CCC, 404

ADVANCE REVIEW COPY

It's important to remember too that human nature has not been completely corrupted. It is wounded and subject to ignorance, suffering, and death as well as inclined to sin. Baptism, by imparting Christ's grace, erases Original Sin,

(CCC, 405).

(CCC, 405).

Sin is an offense against God. It is a failure to respond to his love as Christ has made it known to us. Sin may begin at a personal level but it never ends there. Sin also injures the entire Body of Christ. Therefore, our failures at loving—God, others, and even ourselves—are what Christianity calls sin.

Saint Paul, the Apostle to the Gentiles, wrote the following reflection about his own tendency toward sinfulness:

> I am of the flesh, sold into slavery under sin. I do not understand my own actions. For I do not do what I want, but I do the very thing I hate.
>
> —Romans 7:14-15

Saint Paul speaks for all of us when he admits to giving in to what he calls the "sin that dwells within me" (Romans 7:20). The pull of sin is a powerful force within us. Our wounded nature occurs not through God's handiwork but through human beings abusing their freedom and disobeying him.

Original Sin has wounded human beings and cries out for a redeemer to restore the human condition back to its original state. As creation first occurred at God's hands, so new creation occurs through a Redeemer—Jesus Christ, who is one with the Father and the Holy Spirit. Therefore, Adam and Eve's sin leads directly to Jesus' Paschal Mystery, which won redemption for humanity. This is the Good News. Living as Christ taught us is the Way. This is what frames our commitment to moral living.

Describe What was the state of original innocence?

Explain What were the consequences of the sin of our first parents?

SECTION 1 REVIEW

QUICK REVIEW

1a. Recall Describe human life before the Fall.

b. Link Why couldn't the ancient Israelites comprehend the meaning of Original Sin?

2a. Show How does Original Sin plague the world?

b. Describe What has God revealed about how Original Sin is transmitted to all people?

c. Link How did Saint Paul describe sin?

3a. Recount Why is there sin in the world?

b. Restate How are the actions of Adam and the actions of Christ connected?

Listen and Discuss Discuss the effects of Original Sin.

- Write several short observations before beginning the discussion.
- Share your thoughts, and then listen to those of your classmates.
- Report your groups' main points to the entire class.

Pray Compose a short prayer thanking Jesus for redeeming mankind.

SELF-ASSESS

Which statement best reflects where you are now?

☐ I'm confident enough about the material in this section to be able to explain it to someone else.

☐ I have a good grasp of the material in this section, but I could use more review.

☐ I'm lost. I need help catching up before moving on.

Sin and the Mercy of God

KEY TERMS IN THIS SECTION

venial sin an action that weakens our relationship with God;

(CCC, 1855)

mortal sin an action so destructive that it mortally wounds our relationship with God; complete rejection of God;

(CCC,

1855) It turns us away from God by preferring an inferior good to God

sin of commission purposely doing an action that is harmful to oneself or another thereby violating charity and offending God

sin of omission not doing an action that is called for. This violates charity and offends God and neighbor

Hell

(CCC, Glossary, p. 881)

The Catholic Church's role is to carry on the saving mission of Christ. The Church is the light for our way, especially when we have to confront evil and try to avoid sin. We need to see clearly in order to journey safely toward God. So to live a moral life, we must learn how sin works and how it can plunge us into darkness.

Sin is not just an unfortunate choice. The *Catechism* makes it clear:

QUOTATION TO BE
INCLUDED IN FINAL PRINTING.

—CCC, 1849

Saint Paul lists many kinds of sin in his Letter to the Galatians. We ought to recognize these sins because those who commit sins of the flesh will not inherit the Kingdom of God. He condemns fornication, impurity, licentiousness, idolatry, sorcery, enmities, strife, jealousy, anger, quarrels, dissensions, factions, envy, drunkenness, carousing, and other things like these (see Galatians 5:19-20).

" By contrast, the fruit of the Spirit is love, joy, peace, patience, kindness, generosity, faithfulness, gentleness, and self-control. There is no law against such things.

—Galatians 5:22-23

Sin offends God and turns our hearts away from his love. It keeps the Fruit of the Holy Spirit from growing in our lives. It echoes the sin of our first parents:

QUOTATION TO BE
INCLUDED IN FINAL PRINTING.

—CCC, 1850

Television and the media can be positive forces in our lives unless we gain a perverse attachment to them.

ADVANCE REVIEW COPY

PRIMARY SOURCES

Pope Benedict XVI spoke to the young people of Malta on Valetta Waterfront in April 2010. He retold the account of Saint Paul, once a persecutor of Christians who, on his way to Damascus, had a powerful encounter with Christ. Saint Paul was transformed by the Lord so that for the rest of his life he served as a disciple, Apostle, and missionary in places like Malta. Here is an excerpt of what the Pope said to the young people.

"Every personal encounter with Jesus is an overwhelming experience of love. Previously, as Paul himself admits, he had 'persecuted the church of God violently and tried to destroy it' (Gal 1:13). But the hatred and anger expressed in those words was completely swept away by the power of Christ's love. For the rest of his life, Paul had a burning desire to carry the news of that love to the ends of the earth.

"Maybe some of you will say to me, Saint Paul is often severe in his writings. How can I say that he was spreading a message of love? My answer is this. God loves every one of us with a depth and intensity that we can hardly begin to imagine. And he knows us intimately; he knows all our strengths and all our faults. Because he loves us so much, he wants to purify us of our faults and build up our virtues so that we can have life in abundance. When he challenges us because something in our lives is displeasing to him, he is not rejecting us, but he is asking us to change and become more perfect. That is what he asked of Saint Paul on the road to Damascus. God rejects no one. And the Church rejects no one. Yet in his great love, God challenges all of us to change and to become more perfect.

"Saint John tells us that perfect love casts out fear (cf. 1 Jn 4:18). And so I say to all of you, 'Do not be afraid!' How many times we hear those words in the Scriptures! They are addressed by the angel to Mary at the Annunciation, by Jesus to Peter when calling him to be a disciple, and by the angel to Paul on the eve of his shipwreck. To all of you who wish to follow Christ, as married couples, as parents, as priests, as religious, as lay faithful bringing the message of the Gospel to the world, I say, do not be afraid! You may well encounter opposition to the Gospel message. Today's culture, like every culture, promotes ideas and values that are sometimes at variance with those lived and preached by our Lord Jesus Christ. Often they are presented with great persuasive power, reinforced by the media and by social pressure from groups hostile to the Christian faith. It is easy, when we are young and impressionable, to be swayed by our peers to accept ideas and values that we know are not what the Lord truly wants for us. That is why I say to you: do not be afraid, but rejoice in his love for you; trust him, answer his call to discipleship, and find nourishment and spiritual healing in the sacraments of the Church."

➚ Go to the student site at
hs.osvcurriculum.com

When have you felt at odds with today's culture?

Why do you think the Scriptures use the phrase "Do not be afraid" so much?

How can you bring the culture around you into a better relationship with Jesus Christ?

Pope Benedict XVI prepares to address young people in Malta in April 2010.

The root of sin is in our hearts. Evil thoughts are where sin grows.

QUOTATION TO BE
INCLUDED IN FINAL PRINTING.

(CCC, 1853).

We can see how sin manifests its violence by looking at Christ's Passion. When Jesus' mercy is about to conquer it, sin shows itself most clearly in many forms, including unbelief, murderous hatred, mockery, the cowardice of Pilate, the torture of Jesus, Judas' betrayal, Peter's denial of Jesus, and the flight in fear of the Apostles.

QUOTATION TO BE
INCLUDED IN FINAL PRINTING.

(CCC, 1851).

The Catholic Church teaches that

(CCC, 1854). Sins can be viewed according to their degree of seriousness—less serious sins are called **venial sins**; the most serious sins are called mortal, deadly, or grave sins. While venial sins are like wounds to our relationship with God, **mortal sins**—as the term implies—are destructive because they mortally wound our relationship with God.

In addition, we can classify sin as doing something wrong—a **sin of commission**—or not doing something that we should do—a **sin of omission**. Persons, places, or things that can lead us into sin because of our weakened human situation are called occasions of sin. For example, a recovering alcoholic who frequents a bar is in a place where he would be tempted to sin.

QUOTATION TO BE
INCLUDED IN FINAL PRINTING.

—CCC, 1853

Other ways to classify sins is whether they relate primarily to our relationship with God, our neighbor, or ourselves. Then they can be divided into whether they are physical sins, spiritual sins, or sins in

(CCC, 1853). Sin originates in our hearts, and is freely chosen. Goodness and love also come from the heart.

This discussion of sin is meant to loosen its power over us. We seek to identify and acknowledge sin insofar as it prevents us from cooperating with the Holy Spirit at work in us.

Define What is sin?

Recall What are some ways we can classify sin?

Mortal Sin

When we talk about our Christian life and the place of sin in our life, we are talking about our relationship with God. Mortal sin deprives a person of sanctifying grace or the state of grace.

A sin is mortal when it meets three conditions: it must involve   it must be done with full knowledge, and the one performing the action must do so deliberately with full consent of the will (CCC, 1857). The *Catechism* points out that

(CCC, 1861). In other words, we have the freedom to reject God completely and forever. Freely and forever saying no to God's love results in our exclusion from God's eternal presence in Heaven and our living forever without God's presence in **Hell**.

Mortal sin contradicts the love of God and the love of neighbor.

QUOTATION TO BE
INCLUDED IN FINAL PRINTING.

(CCC, 1856). When mortal sin takes place, a new initiative of God's mercy and a conversion of heart is necessary. This is normally done through the Sacrament of Reconciliation.

(CCC, 1861). God wants all of us with him forever, and thus repentance and God's forgiveness are always available to those who truly seek eternal life with God. This is why mortal sins must be confessed in the Sacrament of Reconciliation. Finally, we need to keep in mind that although we can judge an action to be a grave sin:

(CCC, 1861).

ADVANCE REVIEW COPY

Venial Sin

Many of our sinful actions are not so serious as to be considered mortal. However, the smaller sins we commit do weaken our relationship with God. Venial sins often result from bad habits or laziness. Repeated venial sins weaken our charity and ability to avoid sinning in the future. They manifest a disordered attachment to created goods and impede our growth in virtue and the practice of morally good actions. Venial sin doesn't take away sanctifying grace. But unless we work at overcoming venial sins, we could eventually find ourselves turning completely away from God through mortal sin (see CCC, 1863). Saint Augustine emphasizes the hope we find in the Sacrament of Penance.

QUOTATION TO BE
INCLUDED IN FINAL PRINTING.

—CCC, 1863

We commit venial sins when to a lesser degree we do not observe the moral law or when we disobey QUOTATION TO BE INCLUDED IN FINAL PRINTING. (CCC, 1862).

Jesus tells us that all sins can be forgiven except one. "Whoever blasphemes against the Holy Spirit can never have forgiveness, but is guilty of an eternal sin" (Mark 3:29). The *Catechism* explains it this way:

QUOTATION TO BE
INCLUDED IN FINAL PRINTING.

—CCC, 1864

Sin has to do with the way we treat God in our relationships with him and our neighbor; it does not describe his relationship with us. We may do many things to reject God, but he never rejects us. We look to Jesus who died for us on the Cross, and we know that God is ever-faithful to us—ever-forgiving, and ever-loving.

DISCUSS

- Choose one of the capital sins to research in terms of its impact on society. How do we see the presence of avarice, anger, gluttony, etc., in the news or crime reports?
- Discuss a sin of omission that might be particularly common among teens. Brainstorm ways to address this sinful refusal to do what is right.

The Effects of Sin

When we look at the effects of sin, we can see how they can block our way to eternal happiness with God. Our actions flow from who we are. In the words of the *Catechism*,

QUOTATION TO BE
INCLUDED IN FINAL PRINTING. (CCC, 1865).

We need to examine our overall life patterns, ascertain the fundamental direction of our lives, and determine whether we are heading in the direction God wants for us. Our actions make a statement about where we are going. It's helpful at times to step back and look at the patterns of behavior that we have established for ourselves.

There are capital sins, sometimes called the deadly sins, that give rise to other sins. The seven capital sins are pride, avarice, envy, wrath, lust, gluttony, and sloth (see CCC, 1866). The *Catechism* points out that Scripture describes many sins and provides lists of them. One we already discussed is from the Letter to the Galatians (see CCC, 1852). There are also the sins that Scripture says cry out to Heaven. These include the killing of Abel by his brother Cain, the sin of the Sodomites, the oppression by Egypt of the ancient Hebrew slaves; and injustice toward the migrant, the widow, the orphan, and the laborer (see CCC, 1867).

We have discussed sin as a personal act, but we also have responsibility for others' sins when we have cooperated in these sins in the following ways:

- QUOTATION TO BE INCLUDED IN FINAL PRINTING.
- QUOTATION TO BE INCLUDED IN FINAL PRINTING.
- QUOTATION TO BE INCLUDED IN FINAL PRINTING.
- QUOTATION TO BE INCLUDED IN FINAL PRINTING. (CCC, 1868).

Social ANALYSIS

" Do not conform yourself to this age but be transformed by the renewal of your mind, that you may discern what is the will of God, what is good and pleasing and perfect. "

—Romans 12:2

You know Christ has called us to work with God as he builds his Kingdom here on Earth. The practice of social analysis helps us become aware of the world around us and meet the needs of our time. This practice challenges us to *pay attention* to the concerns and behaviors beyond our own. This spiritual practice is related to what the bishops of our Church call "faithful citizenship."

When you practice social analysis you try to see things through Christ's eyes and support the actions and values he would support. To live our faith fully, we are expected to be aware of the world around us and how others live.

The hectic pace of your life doesn't make this practice easy. You are too busy to pay attention to anything but the stuff you have to deal with in your own life. And since we get information so rapidly, we quickly think we understand something – when in fact we don't know enough.

Many people have come up with concrete ways to practice social analysis. Here's one way to do it: **Look**, **Listen**, **Ask**, **Act**.

Look up from your own preoccupations. Look into the issues people are discussing. Look beyond standard sources of info.

Listen before you make up your mind. Listen to what people you trust are saying. Listen for what the Bible and the Church say.

Ask questions: What causes this? Who's proposing what response? Ask yourself: What do I think? Why do I think this way? What don't I understand? Ask: Who gets hurt? Who gets helped?

Act by expressing your opinion. Act on the situation when you can. Act locally. Act with a group to get more done. Act by praying for those involved.

WWJD?

What issues or situations might deserve social analysis from you at the time?

When can you get to it? What are your first two steps?

ADVANCE REVIEW COPY

From individual sins arise social situations, institutions, or groups that act in variance with God's designs. They may contain policies and practices that lead to situations of injustice. These

(CCC, 1868). Personal sins predispose us to and lead us to these sort of social sins.

QUOTATION TO BE
INCLUDED IN FINAL PRINTING.

—CCC, 1869

We sin when we act contrary to God, who dwells in us, and when we violate people around us. When we choose not to love others, we affect our relationship with God.

REFLECT

Awareness of sin is important to live the moral life.

- How has this section helped you become aware of sin in your life and in the world?

- How can this awareness of sin impact your relationship with God?

So when you are offering your gift at the altar, if you remember that your brother or sister has something against you, leave your gift there before the altar and go; first be reconciled to your brother or sister, and then come and offer your gift.

—Matthew 5:23-24

Recall After a mortal sin has been committed, what is necessary to restore our relationship with God?

Identify In what ways can we be responsible for other people's sins?

SECTION 2 REVIEW

QUICK REVIEW

1a. Define How do you define sin?

b. Link What similarity does sin today have with the sins of our first parents?

c. Explain How did sin manifest itself during Jesus' Passion?

d. Describe How does the Church classify sins according to their gravity? What kinds of sins are there?

2a. Compare and Contrast How are mortal sin and venial sin alike and different?

b. Recall What does mortal sin do to a person who commits it?

c. List What are the criteria for mortal sin?

3a. Consider Why do people commit venial sins?

b. List When are we responsible for others' sins?

Listen and Discuss With a small group of classmates, discuss occasions of sin.

- Why are the occasions of sin different for different people?

- What are some common occasions of sin among young people today? Remember to keep your discussion in the abstract and not point to particular people's weaknesses.

- What are some ways to avoid occasions of sin?

Pray Compose a short prayer asking the Holy Spirit to help you avoid occasions of sin.

SELF-ASSESS

Which statement best reflects where you are now?

☐ I'm confident enough about the material in this section to be able to explain it to someone else.

☐ I have a good grasp of the material in this section, but I could use more review.

☐ I'm lost. I need help catching up before moving on.

Freedom and Morality

KEY TERMS IN THIS SECTION

apathy an attitude of not getting involved, not caring, not acting when action is called for

Along with the advantages of today's technology, we face challenges from immoral situations on the Internet, social media, among friends, and at work. Living a moral life is as challenging today as it has ever been.

God calls us to live a moral life and gives us the grace to do so. Living by the dictates of the Ten Commandments and the Beatitudes enables us to lead a morally upright life by uniting ourselves with Christ's Paschal Mystery. Jesus' suffering, Death, Resurrection, and Ascension into Heaven show his love for us, challenge us to love in a morally upright way, and invite us to share real happiness that can be found in following him.

Living in a moral way is difficult because human nature, wounded by Original Sin, often pulls us in a different direction. Temptations to greed, pride, lust, and other sins of the senses can steer us off the road that we must take to live a moral life. The next two sections of this book consider some of these challenges. They may come from friends, family members, the social media, the Internet, or peers who tell us that:

- we don't need God to help us decide what is right or wrong, because we are created free and can make up our mind.

- we should not judge another person's actions as right or wrong, because morality is relative, everyone has a conscience, and can decide for oneself what is right or wrong.

- we need not take the Catholic Church's teachings seriously because it is not her role to impose moral teachings on the world.

- we can pick and choose what Church teachings to follow, thus limiting the role of God and the Church in our lives, because we control our lives as free people.

- we need not worry about helping others until we first take care of ourselves and our loved ones.

Right and Wrong

Some people may jump to the conclusion that since God created us free, we can decide on our own what is right and wrong. Freedom, as we've learned, is more than getting to choose or do whatever you want to. Freedom is a gift to us as creatures that can reason and practice

Life today presents us with challenges and temptations.

ADVANCE REVIEW COPY

free will. Freedom is the power to act or not to act through our deliberate decisions. We are responsible for them. Until freedom binds itself definitively to God, who is the ultimate good, there is the possibility of

(CCC, 1732). This freedom characterizes proper human actions.

QUOTATION TO BE INCLUDED IN FINAL PRINTING.

(CCC, 1733).

We have to remember that we are responsible for all of our actions done voluntarily. In addition, an action can be indirectly voluntary if

(CCC, 1736).

An example would be an accident that happened because we ignored a speed limit or some other traffic law.

Right to Exercise Freedom

We have reiterated that every one of us is created in the image and likeness of God, and therefore has the right to be treated as a free and responsible person. We owe each other this respect. Some nations have treated the exercise of freedom as a right, and an inalienable requirement of the dignity of people.

(CCC, 1738).

The Catholic Church and other religions have been concerned about an erosion of religious freedom. Catholic dioceses and organizations in the United States sued the federal government in 2012 asking that the government protect the right to exercise religious freedom. Specifically, the lawsuit centered on new government regulations that would require insurance plans to cover contraception and abortion-inducing drugs, both of which are contrary to Catholic Church teaching. In previous laws, there was always a clause to allow those who opposed this coverage for religious reasons to opt out and follow their right to exercise freedom of conscience.

In the Bill of Rights, the very first freedom guaranteed by the U.S. Constitution is religion: "Congress shall make no law respecting an establishment of religion, or prohibiting the free exercise thereof."

Archbishop William E. Lori of Baltimore said the Catholic Church has always promoted the free exercise of religion and social justice policies that benefit the common good of everybody—individuals and groups. He explained that the common good protects families, churches, and institutions that stand between the power of government and the individual's conscience. He said government has the responsibility to recognize this role to protect the common good. Religious institutions, he said, serve not only their own members, but also the rest of society.

"[P]rotecting the rights and human dignity of individuals and serving the common good through a network of organized charities and schools are a deeply engrained part of the Church's mission, not a sideline, not a secular business component, and not an optional extra. The Church serves those in need not because *they* are Catholic but because *we* are. The Church has done this from the beginning even when her members suffered persecution at the hands of Roman Emperors.

—Archbishop William E. Lori, Rome, June 2012

Education for Freedom

We first learn to exercise our freedom as we grow up in our families. Recall that the family is a basic unit of society, where parents are

(CCC, 2207). The family is where religious education and moral values are initially formed. The authority, stability, and relationships of a family are the basis for freedom, security, and fraternity in our larger society. Family life prepares us for life as adults.

QUOTATION TO BE INCLUDED IN FINAL PRINTING.

(CCC, 2207).

We can learn from what our parents teach us as well as from the good examples they provide. Parents aren't perfect and they should acknowledge their own failings in such a way that children can learn from their mistakes as well. As we grow in our family setting, we should learn the correct ways to reason and exercise our freedom.

At the same time, the Church warns about the mistaken concept of moral permissiveness often seen in today's society. Moral permissiveness is tolerating behaviors that are morally wrong, and it is an abuse of freedom. To have true freedom, we must be educated in the moral law with a well-formed conscience. This begins with the family and continues into adulthood as part of our individual responsibility. Using freedom to do whatever we want robs us of freedom. We become slaves to our own harmful desires and bad habits.

The grace of Christ, however, increases our freedom because we gain through it a sense of the truth and goodness of God that he has placed in our hearts. As discussed earlier, the more open we are to God's grace, the more we grow in inner freedom. We will have spiritual confidence as we face the pressures of life. Through grace, the Holy Spirit educates us in spiritual freedom. We become prepared to do the work of the Lord in the world (see CCC, 1742).

Explain How is freedom more than getting to decide whatever we want to?

Recall How are we responsible for indirectly voluntary actions?

The Church and Natural Law

When the world's Catholic bishops convened in Rome from 1962 to 1965 for the Second Vatican Council, they were particularly concerned about threats to human dignity. Many knew firsthand the dehumanizing nature of fascism, Nazism, and communism. They were also concerned about more subtle attacks on human dignity evident in capitalism, individualism, and consumerism.

The Second Vatican Council document titled, *Gaudium et Spes*, is also called as the "Pastoral Constitution on the Church in the Modern World." It teaches that conscience represents an essential element of human dignity that should be cultivated and followed in moral decision-making (see *Gaudium et Spes*, 16).

The document summarizes the Catholic Church's understanding of moral conscience as an exercise of free will. It is a human action grounded in our human dignity that is itself the action of a judicious and loving God. The Church affirms the importance of conscience in order to live a moral life and reach eternal happiness in Heaven. Here is what Church documents have stated in response to three fundamental questions about conscience.

- Are we called upon to act and live conscientiously, that is, in accord with goodness and truth? The *Catechism* states,
  QUOTATION TO BE INCLUDED IN FINAL PRINTING. (CCC, 1778).

- Should we think through our decisions and not act solely out of blind obedience or on whim and feelings? "Hence, the more a correct conscience prevails, the more do persons and groups turn aside from blind choice and endeavor to conform to the objective standards of moral conduct" (USCCB, *The Role of the Conscience*, p. 1).

- Should we act according to the dictates of an informed and developed conscience in our moral decision-making?
  QUOTATION TO BE INCLUDED IN FINAL PRINTING. (CCC, 1782).

We have the freedom from God to choose what is right, true, and good as well as resist temptation to sin. It is not a matter of doing whatever we want. Recall how the *Catechism* describes our conscience:

QUOTATION TO BE
INCLUDED IN FINAL PRINTING.

—CCC, 1776

God created us with the power of freedom. We are free to act as we choose, but our freedom is limited (see CCC, 1739). As long as our freedom is not linked definitively to the ultimate good, which is God, then there is the possibility of

ADVANCE REVIEW COPY

choosing between good and evil. If we are completely bound to God, we could only choose good. Until we get to that point, we must continue our lifelong pattern of growing in perfection or of making bad choices and sinning.

QUOTATION TO BE
INCLUDED IN FINAL PRINTING.
(CCC, 1732).

Freedom then means we follow the natural moral law that God has planted in our hearts. Our sins take away freedom whereas moral acts increase it. This is why the Church teaches that true freedom is choosing what is good and just. Choosing to do evil actions abuses the freedom we've been given (see CCC, 1733).

We have learned that the natural law

QUOTATION TO BE
INCLUDED IN FINAL PRINTING.
(CCC, 1954). Through this ability that God placed in us to understand and reason, we use our human reason to direct us to make good decisions and to avoid sinful ones.

We refer to the true natural law as *right reason*. Right reason indicates our duty and prohibitions. We cannot replace it or completely ignore it. Applying natural law can demand a lot of reflection taking into account conditions, circumstances, places, and time. Still, natural law is key to living a moral life as it connects us to each other and gives us common principles (see CCC, 1957). It is a foundation for individual character and freedom and cannot be destroyed or taken from human hearts.

Character development leads to authentic freedom. It's important to speak about authentic freedom since today the definition often gets blurred.

(CCC, 1744).
Freedom and responsibility, however, can be diminished by

(CCC, 1746).

- Ignorance is lack of knowledge, education, or comprehension.
- Duress means threats and/or unlawful or forcible restraints.

- Fear can be brought about by real and imagined dangers.
- Psychological factors include mental and emotional problems or limitations.
- Social factors include the violation of economic, political, and other conditions needed for the exercise of freedom.

The   is inherent in our dignity as humans (CCC, 1747). Put simply, authentic freedom includes having a sense of who we are called to be and what we are called to do. Freedom includes having the stamina, the skills, and the inner strength to work toward achieving our goals.

We know that not everyone understands the natural law written in our hearts. We must not remain ignorant and strive to form our conscience well. We need God's grace and revelation to know every moral or religious truth that can be known (see CCC, 1960). To sum it up, freedom is found in following the natural law that God has planted in our hearts.

Name When are we obligated to follow what we know to be just and right?

Describe What happens when our freedom is not linked definitively to God?

Becoming Free From Sin

What about when we see someone doing something wrong? Is it wrong to judge their action and tell them about it? No, in fact, we have the responsibility to do so. The right way would be to exercise the virtue of prudence, seek the wisdom of the Holy Spirit, and sometimes even to discern the situation with a competent person (see CCC, 1788).

REFLECT

Think about a time when you felt very free.

- Were there events that seemed to create that sense of freedom?
- How did you react and grow from the experience?

Saint Mary Faustina

(1905–1938)

Leading a moral life creates the need to seek mercy from God and others as well as to practice mercy toward others. While the concept of Divine Mercy was not new, Saint Mary Faustina, the first saint of the new millennium, tremendously increased the devotion to Divine Mercy.

Through communication with Christ, Saint Faustina has brought to the world the great message of God's mercy so that we can know how to live the Christian moral life with an attitude of mercy toward each other.

Saint Faustina was born with the name Helena Kowalski on August 25, 1905, in Glogowiec, Poland. She was the third of ten children born into a family of peasants. In 1925, Helena joined the Congregation of the Sisters of Our Lady of Mercy and took the name Sister Mary Faustina. She didn't have much education and led a life performing daily tasks and observing the rule of religious life, which hid an inner spiritual life and an extraordinary union with God. She contemplated and studied the mystery of God's mercy, which helped Sister Mary Faustina develop trust in God and to have mercy toward others.

Sister Mary Faustina kept a diary of communication with and reflections on Christ. In an excerpt from Diary 1242,

ADVANCE REVIEW COPY

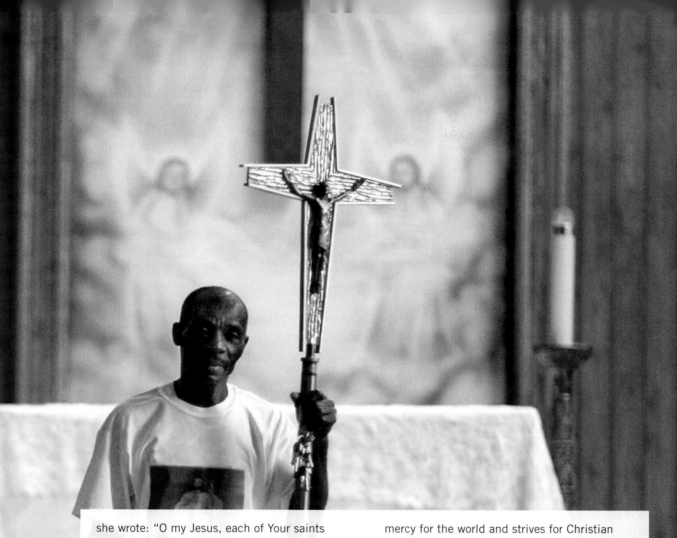

she wrote: "O my Jesus, each of Your saints reflects one of Your virtues; I desire to reflect Your compassionate heart, full of mercy; I want to glorify it. Let Your mercy, O Jesus, be impressed upon my heart and soul like a seal, and this will be my badge in this and the future life."

At the convent, Sister Faustina experienced extraordinary gifts, but she wrote that her holiness and perfection came only from the union of her will with the will of God. The Lord wanted to heal the human race rather than punish us, and he chose Sister Mary Faustina to convey his message about his mercy.

Her mission included:

- reminding the world of the truth of our faith about the merciful love of God toward all human beings

- asking for God's mercy for the whole world and particularly for sinners, among others through the practice of new forms of devotion to the Divine Mercy presented by Jesus

- initiating the apostolic movement of the Divine Mercy which proclaims and prays for God's

mercy for the world and strives for Christian perfection

Sister Mary Faustina died of tuberculosis on October 5, 1938, in Krakow, Poland. She was 33 years old. The Divine Mercy movement has grown ever since, and her diary has been translated into many languages. Saint Mary Faustina was canonized by Blessed Pope John Paul II on April 30, 2000. The second Sunday of Easter is Divine Mercy Sunday.

Think About It What part has mercy played in your life? When has the Divine Mercy of Christ been offered to you? How does mercy help us heal as humans? How does mercy strengthen our relationship with God and with each other?

Go to the student site at
hs.osvcurriculum.com

We must encourage each other to live a life free from sin. We must be willing to say that something is sinful. Correcting others in this way is an act of charity (see CCC, 1793). In order to do that, we must be aware of what sin is, what causes it, and what are its consequences. We would warn someone if they were doing something dangerous, and it is the same way with sin because while it may not hurt them physically, the spiritual consequences are dire (see CCC, 1787).

We have to correct our conscience when we become aware of its errors. We will grow in charity because charity comes from a good and pure conscience enlightened by faith.

QUOTATION TO BE
INCLUDED IN FINAL PRINTING.

—CCC, 1794

The Sacrament of Reconciliation restores our relationship with God.

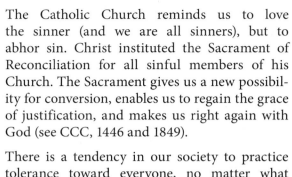

The Catholic Church reminds us to love the sinner (and we are all sinners), but to abhor sin. Christ instituted the Sacrament of Reconciliation for all sinful members of his Church. The Sacrament gives us a new possibility for conversion, enables us to regain the grace of justification, and makes us right again with God (see CCC, 1446 and 1849).

There is a tendency in our society to practice tolerance toward everyone, no matter what they do. This distorts the meaning of tolerance because moral actions must always be measured with truth. Still, we have studied the need to avoid rash judgment. In fact, we need to give people the benefit of the doubt when don't have the whole story.

QUOTATION TO BE
INCLUDED IN FINAL PRINTING.

(CCC, 2478). We also need to avoid thinking of ourselves as better than others, since we all sin and all have room to grow in perfection.

Most of us don't want to tell other people that their choices and actions aren't pleasing to God. As we just mentioned, in our modern society, a dangerous sort of moral relativism is common so we must understand what it means. This belief suggests that everyone has his or her own unique moral code and that morality is relative, varying from situation to situation and depending only on choice. Moral relativism leads to chaos and denies the existence of a universal moral code. Moral relativism says, "What's wrong for me might be OK to you."

We must always seek the truth, but also decide when to share that truth. Not everyone has a right to know all of the truth in every situation. We must act with love for others, and that requires us to decide whether to share with the truth with someone who asks (see CCC, 2488). Love and respect should dictate the response to an inquiry to the truth, but there are reasons to withhold information as well.

QUOTATION TO BE
INCLUDED IN FINAL PRINTING.

(CCC, 2489).

ADVANCE REVIEW COPY

The account of the woman caught in adultery is an example of loving the sinner.

Read John 8:1-11.

- How does Jesus show love the sinner in this passage? Is it only for the woman caught in adultery? Explain.

- How could Jesus be speaking to you in the last verse?

The *Catechism* teaches too that the duty to avoid scandal can be a reason for discretion with sharing truth.

QUOTATION TO BE INCLUDED IN FINAL PRINTING.

(CCC, 2489).

This teaching on secrecy is very important for the Sacrament of Reconciliation. The priest cannot reveal what is told to him in confession for any reason. This is called the Seal of Confession. What is told to the priest is "sealed" in his heart and can never be disclosed. Divulging any confession would be a crime against Canon Law.

There are also reasons for professional secrets in government and the workplace. People like government officials, military personnel, doctors, counselors, and lawyers must keep confidential information secret except when it could cause very grave harm to the person who shared the information, the person who received it, or a third party (see CCC, 2491). In everyday life, we must observe appropriate caution regarding other people's private lives. A balance here must be struck between the common good and respect for individual lives.

QUOTATION TO BE INCLUDED IN FINAL PRINTING.

(CCC, 2492).

Traditional Sources of Morality

The decisions that affect our moral life should not be made quickly or without forethought. Being alert to the many factors involved will improve our moral decision-making.

We have the freedom and the wisdom to judge whether an act is good or bad. That wisdom comes from God and his natural law within us. We know that we are endowed with a conscience, and God has given us the Ten Commandments, the Beatitudes, the life and witness of Jesus Christ, and the grace of the Holy Spirit. God has also given us the Church to teach about faith and morals. The Church identifies three traditional sources of morality—the object chosen, the intention, and the circumstances surrounding the act—to help us in the important human task to judge the goodness or evil of an act. It is important to our moral life that we understand this process.

The object chosen refers to the act that we do. Good acts involve feeding the poor, refusing to ridicule a classmate, visiting the sick, telling the truth, and so on. Bad acts involve selling drugs, murder, stealing, deliberately harming another person's reputation, and so on.

The intention refers to our motive or intention in performing an act. It is determined by its end or purpose. Giving a blanket to a homeless person because we are concerned for his well-being is a good act with a good intention. Cleaning a neighbor's house because we want to steal from that neighbor is an example of a good object (or an objectively good action) done with an evil motive or purpose. Murdering a tyrannical dictator because we want to free a nation from oppression is an evil act for what appears to be a good intention. But we cannot justify an evil act performed for good reasons. An evil act is always evil, even when we believe some good could come from it.

The circumstances of an act refer to conditions surrounding the act that affect its goodness or evil. Certain factors can

QUOTATION TO BE INCLUDED IN FINAL PRINTING.

(CCC, 1754). Thus, there are factors that come into play when judging the goodness and evil of an act. Fear, ignorance, and pressure are some examples of these mitigating factors.

We must always recognize that

QUOTATION TO BE INCLUDED IN FINAL PRINTING.

(CCC, 1760). However there are certain acts that are always wrong to choose, such as blasphemy and perjury, murder and adultery.

(CCC, 1761).

Moral decision-making is a matter of judgment, and we have learned what the process takes. Certain practices, especially prayer, can help us make the step from discernment to judgment. During decision-making, prayer adds an important dimension to the process. In prayer, we seek to diminish our self-absorption in order to be more open to God and to his will. Indeed, the goal of every aspect of our moral decision-making is to make the best judgments that we can—that is, judgments in line with the values and teachings of Jesus.

In the Gospels, Jesus sums up the Law in terms of a loving relationship with God and with our neighbor (see Matthew 22:36-40). Therefore, in determining sin from a Gospel-based perspective we need to ask: What effect do my actions have on my relationship with God? How do my actions harm or enhance the people around me and the quality of my relationship with them?

> No one has a right to sit down and feel hopeless. There's too much work to do.
>
> —Dorothy Day, in Peace Prayers (Harper San Francisco, 1992)

The Gospels speak about what we need to *do* as well as about what we should avoid doing. Certainly, we need to avoid wrongdoing. However, we must not overlook positive contributions that we can make in our moral life. In this light, **apathy**—not getting involved, not caring, and not doing what needs to be done—can be sinful. Visiting a friend in the hospital and helping someone who urgently needs help are expressions of our moral life. Not to do these things, as we have discussed, could be considered committing sins of omission.

> When the Nazis came to get the Communists, I was silent because I was not a Communist. When they came to get the Socialists, I was silent. When they came to get the Catholics, I was silent. When they came to get the Jews, I was silent. And when they came to get me, there was no one left to speak.
>
> —Martin Niemoeller in Robert Ellsberg, All Saints (New York: Crossroad, 1997).

REFLECT

Complete each of the following sentences.

Three people with whom I relate on a regular basis are . . .

I enhance their lives when I . . .

I would describe the quality of my relationships with them as . . .

I would harm their lives if I . . .

Bearing Witness to the Truth

When Jesus was being interrogated by Pontius Pilate, he stated his reason for coming into the world: "to testify to the truth. Everyone who belongs to the truth listens to my voice" (John 18:37). Jesus' reason for being, his entire life, was to be a witness to truth. The word *martyr* means witness. Early Christians who recognized Christ's truth refused to deny him. As a consequence many were killed, proclaiming a message of truth by their very blood. We know these witnesses who kept the light of truth alive as the great martyrs of the early Church.

Jesus calls his followers to be witnesses to the truth, by which all moral actions must be measured. Truthfulness is the virtue by which we are true in what we do and truthful in what we say. We are truthful when we choose not to be hypocrites, liars, or frauds. By acting truthfully, Jesus and the martyrs paid with their lives. Today our truthfulness can occasionally exact a heavy price from us, and yet we suffer an even worse fate if we don't align ourselves with truth. Living a lie kills the spirit. Even laziness in the pursuit of truth wounds the soul.

By our very nature, we are inclined toward the truth. Our dignity as human beings requires us to seek the truth and, once we know it, to act in accordance with it. Even though people lie, it's important to realize that telling the truth is the natural human behavior. This will help us in discerning the actions of others, and having the courage to share the truth with them.

Another way to help identify the true moral goodness of an action is to imagine possible effects of different choices that we might make. Our present actions are the seeds out of which future consequences grow.

ADVANCE REVIEW COPY

DISCUSS

What are ways that you and your classmates might approach one of your peers who is clearly involved in sinful behavior? Make a list of "strategies."

Remember, though, that consequences alone do not determine whether an act is good or evil. The consequences of a moral act can, however, increase or decrease the goodness or evil chosen. We cannot know beforehand all that will result from our actions. However, we can envision possible effects. For instance, the excuse "I didn't mean it!" rings hollow from someone who frequently posts objectionable pictures or comments online. Similarly, someone who consistently drives recklessly should not be surprised when an accident happens. In each case, the people involved would benefit from considering possible effects of their actions.

The fast pace of our modern world makes it hard to pay attention to what might be the effects of our actions. A philosophy that states, "If it can be done, then do it" has led to scientific and technological developments, but these developments and their effects have not always benefited humanity. For example, it is unclear what long-term effects will result from genetic manipulation. We would not be acting conscientiously if we didn't attempt to determine the possible repercussions.

Issues such as these, as well as many of our everyday decisions, remind us that our actions have consequences. We are shortsighted when we fail to consider probable effects of our actions. That helps in determining when to intervene if someone's actions are wrong.

Explain How is judging other people's actions and correcting them an act of charity?

Identify Where does our wisdom come from to judge whether an act is good or sinful?

SECTION 3 REVIEW

QUICK REVIEW

1a. **Define** What is freedom?

b. **Explain** How does grace increase our freedom?

c. **Recall** What is moral conscience, according to Catholic teaching?

d. **Name** When does freedom lead to perfection and how can it be diminished?

2. **Distinguish** What is the difference between freedom and license?

3a. **List** What responsibility do we have when we see someone doing something sinful?

b. **Tell** Why is it OK to be silent with the truth sometimes?

4a. **Recall** What are the three sources of morality?

b. **List** What is required of a morally good act?

c. **Describe** How does prayer assist in good decision-making?

d. **Contrast** How does apathy counter positive contributions in our moral life?

5a. **Name** What is the one thing by which all moral actions must be measured?

b. **Analyze** Explain why this statement is true: Consequences do not determine the goodness of an act.

ACT

Write a list of issues that you think a scientist should consider before embarking on an experiment that involves genetic manipulation.

- Consider researching procedures followed in such experiments.
- Talk with your science teachers about the results of such experiments.
- With a group of classmates, compile a list of the issues that you raised individually.

SELF-ASSESS

Which statement best reflects where you are now?

☐ I'm confident enough about the material in this section to be able to explain it to someone else.

☐ I have a good grasp of the material in this section, but I could use more review.

☐ I'm lost. I need help catching up before moving on.

Dignity and Moral Law

Human dignity and the moral law revealed by God are meant for every person. The *Catechism* makes these points about the dignity of the human person:

- Our dignity is rooted in our creation in the image and likeness of God

- Our dignity is fulfilled in our life's work toward eternal happiness with God

- We must freely direct ourselves to fulfilling this vocation

- Through our own chosen actions, we either do or do not conform to the good promised by God and confirmed by our moral conscience

- We make our own contributions to our inner growth by orienting our whole lives toward it

- With the help of grace, we grow in virtue

- We avoid sin, but when we do sin, we entrust ourselves like the Prodigal Son to the mercy of God (see CCC, 1700)

Everyone has the ability to understand the Catholic Church's basic moral teaching because God has written the natural law on our hearts. The natural law, which the *Catechism* calls (CCC, 1959) provides three things:

- It provides the foundation for the moral rules to guide our choices

- It provides the moral foundation for building the human society

- and it provides the basis for civil law (see CCC, 1959)

While natural law is written on our hearts, remember it is not clearly or immediately understood by everyone.

QUOTATION TO BE
INCLUDED IN FINAL PRINTING.

—CCC, 1960

This Salvador Dali painting titled, *St. John of the Cross*, shows Jesus bearing the sins of the world from a unique perspective.

DISCUSS

View the painting, *Christ of St. John of the Cross*, by Spanish painter Salvador Dali in 1951. Inspiration for the unique perspective of Christ, Dali said, came to him in a dream. Discuss and share ideas about: the unusual perspective of the central figure – Jesus; the meaning of the lake, a fishing boat and fishermen in the painting, the absence of nails, blood, crown of thorns usually associated with Christ on the Cross.

ADVANCE REVIEW COPY

Giving Alms

The root of the word "alms" comes from the Old English word "aelmesse" or "aelmes" which means "pity" or "charity" given to the poor. In the Old Testament's *Book of Deuteronomy*, the ancient Jews were told to set aside a tithe or tenth of their crops and produce every three years. The tithe was stored in warehouses for the priests, as well as for the aliens, orphans and widows of their communities. The Book of Psalms is filled with praise to God for sustaining the poor.

The Book of Proverbs of King Solomon, son of King David, reminded the Jewish community about giving generously to the poor. "If you close your ear to the cry of the poor, you will cry out and not be heard" (Proverbs 21:13). In the New Testament, the mandate for almsgiving was made even stronger through Jesus' teaching. In the Gospel of Luke, Jesus told his followers, "'Whoever has two coats must share with anyone who has none; and whoever has food must do likewise'" (Luke 3:11).

One of Jesus' parables was about the rich man and the poor man, Lazarus. Before his death, Jesus said, Lazarus slept by the door of the rich man who was apparently a faithful Jew. But, the rich man was absolutely blind to the poor man and his need, Jesus said. Lazarus would "gladly have eaten his fill of the scraps that fell from the rich man's table." The rich man not only didn't give what he could easily afford, he also completely ignored the presence of the desperately needy man, right on his doorstep. In the parable, Jesus makes it clear that the rich man was condemned for his lack of charity and compassion. Lazarus went to Heaven (see Luke 16:19-31).

Prayer, fasting, and almsgiving can represent spiritual conversion to ourselves, toward God, and to others.

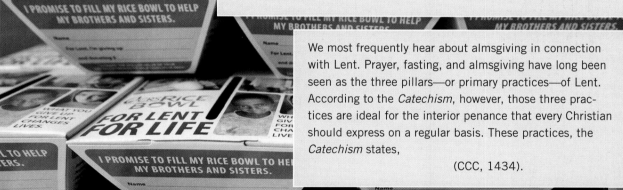

We most frequently hear about almsgiving in connection with Lent. Prayer, fasting, and almsgiving have long been seen as the three pillars—or primary practices—of Lent. According to the *Catechism*, however, those three practices are ideal for the interior penance that every Christian should express on a regular basis. These practices, the *Catechism* states,

(CCC, 1434).

How do we know from the Old Testament that the Law of Moses required the Israelites to help the poor and needy in their communities?

What are the three "pillars of Lent?"

What national and international Catholic organizations serve to meet the needs of the poor?

My Faith

Essentials for a Moral Life

The Old Testament prophet Micah wrote to the People of God:

"He has told you, O Mortal, what is good; and what the LORD requires of you but to do justice, and to love kindness and to walk humbly with your God?"

—Micah 6:8

Take some time with each of these three instructions. They are not meant to cover all God's expectations of us, but they do help us frame up some essentials about the moral life.

Act justly: How would you rate yourself on this? When have you done this well? When have you acted unjustly? What does it take to make this a normal way of life for you?

Love mercy: Would you say that the way you act shows that you love mercy? Why or why not? When have you demonstrated that you love mercy? When have you encouraged someone else to love mercy? When have you desperately needed someone to love mercy but they did not? Who needs you to increase the way you love mercy?

Walk humbly with God: How well do you walk with God in the first place? How humble are you in your relationship with God?

Which of these three instructions from Micah stand out to you the most and why?

Take some time to write yourself some notes.

These My Faith reflections are private. You may choose to include any or none of this in the report you give at the end of the course.

Discipleship ... within the Body of Christ ... for the glory of God and the good of the world.

ADVANCE REVIEW COPY

The Catholic Church teaches what God has revealed about how to live and act and how to treat one another. This is not the Church imposing her views on others. Regarding public policy, the Catholic Church promotes universal moral law and the common good, not her Church rules and disciplines.

The Beatitudes, for example, were given as a response to our longing for happiness. They portray the charity of Christ.

QUOTATION TO BE
INCLUDED IN FINAL PRINTING.

(CCC, 1717). The Beatitudes give us the answer to why we exist, and also tell us how we can reach eternal happiness with God. Since God has put us in the world to know, love, and serve him, the Beatitudes are given to us as a way to meet this calling to eternal happiness (see CCC, 1721).

QUOTATION TO BE
INCLUDED IN FINAL PRINTING.

—CCC, 1723

The Beatitudes are gifts for all people as are the Ten Commandments, the teaching of the Apostles, and the natural moral law. They describe the way that leads to the Kingdom of God. Those who know these revelations must work on them with the grace of God, step by step, in their everyday actions.

The Church teaches that all people must make up their own minds and make their own decisions, but the key is that our moral decisions and actions must be based on an increasingly informed and educated conscience. The Church's role in this is to teach what is right and wrong in an effort to help people educate

GO TO THE SOURCE

Jesus teaches that real love is measured by the degree of generosity we have in giving to and doing for others.

Read Mark 12:38-44.

- Who today resembles the scribes that Jesus describes?
- What was the difference between what the widow put into the collection compared with what others gave?
- When have you sacrificed and given something out of love for others?

their consciences correctly. We always have to remember that God knows, sees, and understands more than any of us. We are limited. We cannot know everything or be in control of everything, but God can see, know, and understand more than we can ever know. It is through our imperfections that human beings come to tragic conflicts (see CCC, 2317). The only way for us to overcome our tendency to sin is through Christ's salvation (see CCC, 619).

QUOTATION TO BE
INCLUDED IN FINAL PRINTING.

—CCC, 620

We have all heard the saying that charity begins at home. This doesn't mean we only help others once we have enough to take care of ourselves and our families? Concern for others and human dignity is a constant characteristic of a disciple of Christ.

Recall What three things does natural law provide?

Identify What gives us answers to the question of why we exist and how we can reach eternal happiness?

QUICK REVIEW

1a. **Explain** Why is an informed conscience important?

b. **Summarize** What does the Catholic Church teach about human dignity?

c. **Tell** How do the Beatitudes help answer why we exist and how to reach eternal happiness?

d. **Connect** How do God's gifts sustain hope for us in our daily lives?

e. **Identify** What must our moral decisions and actions be based on?

2a. **Analyze** Why are almsgiving and tithing important?

b. **Analyze** How has technology affected moral life?

ACT

Investigate websites for Catholic service organizations.

• Work with a classmate to research such Catholic organizations.

• Share your research results with the class.

SELF-ASSESS

Which statement best reflects where you are now?

☐ I'm confident enough about the material in this section to be able to explain it to someone else.

☐ I have a good grasp of the material in this section, but I could use more review.

☐ I'm lost. I need help catching up before moving on.

ADVANCE REVIEW COPY

PRAYER

We thank you, Lord Jesus,
because the Gospel of the Father's love,
with which you came to save the world,
has been proclaimed far and wide in America
as a gift of the Holy Spirit
that fills us with gladness.

We thank you for the gift of your Life,
which you have given us by loving us to the end:
your Life makes us children of God,
brothers and sisters to each other.
Increase, O Lord, our faith and our love for you,
present in all the tabernacles of the continent.

Grant us to be faithful witnesses
to your Resurrection
for the younger generation of Americans,
so that, in knowing you, they may follow you
and find in you their peace and joy.
Only then will they know that they
are brothers and sisters
of all God's children scattered
—throughout the world.

You who, in becoming man,
chose to belong to a human family,
teach families the virtues which filled with light
the family home of Nazareth.

May families always be united,
as you and the Father are one,
and may they be living witnesses
to love, justice and solidarity;
make them schools of respect,
forgiveness and mutual help,
so that the world may believe;
help them to be the source of vocations
to the priesthood and the consecrated life,
and all the other forms
of firm Christian commitment.

Protect your Church and the Successor of Peter,
to whom you, Good Shepherd, have entrusted
the task of feeding your flock.
Grant that the Church in America may flourish
and grow richer in the fruits of holiness.

Teach us to love your Mother, Mary,
as you loved her.
Give us strength to proclaim
your word with courage
in the work of the new evangelization,
so that the world may know new hope.
Our Lady of Guadalupe, Mother of America,
pray for us!
—Blessed Pope John Paul II, Mexico City, January 22, 1999

ADVANCE REVIEW COPY

VOCABULARY

Use each of the following terms in a sentence that shows you know what the term means in the context of the chapter. You may include more than one term in a sentence.

original innocence	sin of commission
Original Holiness	sin of omission
Original Justice	Hell
self-assertion	freedom
venial sin	apathy
mortal sin	

PEOPLE AND TERMS

Define each person or term in the context of the chapter.

1. the Fall
2. Saint Paul
3. Book of Genesis
4. Letter to the Galatians
5. Christ's Passion
6. occasions of sin
7. Pope Benedict XVI
8. capital sins
9. Second Vatican Council
10. *Gaudium et Spes*
11. license
12. moral relativism
13. martyr
14. natural law
15. Saint Mary Faustina
16. almsgiving

UNDERSTANDING

Answer each question and complete each exercise

SECTION 1

1. **Identify** Describe the state known as original innocence.
2. **Name** What are three temptations that have plagued mankind since the Fall?
3. **Define** What is Original Sin?
4. **Link** How is Original Sin transmitted to all humans?

SECTION 2

5. **Explain** Why is mortal sin diametrically opposed to the obedience of Jesus?
6. **Elaborate** What are the classifications of sin?
7. **Describe** When mortal sin takes place, a new initiative of God's mercy and a conversion of heart is necessary. How is this done?

SECTION 3

8. **List** What forces in the world work against human dignity?
9. **Explain** How is freedom impacted by goodness and sin?
10. **Recall** Why do humans seek truth?
11. **Identify** Explain Saint Mary Faustina's mission.

ADVANCE REVIEW COPY

12. **Recall** What three things does natural law provide?
13. **Explain** Where is true happiness found and where is it not found?
14. **Name** What is the key to good moral decision-making?

CONNECTING

Visual This image shows Satan tempting Jesus.

What can this image mean for today's humanity? Describe how Jesus looks in this image? How can this picture help you when you are facing temptation?

Challenge You and your friend Charlie are looking at your friend Claire's Facebook page, when Charlie tells you to leave a mean message for Claire.

You: Why would I do that?

Friend: Just to be funny. I have a secret page under another name, and we can use that page to leave her the message.

You: No. I'm not gonna do that.

Friend: Why not? I promise you won't get caught.

You: It doesn't matter whether I get caught or not. That doesn't make it a good thing to do.

Friend: Come on. Everybody does this. It's just a game.

- What is your next reply?
- Then continue the conversation anticipating at least two more questions that Charlie might ask and how you would answer. Use information from the chapter in your answer.

Question After working through this chapter, what advice would you give someone who thinks that the end justifies the means?

Imagine You have the ability to design a smartphone app that will help people make moral decisions.

- What would the first two or three screens for the app look like?
- What pieces of data would you include in its programming to help people make good decisions?
- What questions would you have the app ask users?

SELF-ASSESS

On Your Own Make a list of the most important things you learned from this chapter.

Select three things that represent your growth in understanding as you worked through this chapter. Write a paragraph explaining your choices.

With a Partner List what you found most helpful or interesting in this chapter as well as any other questions that have surfaced.

Love of God

Go to the student site at
hs.osvcurriculum.com

ADVANCE REVIEW COPY

ADVANCE REVIEW COPY

YOU WILL

- Identify the benefits of God's laws.
- Examine why the ancient Israelites needed God's Law to guide them.
- Explore Jesus' interpretation of the Ten Commandments.
- Discuss God's power and connect it to the First Commandment.
- Review how faith, hope, and charity guide our lives as Christians.
- Consider the importance of always honoring God's name.
- Identify how honoring the Sabbath renews our mind, body, and spirit.
- Recognize the role of obedience and authority figures in our lives.

Natural Law and God's Law

KEY TERMS IN THIS SECTION

Decalogue name for the "ten words," or the Ten Commandments, that God gave to Moses and the Israelites

All laws find their first and ultimate truth in God's eternal law. Laws are rules that govern our behavior to act for the good of everyone.

QUOTATION TO BE INCLUDED IN FINAL PRINTING.

(*Catechism of the Catholic Church,* 1951). We are the only earthly creatures capable of receiving law from God. With our ability to reason and through revealed truth, we are to govern ourselves in justice and in truth.

This 2004 water color painting shows Moses receiving the Ten Commandments.

God's moral law guides us to live as he intended—doing good and avoiding evil. This divine or eternal law can come to us through human reason. If it does, it is natural moral law. It can also be revealed to us by God. For example, the Law given to the ancient Israelites, namely the Ten Commandments, is revealed law because God gave it to Moses. The new Law of the Gospel is also revealed because Jesus gave it to us. He revealed it by his suffering, Death, and Resurrection, and he preached it in the Sermon on the Mount and the Beatitudes.

The Beatitudes reveal the goal of why we are here. The ultimate end of our human lives is the call from God to join in his eternal beatitude or happiness. The *Catechism* identifies this call as a vocation for each of us and for the Church as a whole (see CCC, 1719). The moral law given to us either through revelation or natural reasoning does not just list behaviors we shouldn't do. It is firm in teaching us how to act righteously. It tells us what to do to gain eternal life. The moral law promises happiness and in that way leads us to it (see CCC, 1950).

The foundation of the moral law was revealed to the ancient Israelites when God entered into a Covenant with Moses. The Chosen People, now free from Egypt's slavery, were given the Ten Commandments—the **Decalogue**—that would show them that God's laws lead to freedom.

QUOTATION TO BE INCLUDED IN FINAL PRINTING.

—CCC, 2057

ADVANCE REVIEW COPY

More than three thousand years ago, the ancient Israelites—called by God as his Chosen People and enslaved for generations—were suddenly free. They traced their lineage back to a heritage and a homeland known only from stories kept alive by their ancestors. Moses, whom God called to lead them to freedom, was an instrument, a spokesperson of the true God.

Once freed, the Israelites set out in search of their ancestral lands but found themselves wandering in a vast desert. They implored God to remember the covenant he made with their ancestors. God heard their cries and provided them with enough food and water to survive. They didn't have God's revealed law yet, and no guidelines to help them in their covenant relationship with God. Without these, they were in danger of violating the covenant and falling into a new kind of slavery—sin, lawlessness, unbridled license, and the "might makes right" oppression that they thought they had left behind.

Moses and the People realized that they must adhere to the covenant that God had made with their ancestors, for without the covenant they would neither survive nor thrive. Only divine intervention could:

- make them into a unified people
- guide them on the right path
- clarify proper relations among them
- preserve their covenant faithfulness to their God

Only clear guidelines, a set of rules that apply to everyone, could achieve these goals. Moses asked God to provide laws to guide the newly formed community. Moses' prayers were answered when, while on a mountain in the desert, he received two stone tablets on which

REFLECT

The Ten Commandments reveal things about God to us.

- What do the moral guidelines of the Ten Commandments tell us about God and what he is like?

The Ten Commandments

1. I am the Lord your God, you shall not have strange gods before me.
2. You shall not take the name of the Lord your God in vain.
3. Remember to keep holy the Lord's Day.
4. Honor your father and your mother.
5. You shall not kill.
6. You shall not commit adultery.
7. You shall not steal.
8. You shall not bear false witness against your neighbor.
9. You shall not covet your neighbor's wife.
10. You shall not covet your neighbor's goods.

were written God's Law. Today we know them as the Decalogue (ten words), or the Ten Commandments. Over half the world's population accepts these words as being of divine origin. The Ten Commandments tell us the way to live our lives free from the slavery of sin..

"You must diligently keep the commandments of the LORD your God, and his decrees, and his statutes that he has commanded you. Do what is right and good in the sight of the LORD, so that it may go well with you, and so that you may go in and occupy the good land that the LORD swore to your ancestors to give you, thrusting out all your enemies from before you, as the LORD has promised.

—Deuteronomy 6:17-19

The Decalogue was regarded with great reverence by the Israelites who realized that the Commandments spelled out their way to true freedom. During their time of slavery under the Egyptians, they possessed little freedom and were given little responsibility. As slaves, they did only what they were told. With freedom came responsibility. The Commandments guided them in their freedom and directed their newfound responsibility.

In Judaism, the Commandments are a summation of a much larger body of law called the Law of Moses. The Law summed up in the Commandments spells out how the Israelites should observe the covenant by loving God and showing care and concern for one another. Living faithfully to their laws marked them as members of the People of God.

I will praise the name of God with a song;
I will magnify him with thanksgiving. . . .
Let the oppressed see it and be glad;
you who seek God, let your hearts revive.
For the LORD hears the needy,
and does not despise his own that are in bonds.
Let heaven and earth praise him,
the seas and everything that moves in them.
For God will save Zion and rebuild the cities of Judah;
and his servants shall live there and possess it, . . .
and those who love his name shall live in it.

—Psalm 69:30, 32-36

- To which of the Ten Commandments does this Psalm connect?

- What does praising and loving God lead to?

'You have heard that it was said to those of ancient times, "You shall not murder" . . . But I say to you that if you are angry with a brother or sister, you will be liable to judgment.'

—Matthew 5:21-22

Explain How does following God's Law lead to freedom?

Analyze Why did the ancient Israelites need the Ten Commandments to guide their lives?

Divine Providence

Everyone can relate to the excitement of learning something new. It could be anything from solving a difficult math equation to finally mastering the backstroke. It could be figuring out how to play a tricky percussion solo, or learning how to merge into busy traffic in a way that doesn't stress us out.

To help us do these things, our parents, teachers, and coaches taught us skills. They showed us how things worked, and how we could work together with other people. God, our Father and Creator, is the ultimate teacher. His lessons go deeper and touch our hearts, souls, and minds.

Even though God gave the Ten Commandments to Moses and the Israelites more than 3,000 years ago, there's nothing outdated about them. For centuries, these Commandments have continued to guide the ethical conduct and worship of both Jews and Christians.

God's laws are perfect guides. We are created by God, and he knows exactly what we need to do in order to live our lives in happiness and peace. God understands us completely. He sees what we need as individuals, and as members of families, communities, and of his Church. After the Fall, our all-knowing God knew that his sons and daughters would need direction.

God's laws show us how he knows us through and through, and they reveal him to us.

QUOTATION TO BE
INCLUDED IN FINAL PRINTING.

(CCC, 2059).

Moses was given the Ten Commandments, but Jesus gave us a new way to interpret that Law. He summed up our duties to God with the two Great Commandments—love for God and love for each other (see CCC, 2083). Jesus did not change the Old Testament Commandments or lessen them in any way, but he gave them their full meaning in the New Covenant of love. The Commandments are now fulfilled with Jesus' two-part, but single command to love. It is a much greater challenge that Jesus teaches.

ADVANCE REVIEW COPY

God reveals what we have to do, and what we need to avoid.

QUOTATION TO BE
INCLUDED IN FINAL PRINTING.

(CCC, 1975).
Promised beatitude in this quotation refers to eternal happiness with God in Heaven. In Jesus, God sent humanity a perfect teacher and model who brought about the Kingdom on Earth.

The Church reminds us that receiving law from God is actually a privilege. We can reason, and we are capable of understanding and discernment. God gave us a free will. We are free to reject God's Law or obey it. Obedience is the essential and virtuous choice.

As Saint Thomas Aquinas noted, "Obedience unites us so closely to God that it in a way

IDENTIFY

Re-examine the eight Beatitudes. For each of the Beatitudes, take a deeper look and name a moral good that each one encourages.

GO TO THE SOURCE

Humankind passed from paradise and freedom to the slavery of sin, but the first words of the Ten Commandments appropriately address freedom.

Read: Exodus 20:2 and Deuteronomy 5:6.

- These verses say the same thing, but what do they say about freedom.
- Why do you think this was first?

transforms us into Him, so that we have no other will but His. If obedience is lacking, even prayer cannot be pleasing to God" (*Summa Theologiae*).

(CCC, 1950). It is God's fatherly instruction that offers rules of conduct to reach the promised happiness and also condemns evil actions that turn us away from God's love. Jesus told us that God the Father sent him. "'I came that they may have life, and have it abundantly'" (John 10:10).

God's People needed to learn what living more abundantly really meant. Jesus, whom many called "Rabbi" or "Teacher," spent his public ministry teaching just that. As we discussed in Chapter 1, Jesus summarized this life-giving lesson in the Beatitudes, which are at the heart of his preaching.

QUOTATION TO BE
INCLUDED IN FINAL PRINTING.

—CCC, 1719

In a timeless way, the Beatitudes describe the attitudes and the behaviors that the followers of Jesus must have. But Jesus made it clear that this teaching would not replace observance of the Commandments. "'Do not think that I have come to abolish the law or the prophets'" (Matthew 5:17).

LIST

Identify moral laws that Christians today share with the ancient Israelites.

- What common laws of God do both groups try to uphold, despite the thousands of years worth of changes in history, migration, education, and science?
- Why do you think all of us have held these laws in common for so long?
- What does the timeless value of these laws show you about God's plan for humans?

Jesus wanted the people of his day to look into the deeper meanings of the Law and the Commandments. Any study of morality invites us to do the same—to look into the deeper meaning of what God and the Church are teaching.

The Church also tells us that natural law is a light within us. Human reason, or natural law, has the force of law because of the higher reason behind it—God (see CCC, 1954). Natural law can never be known perfectly because of the presence of sin in the world, which clouds human reason.   the *Catechism* advises,

QUOTATION TO BE
INCLUDED IN FINAL PRINTING.

(CCC, 1955).

Recall According to Saint Thomas Aquinas, how does obedience to God bring us closer to him?

Analyze Why do you think Jesus emphasized that he was not trying to abolish the Law or the prophets?

God's Law Given to Moses

The Ten Commandments are often referred to as the Decalogue, but are also known as the "Ten Sayings," and "the Ten Matters." The *Catechism* adds another name, "the Testimony," because the two tablets given to Moses contained God's testimony, or formal statement (see CCC, 2058).

QUOTATION TO BE
INCLUDED IN FINAL PRINTING.

(CCC, 2062). They are given in detail in the Books of Exodus and Deuteronomy, the second and fifth books of the Bible. The Ten Commandments sum up and proclaim God's Law. Written by God on stone tablets, they were carried for many years throughout the desert. The *Catechism* points out that all moral life takes its meaning from the Covenant with Moses.

In *Exodus*, we read that God gave the Commandments to Moses on Mount Sinai. The stone tables were "written with the finger of God" (Exodus 31:18). The ancient Israelites following Moses tried to live by the Ten Commandments. They saw that the Commandments guided their relationship with God and with other people.

The Ten Commandments are applicable to us today. God established his covenant, and gave us the Commandments. Through the covenant, we are spiritual descendants of the Chosen People who made their way through the Sinai Desert to the Promised Land more than 3,000 years ago.

The Ten Commandments are not extraordinary obligations imposed upon us by a distant God. On the contrary, they are expressions of the natural law, that interior social contract that he has planted within us. The Ten Commandments are a reminder of God's voice within us, telling us of our essential duties toward him and toward our neighbors. By obeying the Commandments in our decision-making, we will be truly alive in God's love both now and forever.

ADVANCE REVIEW COPY

Jesus assures us that we can live out the moral life and contribute to the Kingdom of God when we live in relationship with him. The Church assures us that shaping our lives around the Commandments is possible because

(CCC, 2082).

Recall List at least three names for the Ten Commandments?

Explain How are we connected to the ancient Israelites who lived more than 3,000 years ago?

Jesus knew the Law, and he invites us to reflect its the deepest meaning through the testimony of our lives.

Read Matthew 22:36-40.

- What question is posed to him about God's Law?
- What does Jesus' response focus on?
- How does your life point to the deepest meaning of God's Law?

SECTION **1 REVIEW**

QUICK REVIEW

1a. **Name** What are the two sources of moral law?
  b. **Reflect** What is the ultimate purpose of moral law?
  c. **Retell** What did divine intervention do for the Chosen People?

2a. **Trace** What is the relationship between the Ten Commandments and the two Great Commandments?
  b. **Elaborate** Why do humans alone receive laws from God?

3a. **List** Recall other names for the Ten Commandments.
  b. **Reflect** Why are the Commandments addressed to humans personally?

Listen and Discus Discuss why laws are necessary. Here are some questions to start.

- Do you think that people would keep laws even if laws did not exist?
- What keeps people moral—is it laws or their consciences or something else?
- If conflict exists between human laws and natural law, which takes precedence? Why? What happens when it doesn't? Give an example.

Pray Compose a short prayer reflecting on following the Gospel message of love.

SELF-ASSESS

Which statement best reflects where you are now?

☐ I'm confident enough about the material in this section to be able to explain it to someone else.

☐ I have a good grasp of the material in this section, but I could use more review.

☐ I'm lost. I need help catching up before moving on.

The First Commandment

KEY TERMS IN THIS SECTION

hope

(CCC, Glossary, p. 882)

charity (also called love) the theological virtue representing the core of the Christian life

(CCC, 1822)

sacrilege the act of profaning or disrespecting the Sacraments, the liturgy, or persons, things, or places consecrated to God

simony the buying and selling of spiritual things, such as demanding payment to receive God's forgiveness in the Sacrament of Reconciliation. This is prohibited by the Catholic Church.

acedia spiritual laziness, an uncaring attitude, apathy, boredom, and the

absence of joy

superstition attributing magical power to certain practices (i.e., rubbing a rabbit's foot, carrying a lucky coin) or things (i.e., crystals, tarot cards, statues).

(CCC, Glossary, p. 900)

atheism the denial that God exists in theory or practice

God's First Commandment is a call

(CCC, 2134). This Commandment

(CCC 2088). We do this by prayer: praising him, lifting our hearts and minds to him, spending time with him, being grateful to him for everything that comes our way, and placing our needs before him.

> "'You shall love the Lord your God with all your heart, and with all your soul, and with all your mind.'"
>
> —Matthew 22:37

God has revealed that he is all-powerful, liberating, and loving, as well as kind, merciful, trustworthy, faithful, and unchanging. But God is still Mystery. Nonetheless, we have Sacred Scripture and Sacred Tradition and the person of Jesus to help us understand the one true God and to guide us in our response to him.

With the Son—his Word—and the Holy Spirit—the giver of life—God the Father keeps all creation in existence. We might wonder why he permits moral and physical evil to exist in the world and bad things happen to good people. By sending his only Son into the world, God reveals his ultimate plan for the triumph of good over evil.

Affirming that God is all-powerful makes a statement about us as well as about him. "'For nothing will be impossible with God'" (Luke 1:37). His presence surrounds us. In the desert, the Israelites gathered manna and other foods that kept them alive. They knew, however, that whatever water and food they found came from God. His all-powerful nature is grounds for our hope. Even our capacity for hope is a gift from him.

ADVANCE REVIEW COPY

The Gift of Faith

The source of our moral life is God's gift of faith. Saint Paul said obedience to our faith is our first obligation (see CCC, 2087). It is the theological virtue by which the grace of the Holy Spirit moves our hearts, opens our minds, and enables us to believe all that he has revealed to us. The First Commandment directs us to protect our faith at all costs.

Faith, then, works on a number of levels:

- it is a grace given to us by God;

- it is a human act, a conscious and free act on our part to respond to God's grace;

- and it is an act of the Church which precedes and makes possible individual faith, supporting and nourishing the faith of all believers.

Only by faith can we come to know and experience God as one as the Holy Trinity—the Father, the Son, and the Holy Spirit. Without faith, we cannot believe in the Trinity and thus, without faith, we are not saved. As Jesus said, "'The one who believes and is baptized will be saved; but the one who does not believe will be condemned'" (Mark 16:16).

We can sin against faith in various ways. One way is through voluntary doubt. This is an intentional disregard for what God has revealed and

GO TO THE SOURCE

The **Letter to the Hebrews** contains a chapter on faith.

Read Hebrews 11.

- How does the chapter define faith?

- What does faith help us to understand?

- Make a list of the people the chapter offers as examples of faith and list the reasons why.

- What is it that will make things "perfect"?

APPLY

- Have you ever experienced a moment of doubt? If so, what caused it? How did your faith bounce back?

- How can deliberate doubt lead to blindness?

for what the Church teaches must be believed. We can also call this disbelief—a voluntary rejecting of a truth of faith. Involuntary doubt refers to a hesitation to believe because of situations that happen or difficulties understanding the mystery of faith. This can challenge our faith.

(CCC, 2088).

There are also four other ways we can sin against faith.

- incredulity is the neglect of revealed truth or the willful refusal to accept what God has revealed

- heresy is the unyielding and persistent refusal of a baptized Catholic to believe a truth of faith which must be held

- apostasy is when someone repudiates the Christian faith or the Catholic Church

- schism is the refusal to submit to the Pope or the communion with the members of the Body of Christ subject to him (see CCC, 2089)

List Name three things in your life that indicate God's presence surrounds us.

Explain Why is faith in God so essential to being a true Christian?

The Gift of Hope

In popular usage, the word **hope** often describes a passive quality and not an active virtue. For instance, in the following popular uses, hope implies passivity—standing by, letting things happen, and not taking charge of the situation:

- I hope it doesn't rain today. I didn't bring a raincoat.

Jesus and Mary offer examples of faith that pushes back against doubt, like light that pushes away darkness.

Read Mark 14:32-38 and Luke 1:26-38.

- What is troubling Jesus?
- What does his prayer reveal about his faith?
- In the reading from the Gospel according to Luke, how does Mary express her faith?
- How does the passage from Luke's Gospel help explain why the *Catechism* refers to Mary as   (CCC, 511)

- I hope we don't have a test today. I didn't study.
- I hope my parents don't notice the scratch on the car.

In these uses of the word, hope really means wish, since none of the statements imply any sense of taking action or taking responsibility. By contrast, hope as a virtue implies trusting in God and cooperating with his grace.

> " May the God of hope fill you with all joy and peace in believing, so that you may abound in hope by the power of the Holy Spirit.
>
> —Romans 15:13

The First Commandment is meant to steer us away from the sins against hope—despair and presumption. Despair arises when we stop hoping for our salvation or for help in reaching it. Some people despair by giving up hope for the forgiveness of their sins.

(CCC, 2091).

Saint Paul's Description of Love

The famous description of love from Saint Paul's Letter to the Corinthians offers sixteen characteristics of what love is and what it is not.

- Review each of these characteristics and circle the ones that describe you the most. Then underline two you would like to develop.

Love IS	Love IS NOT
Patient	Envious
Kind	Boastful
Rejoicing in the truth	Arrogant
Bears struggles, disappointments	Rude
Believes in God, Church, others	Insisting on having your own way
Hope-filled	Irritable
Endures all things	Resentful
Never-ending	Rejoicing in wrongdoing

- What insights do you have after this exercise?
- What do you want to ask God for or talk about with him?

ADVANCE REVIEW COPY

DESCRIBE

The *Catechism* uses the following terms to help us appreciate how hope can motivate us to act morally: desire, trust, response, inspiration, a cure for discouragement, and expectation.

- How do these terms connect with hope in your life?
- Write a story of someone who is losing hope. In the story, what do you say to this person to help renew his or her hope?

> Love is patient; love is kind; love is not envious or boastful or arrogant or rude. It does not insist on its own way; it is not irritable or resentful; it does not rejoice in wrongdoing, but rejoices in the truth. It bears all things, believes all things, hopes all things, endures all things. Love never ends. . . . And now faith, hope, and love abide, these three; and the greatest of these is love.

—1 Corinthians 13:4-8, 13

Presumption, on the other hand, can occur first when people have hope only in themselves and in their capacity to save themselves. Secondly, they may presume on God's power or mercy hoping to be forgiven without repentance or changing their sinful ways (see CCC, 2092).

Hope is the virtue by which we strive for eternal life and happiness with God. Hope is trusting in Christ, trusting not on our own resources but on the grace of the Holy Spirit. Hope means trusting in God, in everything that Christ has promised, and in the help of the Holy Spirit. Hope focuses on obtaining eternal happiness in Heaven and receiving the help from God (grace) to achieve it. Jesus taught that this kind of hope is part of the Kingdom of God.

Recall When can despair arise?

Analyze How is hope an active, rather than a passive, virtue?

The Gift of Charity

Charity is the cornerstone of all virtues and the greatest of the theological virtues. We are called by the First Commandment to love God. Nothing should come before him, and Jesus went further by saying we should love God with everything we have.

Jesus also told us the second Greatest Commandment is to love one another. One of the most beautiful descriptions ever written about charity, meaning love, is found in the thirteenth chapter of Saint Paul's First Letter to the Church at Corinth:

Every other virtue that we practice represents some dimension of Christian love. Love, like hope, can be misunderstood. It is not infatuation. Nor is it a passive kind of love. Love is about giving to—and caring for—someone other than ourselves. The *Catechism* defines love in the words of the Saint Thomas Aquinas:

(CCC, 1766).

And, like hope, love can be misdirected. Love is misdirected when we let ourselves be abused or manipulated by someone because we love them. Love is misdirected when we justify some of the hurtful things we say and do to someone because we love them. Nothing is greater than love. With love, we live like God intended. When we love, we have inner joy and inner peace.

My Faith

Living the Theological Virtues

Think about the First Commandment and the virtues of faith, hope, and love. Which of these following statements are the strongest dimensions of your spirituality? How true are each of these statements about you? Rate each on a scale of 1-5 with 1 being "not true" and 5 being "very true."

- The most important thing for me is to be a good person. _____
- I pray a lot. _____
- My relationship with God helps me cope with life's ups and downs. _____
- I'm always interested in learning more about God. _____
- I pay attention when others need help and I step up. _____
- My relationship with God helps me heal from past hurts. _____
- Others would describe me as caring, sensitive, and kind. _____

What would you say about your tendency toward faith, hope, and love?

Which would you like to strengthen while you are still in high school and how?

You can use any of this My Faith as part of the report you will turn in at the end of this course.

Discipleship ... within the Body of Christ ... for the glory of God and the good of the world.

ADVANCE REVIEW COPY

Keeping the First Commandment

Committing to the First Commandment—to love God with all we have—puts our lives on the right spiritual path and opens us up to experience a kind of happiness for which all our souls long. But there are ways to stray from this Commandment.

- We can minimize God's importance. We can be indifferent to him, deny his power, ignore his invitations to love him and others, fail to pray, dismiss religion, and ridicule the Church. We can neglect God by being ungrateful to him for all his gifts to us, we can neglect ourselves as Temples of the Holy Spirit, and we can neglect others in whom Jesus dwells. Letting other things, such as people or material goods, distract us from God's importance is a violation of the First Commandment.

- We can also give ourselves over to distortions of God—false practices and false gods. We can become involved in superstitions like taking seriously such things as tarot cards, palm reading, and other forms of divination and magic that take us away from trusting in God. The First Commandment also condemns irreligion, including tempting God, **sacrilege**, and **simony** (see CCC, 2118).

The First Commandment enjoins us to love God with everything we've got. We sin against this Commandment by violating this love in a variety of ways:

- *indifference* We neglect or fail to consider the importance and power of God's charity through not praying and not loving others

- *ingratitude* We don't give thanks for all we have been given and we don't return God's love

- *lukewarmness* We don't acknowledge God's love or respond to his love or the love of others

- *acedia* Called spiritual sloth or laziness, **acedia** is the refusal to be open to the joy that comes from God

- *hatred of God* We deny God's goodness and we curse God as the one who forbids

REFLECT

We should be aware of straying from the First Commandment.

Which of the five sins against the First Commandment do you think are most common: indifference, ingratitude, lukewarmness, acedia, or hatred of God? Explain.

sins, punishes us for sins, and allows tragedy and hardship in the world (see CCC, 2094)

Adoring God by acknowledging him as Creator and Savior is the fundamental way to strengthen our commitment to the First Commandment and avoid the sins against it. Adoration of God is (CCC, 2096). To adore God is to praise him, expressing

(CCC, 2097). The Catholic Church teaches that faith, hope, and love are accomplished by prayer: lifting our minds toward God with expressions of

(CCC 2098).

God the Father constantly calls each of us to encounter him in prayer. Jesus instructs us in the life of prayer. And the Holy Spirit reminds us with his grace of all that Jesus taught us about prayer. The Holy Trinity thus inspires us to praise and adore God, bless him, entrust our needs to him, ask his intercession for ourselves and others, and give him thanks in our daily prayers.

> Joy has the power to open our hearts, remove fear, instill hope, and foster healing. Joy leads us to wisdom because it connects us to all we are—our mind, heart, power, and spirit. Joy stimulates our immune system, increases our energy, and gives us mental clarity. It helps us heighten our level of consciousness so we can more readily tap our inner wisdom. . . . As our joy expands we feel deeply connected to ourselves and to something bigger than ourselves.
>
> —Charlotte Davis Kasl, *Finding Joy* (New York: HarperCollins), 1994, page xv

Recall Explain how the concept of love can be misunderstood.

List Name and explain the five sins that violate the First Commandment.

Distortion of Religious Practice

An actress says, "Break a leg!" before going on stage. A girl cautions her friend, "Don't walk under that ladder. It's bad luck." Are these examples of superstition?

We perform many rituals that express our belief in God, give us grace, and bring us closer to him. We step over the line into **superstition** when we attribute divine power to external actions and not to God. It can be seen as idolatry. Superstition is a sin against the First Commandment (see CCC, 2111).

Spiritually based ritualistic practices help us to be in touch with God and invite him into our lives. We might light a vigil candle in a church as a ritual accompanying our prayers for a sick friend. If we light candles believing that through such actions we force the issue and bring about a friend's cure, then we have stepped over into superstition. The Sign of the Cross is a rich, meaningful sacramental that Catholics perform. Conceivably someone could treat it magically rather than prayerfully. Horror movies often use Catholic symbols in magical ways, such as using a cross to ward off a vampire.

While superstition relies on magical powers rather than God, tempting him, sacrilege and simony disrespect God. Satan tempted Jesus, who replied with the word of God from Deuteronomy, "Do not put the LORD your God to the test" (Deuteronomy 6:16). Tempting God wounds the respect and trust that we owe God (see CCC, 2119).

We commit sacrilege when we profane or treat with disrespect,

QUOTATION TO BE
INCLUDED IN FINAL PRINTING.

(CCC, 2120). Simony is buying and selling spiritual things, such as demanding money to receive God's forgiveness in the Sacrament of Reconciliation. God's gifts are free. We can only get them from God and without payment (see CCC, 2121).

When people deny the existence of God, it is called **atheism**. Atheism can refer to a variety of false beliefs:

GO TO THE SOURCE

When some of the Israelites lost faith in God in the desert, they built a golden calf to worship.

Read Exodus 32.

- What can we learn from the way the Israelites fell into idol worship?
- What are the "golden calves" of today?

- *practical materialism*, that the material world is all that exists
- *atheistic humanism*, that man is

(CCC, 2124)

- *social atheism*, that religion, of its very nature, deceives people, gives them false hope, and discourages them from working for a better life

The related topic of agnosticism takes on many forms. Someone describing themselves as agnostic may not deny God, but instead talks about a transcendent being that is not involved in our lives and is impossible to affirm or deny (see CCC, 2127).

Belief in more than the one God also goes against the First Commandment. God made this the First Commandment in order to dispel polytheism—the early belief people had in many gods. We cannot believe in, but also cannot venerate, other so-called divinities. Our Triune God is living, and he gives life and his work is experienced throughout history. Scripture gives many instances of people falling into false worship.

We can come to value other things over faithfulness to the one true God. We may not even be aware of how much we adore these things in ways that lead us astray from his path. The *Catechism* lists the following as potential idols for people today: power, pleasure, race, ancestors, the state, and money.

(CCC, 2113).

- What are some positive and some negative uses of religious symbols?
- When is the line crossed that makes religious symbols contrary to the First Commandment?

While the First Commandment condemns idolatry, the Christian veneration of images does not go against it. The reason is that the honor we have goes to the person portrayed in the image.

QUOTATION TO BE
INCLUDED IN FINAL PRINTING.

(CCC, 2132).

Contrast What is the difference between lighting a vigil candle as part of your prayer for a sick friend and believing that lighting a vigil candle will cure your friend?

Define What is sacrilege?

SECTION 2 REVIEW

QUICK REVIEW

1. **List** How do we observe the First Commandment?

2a. **Define** What is faith?
 b. **Contrast** What is the difference between heresy, apostasy, and schism?

3a. **Explain** How can hope appear to be a passive virtue?
 b. **Support** Why is trust in God an integral part of hope?

4a. **Analyze** Why is charity the central Christian virtue?
 b. **Explain** Why is "selfish love" a contradiction in terms?

5. **Connect** How do we benefit from our adoring God?

ACT

Make a list of the ways that you can adore God.
- What do you do every day already?
- Which additional ways of adoring God would fit into your life?

Pray Compose a short prayer thanking God for the gift of faith.

SELF-ASSESS

Which statement best reflects where you are now?

☐ I'm confident enough about the material in this section to be able to explain it to someone else.

☐ I have a good grasp of the material in this section, but I could use more review.

☐ I'm lost. I need help catching up before moving on.

ADVANCE REVIEW COPY

Second and Third Commandments

KEY TERMS IN THIS SECTION

blasphemy speech or action that shows disrespect or contempt for God or persons or things dedicated to God

perjury making a promise under oath with no intention of keeping the promise; lying under oath

The Second Commandment requires us to have respect for God's name. As we learned from the First Commandment, God's name is sacred and meant for adoration. Therefore, we are not to speak his name except to bless, honor, and praise him (see CCC, 2143). Uttering obscenities involving God's name, cursing someone using the name of the Lord, or employing God's name in crude language defile and cheapen that which is most sacred to our faith.

> You shall not make wrongful use of the name of the LORD your God, for the LORD will not acquit anyone who misuses his name.
>
> —Exodus 20:7

Our speech reflects what we value and honor. We communicate through language, and we communicate our values through language. Likewise, our language about God reflects the amount of value and honor we place on God. Without a profound respect for the holy God and a profound respect for the sacredness of creation, all the other Commandments are groundless. For example, killing is wrong because human life is sacred. Indeed, when we speak reverentially about God and his creatures we contribute greatly to the spirit of holiness without which our world could not survive. In a sense, all of our speech either witnesses to or mocks God.

Actions opposed to the Second Commandment include the improper use of the names of Jesus and God as well as the Virgin Mary and the saints. Any promises or vows made in God's name must be kept.

(CCC, 2147). Other sins against the Second Commandment include blasphemy and perjury.

QUOTATION TO BE INCLUDED IN FINAL PRINTING.

(CCC, 2162). Blasphemy involves directing toward God words or gestures of malice, hostility, or dishonor. When we consider someone or something to be sacred, we are deeply offended when others speak disrespectfully about them. The Second Commandment demands that we speak out when the name of God, the saints, our Church, or other sacred things are defiled in word and action.

ADVANCE REVIEW COPY

- Restate the Second Commandment in positive terms.

- What does it mean to say that our speech either witnesses to or mocks God?

- How is speaking with reverence essential to being a full and complete human being?

- Some magazines, comedians, and television shows poke fun at what we hold sacred. This can be helpful when they expose our idol worship as misguided. It's another matter when it shows disrespect for that which is truly holy. Give examples to illustrate the difference between exposing false gods and disrespecting the true God.

QUOTATION TO BE
INCLUDED IN FINAL PRINTING.

—CCC, 2151

Perjury is another violation of the Second Commandment. We commit perjury when we falsely give our word under oath or make a promise under oath that we do not intend to keep. Perjury is an offense against the Second Commandment because of the nature of an oath. Taking an oath is swearing, with God as our witness, to the truth of what we say. By making such an oath, we are calling upon the Lord's name and truthfulness as a pledge of our own truthfulness.

We are literally, then, taking the Lord's name in vain when we make a false, deceptive, or dishonest statement under oath. By lying under oath, we are calling upon God to be a witness to our dishonesty.

(CCC, 2152).

Jesus talked about the Second Commandment when he said, "'Again, you have heard it said to those of ancient times, "You shall not swear falsely, but carry out the vows you have made to the Lord." But I say to you, Do not swear at all . . . Let your word be "Yes, Yes" or "No, No"; anything more than this comes from the evil one'" (Matthew 5:33-34, 37). Jesus' statement does not prohibit us from taking oaths for serious and right reasons, such as in court. Jesus wants our

honesty to be such that no one need ever doubt it or have a need to put it to a test. He commands us to be truthful in all speech.

In the film *A Man For All Seasons*, Saint Thomas More is imprisoned because he refuses to swear to an oath that goes against his faith. His family implores him to simply take the oath so he can be released from jail, but he cannot. Saint Thomas explains his feelings to his daughter: "When a man takes an oath, Meg, he's holding his own self in his own hands. Like water. And if he opens his fingers *then*—he needn't hope to find himself again."

Analyze How does blasphemy harm our relationship with God?

Explain Why is taking an oath a truly serious matter?

Remembering the Sabbath

The Third Commandment recalls the holiness of the Sabbath Day, which was the seventh day of creation when the Lord rests. The Sabbath recalls creation, memorializes Israel's liberation from slavery in Egypt, and signifies the everlasting covenant with Israel (see CCC, 2170-2171).

> Remember the sabbath day, and keep it holy. Six days you shall labor and do all your work. But the seventh day is a sabbath to the LORD your God; you shall not do any work.
>
> —Exodus 20:8-10

GO TO THE SOURCE

Some in his time questioned Jesus' actions on the Sabbath and claimed that they violated the Law. But Jesus always respected the holiness of the Sabbath.

Read Mark 2:23–3:6.

- Summarize what Jesus says about the Sabbath.

- Who was the Sabbath made for and what is Jesus' role for the Sabbath?

- What does this say to you about the importance of the Sabbath?

The action of God on the Sabbath is a model for us. We need the day to rest and refresh just as the Lord did as well as to let others rest and recover from everyday work. Jesus was accused of violating the Sabbath law, but he always respected the holiness of the day.

QUOTATION TO BE
INCLUDED IN FINAL PRINTING.

(CCC, 2173).

The Third Commandment enjoins us to be attentive both to our worship and our leisure. Most Christians honor Sunday as the Lord's Day because the Resurrection of Jesus took place on the first day of the week. The timing of the Resurrection recalls the first account of creation, and

(CCC, 2174). For Catholics, it is the first of all feasts and the day of the Lord—Sunday. The first day of creation separated the light from the darkness, and on the same day, our Savior rose from the dead.

QUOTATION TO BE
INCLUDED IN FINAL PRINTING.

—CCC, 2176

Accounts we have of the early Christians indicate that they gathered for the Eucharist on Sundays.

Followers of Christ keep Sunday holy by making it a day of worship. We keep Sunday holy by participating at Mass and by abstaining from activities or work that hinder us from the spiritual observance of the Lord's Day. We live the spirit of Psalm 118:24 that exclaims, "This is the day that the LORD has made, let us rejoice and be glad in it."

QUOTATION TO BE
INCLUDED IN FINAL PRINTING.

—CCC, 2185

One of the five Precepts of the Church requires Catholics to participate at Mass on Sundays and other holy days of obligation. To do that we can participate at a Mass celebrated in a Catholic rite either on the day or the evening of the preceding day (see CCC, 2180).

Participation at Sunday Eucharist is an opportunity to remember and praise God in Christ Jesus. Through Sunday Mass, we strengthen and encourage one another's faith under the guidance of the Holy Spirit (see CCC, 2178). A community gathered at Sunday Eucharist testifies to all humanity that God and the Church are good, worthy of praise, and the hope for the world's salvation. By participating in Sunday Mass, we add our voices to a great chorus praising God throughout the world and in Heaven. Since Sunday Eucharist is so important to the Catholic faith, those who deliberately miss Mass have committed a grave sin (see CCC, 2181).

ADVANCE REVIEW COPY

PRIMARY SOURCES

In his book, *Truth for Your Mind, Love for Your Heart: Satisfying Your Hunger for God,* Father Alfred McBride, O. Praem., points out that:

It should be noticed that God saved Israel before asking her to keep the commandments. The word "saved" here refers to God graciously liberating them from slavery. Israel knew salvation before agreeing to keep the law of God. We often hear that we must keep the commandments in order to be saved. But we must be careful not to think that we earn salvation by keeping the commandments. God first gives us the gift of salvation, and we then respond by keeping the commandments as a sign of our gratitude.

We are first saved from our sins at baptism, which is symbolized by the redemption of the Israelites at the Red Sea. This salvation was actually achieved for us by the death and resurrection of Jesus.

We keep the commandments, moreover, as a sign of our resolution to remain in the process of salvation.

Salvation at the Red Sea was not enough. The march to Sinai was not enough. For even after the giving of the covenant and the agreement to live up to it, there still lay ahead for the Hebrews the journey to the Promised Land. Even after this, life went on, and Israel was expected to live up to the high standards agreed to at Sinai.

A satellite view of the Mediterranean Sea looking east toward Israel and the Middle East.

➜ Go to the student site at
hs.osvcurriculum.com

What truth is Father McBride pointing to here?

Do you view keeping the Commandments as the way to earn salvation? Or are they a way for you to remain in the process of salvation?

especially of noble beings, and knowledge of happiness and misery in the next life

---

Our obligation to attend Mass may be excused for a serious reason, which can include illness or caring for infants. A pastor may also excuse someone from this obligation. Sometimes a sacred minister is not available or some other circumstance makes participation in the Eucharist impossible. In those cases, it is recommended that Catholics take part in the Liturgy of the Word as prescribed by the local bishop. If that is not possible, the faithful can take time to pray personally, with their family, or with a group of families (see CCC, 2183).

In addition to Mass, we keep the Lord's Day holy by allowing ourselves a sufficient amount of leisure time to nurture our cultural, social, spiritual, and family lives. Likewise we should be sensitive to the needs of others and refrain from making unnecessary demands on them that would hinder their observance of the Lord's Day.

The *Catechism* says Christians who can rest on Sundays should remember those who cannot because of poverty or misery.

(CCC, 2186). Catholics can also designate Sunday as a holy day by devoting time for family. The *Catechism* calls for a united effort in sanctifying Sundays and holy days by finding sufficient time for rest and leisure (see CCC, 2187).

The Israelites set an example by taking this Commandment very seriously, limiting the steps they could walk and meals they could cook, etc. Today the Commandment has not changed. Keeping the Lord's Day holy has always involved worship and rest.

Mary, Mother of Jesus

(First Century A.D.)

More than twenty centuries ago, Mary, or "Miriam," as she was called by her parents, was living a quiet life in what is today Israel. Mary's parents were Saints Joachim and Anne. They made sure they and their daughter practiced the Third Commandment to Honor the Sabbath. Like most parents through the ages, they wanted the best for their child and hoped her life would be better than theirs.

When Mary herself became a parent, she helped instruct Jesus about rightful authority. He was a loyal and dutiful son, even on one occasion when his parents felt distress. When Jesus was 12, his family traveled to Jerusalem and when his parents departed, he remained behind in the Temple. Mary and Joseph searched for their son for three difficult days. When the shaken and exhausted Mary was finally reunited with Jesus she said, "Look child, why have you done this to us? Your father and I have been searching for you in great anxiety" (Luke 2:48).

ADVANCE REVIEW COPY

The Church of the Nativity is pictured here in modern-day Bethlehem.

Although Jesus explained that he needed to be busy in his Father's house, he must have also seen that his parents had suffered in fear. Mary and Joseph may not have understood what this meant. As Luke's Gospel adds, "He went down with them and came to Nazareth, and was obedient to them" (Luke 2:51). Even as the only Son of God, Jesus accepted the authority of his parents, Mary and Joseph.

When Jesus began his public life and left home, Mary honored this mission. She knew her Son was God's anointed, the promised Messiah. In Jewish society, it was a son's responsibility to support his widowed mother. Jesus must have provided for Mary. Later, from the Cross, he asked John to care for Mary (see John 19:27). With his last breath, Jesus fulfilled his responsibilities to his loving, grieving mother.

All through her life, Mary honored and lived perfectly in the spirit of the Fourth Commandment.

She knew that God gives laws to guide his children to freedom and happiness, and that the full text of this commandment contains a promise.

"Honor your father and your mother, as the LORD your God commanded you" (Deuteronomy 5:16).

> **Think About It** Name two or three circumstances where you find it most difficult to live by the Third and Fourth Commandments. What quality or virtue in Mary would you particularly like to develop in your life? What activities or efforts could help foster that quality or virtue in you? What trends in American society make it hard for young people to be obedient?

Go to the student site at
hs.osvcurriculum.com

ADVANCE REVIEW COPY

Research the Old Testament practice of keeping holy the Lord's Day as practiced by the ancient Israelites.

- What rules guided the way the Israelites honored this Commandment?
- What happened to those who did not keep holy the Lord's Day?

Failing to pray is also a sin against the Third Commandment. Prayer is a vital necessity for a person trying to live a good and moral life. A life without prayer moves away from God for

(CCC, 2744). Prayer and the Christian life are inseparable.

(CCC, 2745).

The first three Commandments of the Decalogue point directly to our responsibilities toward God. They instruct us to be attentive to how we speak of him. They tell us that if our relationship with God is to remain vibrant we need to keep holy the Lord's Day—the day Christ rose and announced new life for us.

Explain Why is the Jewish Sabbath celebrated on Saturday?

Contrast What is the difference between "holy leisure" and laziness?

SECTION 3 REVIEW

QUICK REVIEW

1a. Summarize What is the Second Commandment about?

b. Link How is perjury an offense against the Second Commandment?

c. Explain How did Jesus expand the Second Commandment?

2a. Define What two human needs are emphasized by the Third Commandment?

b. Link How is recreation like re-creation?

c. Evaluate Should you shop at stores that are open on Sunday? Why or why not?

Listen and Discuss Talk with a group of classmates about keeping the Lord's Day holy.

- Why would the Church require us to worship on Sunday?
- How do you re-create yourself on Sunday?
- Is it harder to set aside time for worship or for relaxation on Sunday? Explain your answer.

SELF-ASSESS

Which statement best reflects where you are now?

☐ I'm confident enough about the material in this section to be able to explain it to someone else.

☐ I have a good grasp of the material in this section, but I could use more review.

☐ I'm lost. I need help catching up before moving on.

ADVANCE REVIEW COPY

The Fourth Commandment

The first three Commandments are about loving and honoring God. The Fourth through Tenth Commandments are about loving and honoring others. After God, we are to honor our father and mother because they loved us into the world and are our first teachers about God. The relationship between child and parent is universal. The Fourth Commandment extends also to honoring and loving our family members, elders and ancestors, and even extends to the relationships between students and teachers, employees to employers, workers to leaders, citizens to their country, and those who govern (see CCC, 2199).

> " Honor your father and your mother, so that your days may be long in the land that the LORD your God is giving you.
>
> —Exodus 20:12

Marriage and the family bring happiness and goodness to the spouses. Marriage is intended for the mutual love of the spouses and for producing and educating children. We form our first relationships in the family. The Catholic Church calls on governments to recognize the importance of the family.

> QUOTATION TO BE
> INCLUDED IN FINAL PRINTING.
>
> —CCC, 2203

Pope Benedict XVI said the family and the Church are called to work more closely in the formation of people and the transmission of the faith. The Second Vatican Council called the family the domestic church. For the common good of the family members as well as the larger society, families have many responsibilities and rights.

The Christian family can serve as a beautiful model of the Trinity. It is a community that shares in the work of creation. Prayer and commitment to Christ should be a normal part of family life. QUOTATION TO BE INCLUDED IN FINAL PRINTING.

(CCC, 2205).

Family Responsibilities

The language of faith comes to us through our parents, who serve as our first contacts with God. The *Catechism* states, however, that (CCC, 239).

Despite human frailty, parents have the following responsibilities toward their children. Parents must:

- educate their children in the ways of faith, prayer, and morals;

- regard their children as sons and daughters of God
(CCC, 2222);

The language of faith comes to us first through our family.

Call to ACCOUNTABILITY

You've seen how the Israelites were held accountable with laws and expectations after they gained their freedom. The Commandments call us to accountability.

Athletes are accountable to their coaches and teammates. Children are accountable to their parents. Parents are accountable to their families. Husband and wife are accountable to each other. Citizens are accountable to the law of the government. Elected officials are accountable to those they represent.

Catholics are accountable to Christ and the Church.

How willing are you to be accountable? The spiritual practice of accountability helps ensure that you live as God intended. You practice accountability when you measure your actions against the standards set by by God and others you respect. You practice accountability when you evaluate your actions to the virtues of Christ. You practice accountability when you submit yourself to the wisdom of the Holy Spirit and those in authority.

You practice accountability when you check yourself—and let yourself be reminded by the promptings of the Holy Spirit—about your responsibilities, commitments, and morals.

Accountability is a spiritual practice that requires humility, honesty, courage, and faithfulness.

Accountability Assessment					
Grade yourself on the way you practice:					
Accountability to God	F	D	C	B	A
Accountability to family	F	D	C	B	A
Accountability to the Church	F	D	C	B	A
Accountability to friends	F	D	C	B	A
Accountability to teachers	F	D	C	B	A
Accountability to yourself	F	D	C	B	A

Write yourself instructions for improving the grade you gave yourself on the above.

ADVANCE REVIEW COPY

Choose five of the following and give a brief explanation or finish the thought. You can apply these to both or one of your parents or your stepparents.

- I admire my parents more than any other people in my life.
- My parents sacrifice a lot for our family.
- My parents and I could improve the way we . . .
- From my parents, I've learned . . .
- When it comes to honoring my parents, I wish I could . . .
- I need to tell my parents that . . .
- If God graded me right now for how well I am honoring my parent, I'd get a . . .

- create a home in which tenderness, mutual affection, forgiveness, respect, fidelity, and service are the norm. The home must be a place where education in faith and virtues can take place, meaning that material needs are subordinate to spiritual ones (see CCC, 2223);

- initiate children into community roles and responsibilities;

- evangelize their children from an early age into the mysteries of the faith and connect them with the life of the Church;

- QUOTATION TO BE
INCLUDED IN FINAL PRINTING.

(CCC, 2253);

- provide good example and provide for the physical and spiritual needs of their children (see CCC, 2228);

- as much as possible, choose a school and educational system that will help in their duty as Christian educators;

- be careful not to pressure their children in their choice of profession or who they will marry, but instead to offer advice, especially in starting a family.

Children have the right and duty to discover their profession and choose their state of life. They should willingly seek advice and counsel from within their trusted parental relationship (see CCC, 2230).

> With all your heart honor your father,
> and do not forget the birth pangs of your mother.
> Remember that it was of your parents you were born;
> how can you repay what they have given to you?
>
> —Sirach 7:27-28

Children should honor their parents because the source of their parenthood is God the Father. It is required by the Fourth Commandment:

QUOTATION TO BE
INCLUDED IN FINAL PRINTING.

(CCC, 2214). Respect for parents comes from the gratitude of being brought into the world and cared for through love. The Book of Proverbs instructs us to listen attentively to the lessons of our parents and keep them in our hearts.

> When you walk, they will lead you;
> when you lie down, they will watch over you;
> and when you awake, they will talk with you.
>
> —Proverbs 6:22

The *Catechism* teaches young people to obey parents as long as they live at home and

(CCC, 2217). Young people should obey reasonable directions of teachers and others who care for them. The Church also notes that if a child's conscience tells him or her that it would be morally wrong to obey some particular direction, then the child should not do so.

The pace and distractions of the contemporary world are not caused by children, but today's children have to deal with the effects of them. A five-year study at a middle school in Wisconsin found that when students ate a healthful diet for a period of time they ended up behaving better in school. The price that families pay for eating unhealthy meals is not just physical but also behavioral, emotional, and perhaps spiritual as well.

GO TO THE SOURCE

Family dynamics were an issue for the first followers of Christ.

Read Ephesians 5:21–6:4.

- What words from this passage stand out for you?
- How would you summarize what Saint Paul is calling for among family members?

The Fourth Commandment implies developing a spirituality of the home. Our homes can be places where we merely spend time, or they can be holy places where the Christian climate is evident, marked by family prayer, a crucifix, a Bible, religious books, and regular Sunday Mass attendance. Following the Golden Rule—treat others as you would have them treat you—is a good starting point for making home a holy place.

Today's parents also have responsibilities for their parents. Adult children are to give emotional, moral, and material support to their parents, making sure they have what they need to maintain their lives and their dignity.

(CCC, 2218).

Respect in the family promotes harmony in all aspects of family life. This includes relationships between brothers and sisters, and the *Catechism* adds that

QUOTATION TO BE
INCLUDED IN FINAL PRINTING.

(CCC, 2219).

Forgiveness plays a vital role in the relationships of family members.

QUOTATION TO BE
INCLUDED IN FINAL PRINTING.

(CCC, 2227).

The *Catechism* also mentions the role of single people in their families. These may be people who don't marry in order to care for parents or other family members, to give themselves to their profession, or to serve people in some other way.

(CCC, 2231).

Contrast How does the Church differentiate between obeying one's parents and obeying one's conscience?

Analyze How can the pace of the modern world get in the way of honoring one's family?

Beyond the Family

The Fourth Commandment applies to relationships outside of the family as well. Parents entrust their children to a variety of caregivers including teachers, coaches, bus drivers, and those in religious life. Adults other than parents play an important function in children's lives. By taking on their profession, they have serious responsibilities as well.

Those who hold positions of public authority are obligated to show respect for the basic human rights of others and to work to ensure the conditions that promote the exercise of freedom. There is a delicate distinction that we mentioned earlier regarding children and authorities. On the one hand, children should obey reasonable directions. On the other hand, if a child is convinced in conscience that it would be morally wrong to obey a particular order, the child must not do so. He or she is to tell a parent or another authority figure.

QUOTATION TO BE
INCLUDED IN FINAL PRINTING.

—CCC, 2212

DISCUSS

- What are some ways that contemporary life builds up and breaks down the family? List at least three examples of each.

Besides personal caregivers, parental figures exist within the broader community to whom people of all ages owe obedience. When a police officer motions the driver of a car to pull over, he or she should do so. The authoritative nature of this profession indicates why "impersonating an officer" is such a serious crime.

Citizens show their responsibility for one another by electing government officials who uphold the common good of society. To this voting responsibility we must bring the light of the Gospel. Otherwise, as history has demonstrated, our society can easily become tyrannical and dictatorial. Therefore, voting and other forms of participation in public life are duties that fall under the Fourth Commandment.

Those who hold authority over others have the responsibility to do so as a service (see CCC, 2235). Those in authority must take into account the needs and contribution of all people under their rule with the goal of peace and harmony. They are to respect fundamental rights of people.

(CCC, 2237).

We have duties as citizens that are governed by the Fourth Commandment. We should regard

Political responsibility, such as voting, must be exercised for the good of the nation and the community.

- Name two authority figures you admire and explain why you do in a paragraph on each.

those in authority as

(CCC, 2238). We, along with public authorities, have the responsibility to contribute to the good of society with truth, justice, solidarity, and freedom.

QUOTATION TO BE
INCLUDED IN FINAL PRINTING.

(CCC, 2240). The Apostles themselves told us to pray for everyone who holds authority.

These responsibilities extend to the family of nations as well. We are to welcome the foreigner or immigrant who seeks security or a better means of life. We can make laws to govern how this takes place, and immigrants in return are expected to respect the

(CCC, 2241).

Finally, citizens are not obligated to obey public authorities when orders are contrary to the moral order, the rights of others, or the teachings of the Gospel.

QUOTATION TO BE
INCLUDED IN FINAL PRINTING.

(CCC, 2242).

In this regard, armed resistance to government oppression is not legitimate unless these conditions exist:

1.   QUOTATION TO BE INCLUDED IN FINAL PRINTING.

2.   QUOTATION TO BE INCLUDED IN FINAL PRINTING.

3.   QUOTATION TO BE INCLUDED IN FINAL PRINTING.

4.   QUOTATION TO BE INCLUDED IN FINAL PRINTING.

5.   QUOTATION TO BE INCLUDED IN FINAL PRINTING.

Elaborate Name some relationships outside of the family to which the Fourth Amendment applies.

Explain How does the Fourth Commandment affect our lives as citizens?

QUICK REVIEW

1a. **Recall** Whom does the Fourth Commandment explicitly tell us to honor?

b. **Compare** How is the family like the Trinity?

c. **List** What are children's responsibilities toward their parents?

2a. **Recall** How does the Fourth Commandment extend beyond the family?

b. **Explain** How did Jesus honor his earthly parents during his life?

ACT

With a group of classmates, write two scenes.

- In the first scene, show an authority figure acting appropriately, with the subordinates responding appropriately.

- In the second scene, show an authority figure acting inappropriately. Have the subordinates responding as they should to an abuse of power.

Pray Compose a short prayer asking God to help authorities behave wisely.

SELF-ASSESS

Which statement best reflects where you are now?

☐ I'm confident enough about the material in this section to be able to explain it to someone else.

☐ I have a good grasp of the material in this section, but I could use more review.

☐ I'm lost. I need help catching up before moving on.

ADVANCE REVIEW COPY

PRAYER

Opening Prayer

We begin in the name of the Father, and of the Son, and of the Holy Spirit. Amen.

Lord God, be our light.
Be the light of forgiveness and love.
Be the light of goodness in us and each other.

Help each of us to see your light in everyone, infused with your image and likeness.

Strengthen us by your life, Death and Resurrection that we may live that passion in our daily lives with one another.

Be our light.
Amen

Closing Prayer

Lord Jesus, you have cleansed us of sin and division;
You have invited us to a new life of love and freedom.

Help us to see and recognize the separation between You and our fellow man.

Help us to see each other as Your children created in Your image and likeness.

Like Onesimus, remind us of our Baptism when you made us Your child;

May it unite us in love which flows from our very lives from You and may it redeem itself in others.

Let us believe that we are truly Your beloved sons and daughters in our hopes, in our loves, in our forgiveness and in our reconciliation.

Jesus, with your Father and the Holy Spirit, bless us and keep us safe.

Be with us now and always. Amen.

ADVANCE REVIEW COPY

TERMS

Use each of the following terms in a sentence that shows you know what the term means. You may include more than one term in a sentence.

hope   simony

charity   atheism

acedia   blasphemy

superstition   perjury

sacrilege

PEOPLE AND IDEAS

Identify what each term means in the context of the chapter.

1. natural moral law

2. Moses

3. Decalogue

4. Law of Love

5. voluntary doubt

6. despair

7. presumption

8. indifference

9. ingratitude

10. acedia

11. practical materialism

12. Saint Augustine

UNDERSTANDING

Answer each question and complete each exercise.

SECTION 1

1. **Explain** How did divine intervention help the Hebrews in the desert?
2. **Reflect** How are the Beatitudes an extension of the Ten Commandments?
3. **Explain** Why is moral law *sensible*?
4. **Link** How are the Ten Commandments and natural moral law related?

SECTION 2

5. **Explain** Why does the First Commandment direct us to protect our faith at all costs?
6. **Explain** How is hope forward looking?
7. **Evaluate** How is charity the starting point for all other virtues?
8. **List** What false beliefs stem from atheism?

SECTION 3

9. **Explain** Why is blasphemy a sin?
10. **Describe** How does perjury lack respect for God?
11. **Reflect** How does the Third Commandment help preserve ritual in our lives?

ADVANCE REVIEW COPY

12. **Explain** Why is the domestic Church important?
13. **Evaluate** What aspects of our society undermine families?
14. **Reflect** When would a child be correct to reject an authority's command?

CONNECTING

Visual Jesus willingly accepted his Cross.

What kind of obedience did Jesus display throughout his Passion? When was the last time you did what you thought was right rather than what you wanted to do?

Challenge You are walking home with a friend who has an idea for a prank to make some young kids think you are both drug dealers. Your friend says you can pretend you have stuff to sell and to ask them for help. The friend says it would be really funny. You object and your friend wants to know why. How do you answer? Be sure to use information from the chapter in your answer.

Question After working through this chapter, what advice would you give someone who wants to know how to show charity to others?

Imagine You are an artist commissioned to design a set of stained glass windows on the virtues of faith, hope, and charity.

- What sorts of images would you use to demonstrate these virtues?
- What colors would you use to convey your ideas?
- Where would you want the finished windows to be placed?

SELF-ASSESS

On Your Own Make a list of the most important things you learned from this chapter.

Select three things that represent your growth in understanding as you worked through this chapter. Write a paragraph explaining your choices.

With a Partner List what you found most helpful or interesting in this chapter as well as any other questions that have surfaced.

CHAPTER 4

- What does this photo say to you?
- How do you practice Jesus' command to love others?

Love of Neighbor

Go to the student site at
hs.osvcurriculum.com

ADVANCE REVIEW COPY

ADVANCE REVIEW COPY

YOU WILL

- Delve deeper into the meaning of love for one's neighbor.

- Explore the Fifth Commandment not to kill.

- Identify the moral principle that connects abortion, euthanasia, and other life issues.

- Review God's plan for sexuality in our lives.

- List offenses against the Sixth and Ninth Commandments.

- Connect the Seventh and Tenth Commandments.

The Fifth Commandment

KEY TERMS IN THIS SECTION

abortion

euthanasia

(Catechism of the Catholic Church, Glossary, p. 864)

(CCC, Glossary, p. 877)

God's Commandments help to rescue all humankind. They direct us to live in relationship with God and each other. The Ten Commandments written in our hearts reveal grave obligations. We cannot manage our world without them. The six remaining Commandments of the Decalogue guide us in "love of neighbor," the second "Great Commandment" that Jesus spoke of in the New Testament.

The Fifth Commandment mandates respect for human life in all stages and situations.

The annual March for Life takes place every January in Washington, D.C.

QUOTATION TO BE INCLUDED IN FINAL PRINTING.

(CCC, 2258).

This Commandment states: "You shall not murder" (Exodus 20:13). When the life of another human being is taken, it means the death of a person made in God's own image and likeness.

QUOTATION TO BE INCLUDED IN FINAL PRINTING. (CCC, 2268).

The first murder is described in Genesis 4 in the Old Testament. Abel was the target of unleashed, violent hatred and scorn. God condemns this first homicide. "'What have you done?'" he says, confronting Cain. "'Listen your brother's blood is crying to me from the ground!'" (Genesis 4:10).

In the New Testament, Jesus delves more deeply into the meaning of this Fifth Commandment. In the Sermon on the Mount, he taught that anger, hatred, and vengeance are the seeds of murder sown in the heart.

QUOTATION TO BE INCLUDED IN FINAL PRINTING.

(CCC, 2262).

The saints of the Church understood that Jesus calls us to live the Commandments and the love that is their foundation. "No one is to be called an enemy," taught Saint Francis of Assisi, who had been a soldier. "All are your benefactors and no one does you harm. You have no enemy except yourselves." This reflects Jesus' further teaching on the Fifth Commandment.

ADVANCE REVIEW COPY

> 'But I say to you that if you are angry with a brother or sister, you will be liable to judgment; and if you insult a brother or sister, you will be liable to the council; and if you say, "You fool," you will be liable to the hell of fire.'

—Matthew 5:21-22

In this chapter, we follow the Fifth Commandment with study of the Sixth and Ninth Commandments, which show us even more of God's plan. We see that chastity means

QUOTATION TO BE
INCLUDED IN FINAL PRINTING.

(CCC, 2337). "Male and female, he created them" (Genesis 1:27). That's who we are as creatures made in God's image and likeness. Sexual expression is truly human when it's expressed in the context of one man and woman giving to each other in a complete and lifelong covenant of marriage.

Learning to see, understand, and respect God's perfect plan for us as men and women protects us from loneliness, selfishness, and fear. In the Seventh and Tenth Commandments that end this chapter, we find that respect for the goods and private property of others brings peace, justice, and charity to our world. As stewards of creation, we can justifiably enjoy the fruits of our own hard work and efforts. But the *Catechism* reminds us that we must look beyond our own goals and personal security. From the beginning, in the Book of Genesis, God teaches

CONNECT

The Commandments, the *Catechism of the Catholic Church* points out,

(CCC, 2072).

- Which of the Commandments have you followed naturally since you were young?
- Which Commandments need more clarification for you?

DISCUSS

- Write down what your group thinks the virtues of temperance, justice, and solidarity mean.
- Then look up a formal definition of each and compare those definitions with those given by your group.
- Come up with three real life examples of each of these virtues being lived out or applied.

that we are our "brother's keeper." Jesus had the same message.

QUOTATION TO BE
INCLUDED IN FINAL PRINTING.

—CCC, 2407

Recall What is the first act of murder chronicled in the Bible?

Analyze How do people build moral good in themselves?

Respect for Life

The Fifth Commandment forbids the deliberate taking of innocent life. The Church offers a way to free us from violence by urgently insisting us to prayer and action (see CCC, 2307).

The consequences of Original Sin unveiled the presence of anger and envy in us. Respect for life was lost, and a seemingly unending cycle of killing resulted as people saw their fellow humans as the enemy. When used as a verb, the word "respect" means to consider worthy of high regard, to esteem; to value highly. What we respect, we naturally protect and nurture. What we protect and nurture, we grow to love.

Our whole human history testifies to a never-ending shedding of human blood, and the taking of innocent human life.

QUOTATION TO BE
INCLUDED IN FINAL PRINTING.

(CCC, 2260).

Murder is wrong because all human life is precious in God's eyes. It also requires us to think creatively about how we can foster a culture of life so that human beings view one another with the spirit of reverence that Jesus asks of us.

Killing the innocent and the righteous is specifically prohibited in Scripture. This theme brings us to questions related to violence and warfare. Is the deliberate taking of life ever justified? Does taking a life always diminish the human family? When people are being killed, is it justifiable to execute the killers?

No country is immune from violence, and the United States has a particularly high rate of violent crime. In some states, we continue to sanction capital punishment—a practice opposed by Church leaders as unnecessary in practically every circumstance today. In our world, leaders of many nations still rely on acts of war to achieve their ends. As with all moral matters, a Catholic looks deeply at these issues, seeking always to determine: *What would Jesus have me do?*

We know that sins against the Fifth Commandment come in endless and horrendous variety. New ways to kill, threaten, or damage human life are always being invented, it seems. Though they may not always end a human life, these sins violate that respect for human life and the person's innate dignity. We will explore these and how the Fifth Commandment mandates respect for the elderly, the handicapped, the dying, and the bodies of the deceased. We will also address questions related to self-defense, safeguarding the life and safety of others, and war.

Abortion and **euthanasia** are two sins against the Fifth Commandment. Both are hotly contested issues in society charged with strong emotions. The Church teaches against these practices in light of their impact on the dignity of the human person.

> When I look at your heavens, the work of your fingers,
> the moon and the stars that you have established;
> what are human beings that you are mindful of them,
> mortals that you care for them?
> Yet you have made them a little lower than God,
> and crowned them with glory and honor.
>
> —Psalm 8:3-5

The killing of unborn children through abortion has become what many people around the world call "a silent holocaust." The term "holocaust" described the genocidal extermination of the Jews in Europe by Hitler's Nazi Germany during the 1930s and 1940s. In 1973, in the landmark *Roe v. Wade* decision, the U.S. Supreme Court ruled that a right to privacy extended to a woman's right to have an abortion. Since that time, an estimated forty million abortions have been performed in the United States alone.

Because of legalized abortion and other attacks on the sacredness of human life, Blessed Pope John Paul II opposed what he called the "culture of death" with what he promoted as a "culture of life." Life was increasingly threatened as the twentieth century came to an end, he said. Those who believed in this Gospel-based "culture of life" could make a difference in the next century.

Blessed John Paul II quoted Saint Edith Stein whom he canonized in 1998. The Saint, known as Sister Teresa Benedicta of the Cross, was a Jewish Carmelite nun who died in 1942 in the death chambers of the Auschwitz Prison Camp run by the Nazis in Poland. "The nation," she said, "doesn't simply need what we have. It needs what we are." The need to be a witness and speak out for the sacredness of life was a central theme of Pope John Paul's papacy.

ELABORATE

- What do you think happens to our society each time the Fifth Commandment is broken?

ADVANCE REVIEW COPY

> The culture of life means respect for nature and protection of God's work of creation. In a special way, it means respect for human life from the first moment of conception until its natural end.
>
> —Blessed Pope John Paul II

Human life is sacred for two reasons: God created us; therefore we have a special relationship with him. Jesus takes this notion even further. Humans are holy because they are creations of God, made in his image and likeness. Jesus wants us to be attentive to the needs of those who are most vulnerable and unable to care for themselves.

Since the first century, the Catholic Church has been very clear about protecting human life from the moment of conception.

QUOTATION TO BE
INCLUDED IN FINAL PRINTING.

(CCC, 2270). Abortion is a sin against the Fifth Commandment that has been described as an abominable crime (see CCC, 2271). Embryonic stem cell research is also a sin against the Commandment because it causes the death of a human life at that early stage.

QUOTATION TO BE
INCLUDED IN FINAL PRINTING.

—CCC, 2322

In this teaching, the Church is not limiting forgiveness and mercy. Instead, she is making a point about the seriousness of the crime, the harm done to the human life that was ended, as well as to the parents and the wider society (see CCC, 2272). The Church calls on governments to protect the right to life of innocent human beings. Unless this protection takes place, the foundations of the state or nation based on law are undermined.

The Church teaches that a human embryo

QUOTATION TO BE
INCLUDED IN FINAL PRINTING.

(CCC, 2274). Prenatal care must be directed toward safeguarding and healing the unborn child. It is morally wrong to do a procedure to determine the health of an unborn child in order to decide if he or she should be aborted.

(CCC, 2274).

The Church also teaches that it is morally wrong

QUOTATION TO BE
INCLUDED IN FINAL PRINTING.

(CCC, 2275).

> For it was you who formed my inward parts;
> you knit me together in my mother's womb.
> I praise you, for I am fearfully and wonderfully made.
> Wonderful are your works.
>
> —Psalm 139:13-14a

Recall About how many abortions have taken place since the 1973 *Roe v. Wade* decision?

Explain What did Blessed Pope John Paul II mean when he used the phrase *culture of life*?

Rejection of Euthanasia

This respect and protection of human life also means rejection of euthanasia. The morality of euthanasia is complicated by questions about when human life ends. In life, our lungs automatically inhale life-giving oxygen, our heart pumps blood throughout the body, and our brain serves as a control center for all the conscious and unconscious activities that keep the body functioning. When a person is dead, these essential life systems no longer function. Thus, the threshold between life and death would seem to be clearly defined. Yet, more and more we are hearing of instances in which this threshold is not so clear.

We face important new moral decisions because of increased complexity in the dying process resulting from improved medical technology.

Saint Vincent de Paul

(1580–1660)

Saint Vincent de Paul was born into a peasant family in a small village in France. He was educated by Franciscans and studied theology at the University of Toulouse before being ordained in 1600. Five years later, while traveling by sea, he was captured by pirates. Vincent was sold into slavery in Tunis. For two years, young Father Vincent was a slave. He prayed to find a way to escape. In 1607, he escaped after converting his owner to Christianity.

After moving to Paris in 1608, Father Vincent met two priests who would spiritually influence him. They helped Vincent see that power and a good income were not the most important goals in life. Through prayer, he recognized that God was calling him to something deeper. His priesthood was an opportunity to serve. In 1613, however, Vincent was named as chaplain and tutor for the wealthy de Gondi family. He was honored to serve the de Gondis, but the cry of the poor was never far away.

At his request, Vincent was finally sent to a poor parish in southeast France. One day, a parishioner came to tell him about a desperately hungry family. At Mass, Father Vincent told their story. In just a day, fifty families took food to the needy family. When Father Vincent later went to see them,

ADVANCE REVIEW COPY

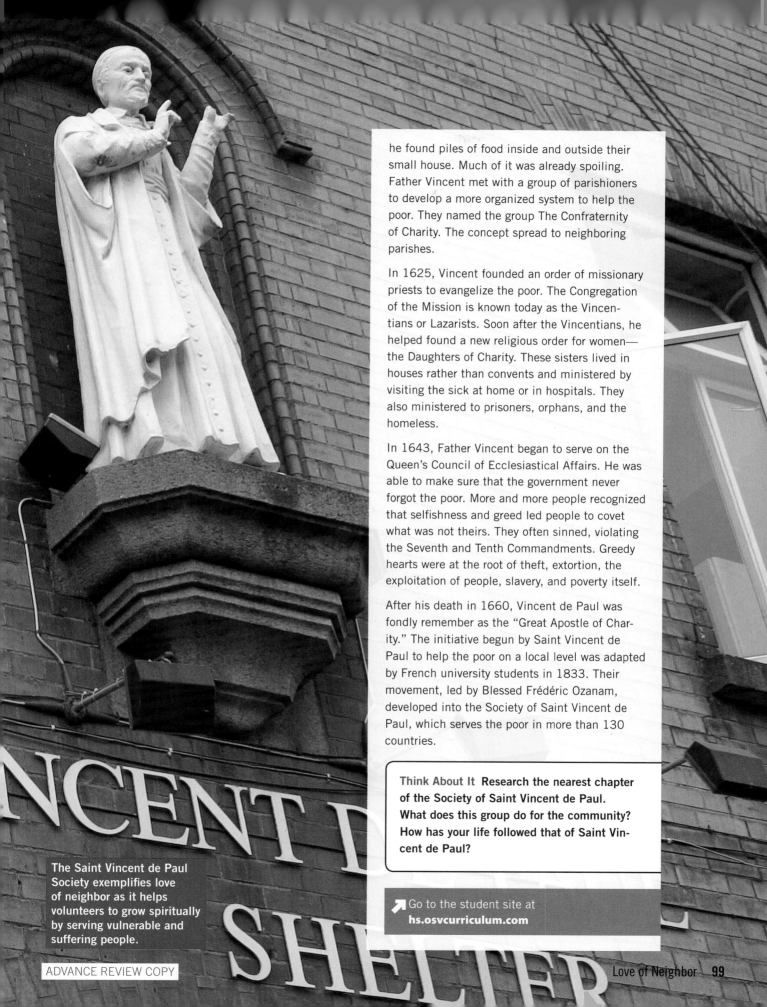

he found piles of food inside and outside their small house. Much of it was already spoiling. Father Vincent met with a group of parishioners to develop a more organized system to help the poor. They named the group The Confraternity of Charity. The concept spread to neighboring parishes.

In 1625, Vincent founded an order of missionary priests to evangelize the poor. The Congregation of the Mission is known today as the Vincentians or Lazarists. Soon after the Vincentians, he helped found a new religious order for women— the Daughters of Charity. These sisters lived in houses rather than convents and ministered by visiting the sick at home or in hospitals. They also ministered to prisoners, orphans, and the homeless.

In 1643, Father Vincent began to serve on the Queen's Council of Ecclesiastical Affairs. He was able to make sure that the government never forgot the poor. More and more people recognized that selfishness and greed led people to covet what was not theirs. They often sinned, violating the Seventh and Tenth Commandments. Greedy hearts were at the root of theft, extortion, the exploitation of people, slavery, and poverty itself.

After his death in 1660, Vincent de Paul was fondly remember as the "Great Apostle of Charity." The initiative begun by Saint Vincent de Paul to help the poor on a local level was adapted by French university students in 1833. Their movement, led by Blessed Frédéric Ozanam, developed into the Society of Saint Vincent de Paul, which serves the poor in more than 130 countries.

Think About It Research the nearest chapter of the Society of Saint Vincent de Paul. What does this group do for the community? How has your life followed that of Saint Vincent de Paul?

➦ Go to the student site at
hs.osvcurriculum.com

The Saint Vincent de Paul Society exemplifies love of neighbor as it helps volunteers to grow spiritually by serving vulnerable and suffering people.

ADVANCE REVIEW COPY

Caring for the elderly meets Jesus' command to love our neighbor.

Church teaching makes a distinction between allowing a person to die and euthanasia. Allowing a person to die means

QUOTATION TO BE
INCLUDED IN FINAL PRINTING.

(CCC, 2278). In this situation, no one wants to cause the person's death. They are accepting their inability to stop it.

For some, euthanasia has come to mean mercy killing—mercifully putting to death someone who is dying or who is experiencing extreme suffering, as we might put to death a dying beloved pet. Blessed Pope John Paul II gave the following definition: "Euthanasia in the strict sense is understood to be an action or omission which of itself and by intention causes death, with the purpose of eliminating all suffering" (*The Gospel of Life*, 65).

In the 1980 *Declaration on Euthanasia*, the Congregation for the Doctrine of the Faith had previously defined it in a similar way. It said "euthanasia is understood as an action or an omission which of itself or by intention causes death, in order that all suffering may in this way be eliminated."

Since it is an act that is directly contrary to the dignity of the human person, euthanasia is a sin against the Fifth Commandment. Notice that Blessed Pope John Paul II referred to "euthanasia in the strict sense." Sometimes people use the term to refer to actions that are not, strictly speaking, euthanasia. The same action may or may not fall under this strict definition of euthanasia depending on the kind of act involved, the intention behind the action, and the circumstance surrounding the action.

Terms used in moral discussions about euthanasia today, include:

- Euthanasia in the strict sense involves taking deliberate steps to end the life of a suffering and incurably ill person. This action may happen with (voluntary) or without (involuntary) the consent of the patient. Regardless of whether the euthanasia was performed voluntarily or involuntarily, in a strict sense euthanasia involves the direct and intentional taking of life. Sometimes this is called active or direct euthanasia.

- Euthanasia in a strict sense can also be extended to mean deliberately not taking steps to prevent a sick person's death, precisely with the desire and intention that this withholding will cause his or her death. An example would be refusing a life-saving surgical procedure for a newborn with Down's syndrome because the parents would prefer the child not to survive. In this instance, although it involves an action not taken, the intention—just like active euthanasia—is to take a life, even if "relieving suffering" or another rationalization is used to try to justify it. This action may happen with or without a patient's consent. It is wrong because the intention is the taking of a life. Sometimes this is called passive or indirect euthanasia.

Hospitals that feature the latest medical equipment have an array of machines, monitors, and other devices available for seriously ill or injured patients. This medical technology can cause some people to fear that, if their health becomes seriously impaired, the decision about whether to live or die will be out of their hands. They imagine with dread the possibility of being kept alive without any hope of serious recovery. With all the medical treatments and equipment available today, the dying person can be forgotten. Keeping the body functioning even at minimal levels can become the driving force behind treatment.

For instance, the body functions of a comatose person with no medical hope of recovery can remain operating almost indefinitely with the help of machines and artificial nutrients.

ADVANCE REVIEW COPY

The *Declaration on Euthanasia* of the U.S. Bishops acknowledges that there are times when modern medical technology and practices will not cure a person but will only delay death indefinitely. In such cases, medical treatments may be discontinued if they do no more than prolong life at great expense or with excessive burden. Such a decision is not "mercy killing" or euthanasia since it allows the natural dying process to occur. The focus is on foregoing excessively burdensome treatment, not on killing the patient (see CCC, 2278).

Excessively burdensome treatment—or what some call extraordinary measures—to keep someone alive in vegetative state, can be confusing when it comes to providing food and water. The Church does not consider artificial nutrition and hydration extraordinary measures, meaning there is an obligation to continue, when possible, giving the patient enough food and water to maintain life.

Medical personnel who work with dying patients often find themselves faced with decisions that rely on subtle but important distinctions. For instance, what is acceptable when a frail and incurably ill person is experiencing pain and has been prescribed medicine to relieve the pain? At some point, increasing the dosage of certain pain medications may hasten or contribute to death. In this situation, it is important to remember that the intention and the method used determine whether the action is euthanasia.

QUOTATION TO BE
INCLUDED IN FINAL PRINTING.

—CCC, 2279

Define What is euthanasia?

Explain How does the *Declaration on Euthanasia* address the issue of a comatose person with no hope of recovery?

QUICK REVIEW

1a. Recall What does the Fifth Commandment mandate?

b. Link Why did Blessed John Paul II speak out on the "culture of life" and "the culture of death"?

2a. Explain What was Jesus' deeper interpretation of the Fifth Commandment?

b. Analyze Why can it be so difficult to follow Jesus' advice of "turning the other cheek?"

3. Recall When do human beings have the right to life?

4a. Apply How should medical professionals determine proper care for dying patients?

b. Consider What do Catholics need to keep in mind about death?

Listen and Discuss Meet with a medical professional who specializes in caring for terminal patients.

• Discuss how Christian and medical ethics are similar.

• Ask whether the person has ever felt a conflict about the care of a dying patient.

• Find out how you can help others who are facing this situation.

Pray Compose a short prayer asking God to help those who are near death today, as well as their loved ones and caregivers.

SELF-ASSESS

Which statement best reflects where you are now?

☐ I'm confident enough about the material in this section to be able to explain it to someone else.

☐ I have a good grasp of the material in this section, but I could use more review.

☐ I'm lost. I need help catching up before moving on.

Defending Life

KEY TERMS IN THIS SECTION

capital punishment the death penalty; state-sanctioned execution of people convicted of murder or other serious crime

scandal wrongdoing that serves to disillusion or harm more vulnerable people;

(CCC, 2284)

The Fifth Commandment's condemnation of murder does not cancel out our right to self-defense. In defending ourselves, we have the right to incapacitate an aggressor, even if that includes delivering a lethal blow.

QUOTATION TO BE
INCLUDED IN FINAL PRINTING.

(CCC, 2263).

To take self-defense one step further: Elected leaders, police officers, military personnel, and all those who have responsibility for the lives of others have a grave duty to defend those who are entrusted to them and to ensure the common good (see CCC, 2265).

When Cain murdered his brother Abel, he was punished but not executed. In fact, God said, "'Whoever kills Cain will suffer a sevenfold vengeance'" (Genesis 4:15). God, then, placed a mark on Cain, so that anyone seeing the mark would know not to kill him.

The teaching of Jesus provides us with even greater insight into the issue of **capital punishment**. Jesus never offers violence as a solution for correcting the ills of society. On the contrary, Jesus reveals God's unconditional love for all people, regardless of their crimes or worthiness. Jesus does not desire the death of sinners but rather that they convert and attain eternal life.

Jesus' focus on mercy is seen when a woman caught in adultery is brought before him (see John 8:1-11). The religious leaders point out that, in the law, Moses commands that such women be stoned to death. The leaders want to know what Jesus thinks about this. He bounces the challenge back to the woman's accusers by saying, "'Let anyone among you who is without sin be the first to throw a stone at her'" (John 8:7). Her accusers walk away until only Jesus and the woman are left alone. Jesus then tells her, "'Neither do I condemn you. Go your way, and from now on do not sin again'" (John 8:11).

> Jesus often shifts focus of judgment to a higher court, a court where there is no need for polygraph, where there is absolute knowledge of evidence, of good deeds and of evil, of things private and things public; a court where there is justice and mercy, both law and grace, wrath and tenderness.
>
> —Cardinal Sean O'Malley, OFM Cap, "The Gospel of Life vs. The Death Penalty" Pastoral Letter on Capital Punishment, February 25, 1999

Sister Lynn Marie D'Souza of the Benedictine Sisters of Perpetual Adoration is a biomedical scientist who helped develop a gluten-free recipe for communion bread.

ADVANCE REVIEW COPY

- What are the laws for the death penalty in your state?
- Research what your local bishops and bishop conference has said about the death penalty in your state?

In 1972, the U.S. Supreme Court declared the death penalty to be unconstitutional. At the time, the country was moving toward the position of most other Western nations who determined that capital punishment was ineffective, unnecessary, and immoral. However, in 1976, the Supreme Court declined to disallow new state laws and procedures, thus making it possible for thirty-eight states to have legalized capital punishment.

The death penalty is acceptable only when society has no other means of defending itself (see The *Gospel of Life,* 56). Blessed Pope John Paul II emphasized that the existence of high-security prisons makes capital punishment unnecessary and immoral in modern societies. Today cases for which no effective alternative exists to capital punishment

(CCC, 2267).

Contrast What is the difference between self-defense and murder?

Explain What is the Church's view of the death penalty?

DISCUSS

List the arguments people sometimes give for and against capital punishment. Give possible pros and cons to each argument.

- Which arguments do you believe are more convincing?
- Which arguments do you believe reflect a Catholic perspective? Explain.

Scientific Research

The Fifth Commandment also extends to the principles of health, science, and threats to the integrity of our bodies. Science and faith are often seen as adversaries, but Blessed Pope John Paul II showed that the two can go hand in hand. "It is science that has shown us how numerous and complex the works of creation are and how seemingly limitless the created cosmos is," the Pope said in a 2002 address. He also warned that the special knowledge accorded to scientists gives them greater responsibility to use it wisely. It must benefit humankind, he said, and be grounded in respect for human life.

The *Catechism* sees scientific research as part of our God-given dominion over creation.

QUOTATION TO BE
INCLUDED IN FINAL PRINTING.

(CCC, 2293). Science and technology then get their purpose from us and find their limits in our moral values.

QUOTATION TO BE
INCLUDED IN FINAL PRINTING.

—CCC, 2295

In other words, we cannot experiment on people if it jeopardizes their lives in a disproportionate way. To preserve the dignity of people, experimentation on any person must have that person's complete and informed consent.

The *Catechism* also discusses the increasingly important issue of organ transplants.

QUOTATION TO BE
INCLUDED IN FINAL PRINTING.

(CCC, 2296). The *Catechism* sees organ donation as a noble act as long as it does not bring about the death of a person.

Scientific research has also helped us understand the dangers of abusing food, alcohol, tobacco, and drugs. The virtue of temperance helps us avoid excesses with these substances. Abusing them is a sin against the Fifth Commandment. We can commit a grave sin when we endanger ourselves or others in a vehicle we are operating on the road, the water, or in the air (see CCC, 2290). The *Catechism* also notes the use of illegal drugs causes very grave damage to ourselves and others and is a grave sin, unless used strictly for therapeutic purposes. Production and distribution of illegal drugs is a scandalous practice (see CCC, 2291).

The Church also teaches that we must give care to those who are dying. Relatives must pray for the dying family member as well as ensure that they receive the Sacraments to prepare them to meet the Lord. Once someone has died, their body must be treated with respect, and burying the dead is one of the corporal works of mercy. Autopsies are allowed for legal or scientific research, and the Church does permit cremation while maintaining faith in the resurrection of the body and as long as the ashes are buried and not scattered or kept somewhere else (see CCC, 2301).

Explain What did Blessed Pope John Paul II say about the special knowledge possessed by scientists?

Summarize What does the *Catechism* teach about organ donation?

The Power of Scandal
The term **scandal** refers to an
(CCC, 2284).
It points to an affront against truth and integrity by people who are entrusted with a responsibility to uphold these virtues.

(CCC, 2326).

QUOTATION TO BE
INCLUDED IN FINAL PRINTING.

—CCC, 2285

Scandal refers to wrongdoing by people who hold some kind of trust and misusing that trust

in such a way that it harms and disturbs more vulnerable people.

For instance, teenagers drinking illegally in front of younger brothers and sisters, presenting it as fun without inherent dangers, adds a dimension of scandal to the behavior even though the older teens have not directly harmed the younger ones. Directly betraying someone's trust—like the adult who sexually abuses a child—or the teen who introduces a younger sibling to alcohol is scandalous also. Scandal is wrong because it models immoral behavior.

Identify When is scandal a grave sin?

Elaborate Name an instance where you witnessed or were effected by scandal. How might that incident have hurt your own efforts to live the moral life?

War and Respect for Life
The Church's moral teaching applies to the question of war the same principles it applies to the question of abortion, euthanasia, capital punishment, and other issues in which human lives are at stake. We are to respect life itself as well as the lives of individuals. War is an assault on human life and brings with it suffering and death, and we should do everything possible within reason to avoid it (see CCC, 2327). Jesus invites us to be peacemakers. To do this, we must struggle for peace, which is always a struggle for life.

Kidnapping and hostage-taking also violate the person and the human community. They threaten the victims with death and subject them to intense stress. In our modern age, we now know that these acts are sometimes connected to terrorism.

QUOTATION TO BE
INCLUDED IN FINAL PRINTING.

—CCC, 2297

ADVANCE REVIEW COPY

THE CONCEPT OF
Just War

Many people have spoken about the concept of just war and the decision to use military force. The Catholic Church places strict conditions on this decision. It calls for thorough, exhaustive, and accurate consideration before using military force. The *Catechism* lists these traditional conditions as:

QUOTATION TO BE INCLUDED IN FINAL PRINTING.

QUOTATION TO BE INCLUDED IN FINAL PRINTING.

QUOTATION TO BE INCLUDED IN FINAL PRINTING.

QUOTATION TO BE INCLUDED IN FINAL PRINTING.

(CCC, 2309).

The U.S. Holocaust Memorial Museum in Washington, D.C., displays the shoes of men, women, and children who died in the Nazi death camps of World War II.

WE ARE THE SHOES, WE ARE THE LAST WITNESSES.
WE ARE SHOES FROM GRANDCHILDREN AND GRANDFATHERS
FROM PRAGUE, PARIS, AND AMSTERDAM,
AND BECAUSE WE ARE ONLY MADE OF FABRIC AND LEATHER
AND NOT OF BLOOD AND FLESH, EACH ONE OF US AVOIDED THE HELLFIRE.

YIDDISH POET MOSES SCHULSTEIN (1911—1981)

Think about the conflicts around the world. How often are these conditions met before military force is used?

How do you know when all other means have been tried to end a conflict before deciding that war is the only alternative?

The Church calls on us to pray for victims of terrorism or torture. She also calls for prayers for the repentance of their tormentors. Sometimes Catholics have not spoken out enough about atrocities such as terrorism and torture occurring in their own countries and around the world. Even so, the Catholic Church has taught mercy as well as forbidding violence and war (see CCC, 2298).

In a 2003 address, Pope John Paul II said: "War is not always inevitable. It is always a defeat for humanity. . . . War is never just another means that one can choose to employ for settling differences between nations. . . . War cannot be decided upon, even when it is a matter of ensuring the common good, except as the last option and in accordance with very strict conditions, without ignoring the consequences for the civilian population both during and after military operations."

Human history is scarred by wars. One thorough statement of Christian teaching on war is the 1983 pastoral letter of the U.S. Catholic bishops, *The Challenge of Peace: God's Promise and Our Response*. The letter discusses the morality of war. It enunciates general principles about war and suggests some specific applications of those principles to our contemporary world.

The Challenge of Peace acknowledges that the use of violence in war is a complex moral issue. For example, the pastoral letter says that: "Even a brief examination of war and peace in the Scriptures makes it clear that it does not provide us with detailed answers to the specifics of the questions which we face today" (*Challenge of Peace*, 55). Although the Bible does not give us definitive answers about war, it does aim us always in the direction of peace. The pastoral letter points us in the same direction when it offers us the following as a first principle regarding war: "Catholic teaching begins in every case with a presumption against war and for peaceful

settlement of disputes" (*Challenge of Peace, Summary*, A1).

According to the bishops, in defending and working for peace, there are two legitimate options: to resist bearing arms or to bear arms. Nonetheless, it's important to keep in mind that both of these options, while in disagreement on means, do agree on the goal—a just resolution of conflict accompanied by the least possible harm to all parties involved. Given this understanding of means and ends, the bishops accept the idea that war is permissible when entered into for defensive purposes. However, it is subject to rigorous restrictions that have been spelled out since the early centuries of Christian history. The *Catechism* calls the arms race of nations one of the   to life on Earth, especially the damage it inflicts on the poor (CCC, 2329). During war, moral law remains valid, and deliberate practices against international law are crimes (see CCC, 2328).

Analyze What did Blessed Pope John Paul II mean when he said that "war is not always inevitable?"

Compare How do the options of choosing to fight in a war and not choosing to fight both aim toward the same goal?

APPLY

Decisions on war are prudential judgments on the application of the Church's principles to concrete threats. The bishops remind us that when it comes to war "the possibility of taking even one human life is a prospect we should consider in fear and trembling" (*Challenge of Peace*, 80).

- Describe the attitude toward war that currently exists in our society.

- How can we change that in light of Church teachings?

No matter what causes us to suffer, we are never without hope in Jesus Christ.

What is Death?

The Book of Genesis says that the first man and woman were immune from death. Original Sin changed that and now we must all suffer death. To atone for the sins of the world, even Jesus died and, by doing so, conquered death and reversed the damage done by the sin of our first parents. Jesus told us:

> 'I am the resurrection and the life. Those who believe in me, even though they die, will live, and everyone who lives and believes in me will never die. Do you believe this?'
>
> —John 11:25-26

We learn that "all of us who have been baptized into Christ Jesus were baptized into his death" (Romans 6:3). Through Baptism, then, we have already died with Christ and are on a pilgrimage to a new life. Death is the end of that pilgrimage, because it is the portal to eternal life with God. As Saint Teresa of Ávila said,

(CCC, 1011). By singular privilege, God exempted Mary, Jesus' Mother, from death. Since she was sinless, at the end of her life on Earth, Mary was taken body and soul into Heaven. Mary's was a singular participation in the Resurrection of Jesus, giving the rest of us the hope of resurrection (see CCC, 966).

Death, nonetheless, inspires some of our worst fears. It is often identified with tragic endings,

the sadness of losing friends and family members, weeping, pain, and helplessness (see accompanying chart on suicide). The suffering often associated with dying should not blind us to the blessings Jesus gave us through his Paschal Mystery. His Passion and Death led to Resurrection—for himself and for us who believe in him. He ascended into Heaven where he sits at the right hand of the Father.

The *Catechism* on Suicide
QUOTATION TO BE INCLUDED IN FINAL PRINTING. (CCC, 2280).
QUOTATION TO BE INCLUDED IN FINAL PRINTING.
(CCC, 2282).
QUOTATION TO BE INCLUDED IN FINAL PRINTING. (CCC, 2283).
QUOTATION TO BE INCLUDED IN FINAL PRINTING. (CCC, 2325).

• What are the prevailing views toward death and dying present in our contemporary society? How are they similar to or different from a Catholic view toward death and dying?

DISCUSS

Do you agree that it is important not to reduce "dying well" merely to dying a painless death? What else might be involved in dying well?

Through our faith, we are concerned about compassionate care and comfort for the dying. Jesus said, "'Cure the sick'" (Matthew 10:8), and the Church strives to do so by caring for the sick and interceding for them in prayer. The Church is concerned about how we can best enable one another to die a happy death. On this point, it is important to recall that, in many languages, the root of the word health is the same as that for salvation. In the end, therefore, being healed means not avoiding death but being saved—life with Christ after death. If we don't distinguish between our concern for healing and Catholic teaching about death and resurrection, we can end up with misguided positions on some important moral dilemmas.

Explain Why should we not fear death?

Analyze Why do you think so many movies, TV shows, and video games are filled with images of death?

SECTION 2 REVIEW

QUICK REVIEW

1a. Explain Why is capital punishment wrong in most situations?

b. Synthesize What does the Church teach about physical experimentation and organ transplantation?

2. Apply Why should war always be the last option to resolve conflicts?

3. Consider What do Catholics need to keep in mind about death?

Listen and Discuss Meet with a veteran who has experienced war.

- Discuss how he or she perceived war before experiencing it.

- Discuss how he or she perceived war afterward.

Pray Compose a short prayer asking God to help those who live in a war zone or must live with the constant threat of terrorism.

SELF-ASSESS

Which statement best reflects where you are now?

☐ I'm confident enough about the material in this section to be able to explain it to someone else.

☐ I have a good grasp of the material in this section, but I could use more review.

☐ I'm lost. I need help catching up before moving on.

ADVANCE REVIEW COPY

Sixth and Ninth Commandments

KEY TERMS IN THIS SECTION

chastity
QUOTATION TO BE INCLUDED IN FINAL PRINTING. (CCC, Glossary, p. 870)

fecundity fruitfulness and the ability to bear children that is a gift of the Sacrament of Marriage; (CCC, 2366).

The Theology of the Body is rooted in a series of more than one hundred talks given by Blessed Pope John Paul II early in his papacy. The phrase *theology of the body* means that our bodies teach us through their very design about God's purpose for us. The Pope's talks were delivered at his Wednesday audiences. The subject matter covered the meaning of the human person, God's original design for sexuality, and the sacramental nature of marriage.

For more than five years, the Pope spoke about the need and desire that human beings naturally have for loving communion. In ways that thoughtful people around the world could understand, he shared good news about what sexual expression really means. This precious gift has been distorted by sin, he explained.

Nonetheless, it has also been restored and renewed through our Redeemer, Jesus Christ.

The Sixth Commandment is "You shall not commit adultery" and the Ninth Commandment is "You shall not covet your neighbor's wife." Today, these Commandments are sometimes seen as warnings what we shouldn't do. In fact, they invite us to learn more about God's gift of sexuality. Relationships that do not take sexuality seriously eventually wound us. God has designed us to be happy and fulfilled when we can give ourselves, as husband and wife, in a mutual, lifelong relationship.

The Catholic Church teaches us who we are and how we can love as God intends us to love. The *Catechism* teaches that these lessons on love begin with lessons in **chastity**.

Relationships must take God's gift of sexuality seriously.

The Virtue and Practice of Chastity

Here's an excerpt from the *Catechism* about chastity:

QUOTATION TO BE
INCLUDED IN FINAL PRINTING.

(CCC, 2339).

Notice some of the words and phrases the Church uses in describing the virtue and practice of chastity: self- mastery; training in human freedom; govern passions ... find peace; dominated by them . . . unhappy; dignity; slavery; and freely choosing what is good.

Which of these words and phrases rings most true to you about chastity? Which of these present you with a challenge? Which one inspires you?

Who or what can help you with the virtue and practice of chastity? Who or what can make it more difficult for you?

Make some notes about your journey of faith and this sacred and powerful virtue called chastity. Then internalize them and pray on them.

You can use any of this My Faith as part of the report you will turn in at the end of the course.

Discipleship ... within the Body of Christ ... for the glory of God and the good of the world.

We become truly free when we have self-control. Nonetheless, self-mastery in the area of chastity

(CCC, 2342). Chastity is a moral virtue in which the Holy Spirit enables us to imitate the purity of Christ. It falls under the cardinal virtue of temperance, in which we practice moderation and self-control. Our ability to reason tempers our passions (see CCC, 2341).

We grow in chastity in stages that are marked by imperfection and too often by sin.

QUOTATION TO BE
INCLUDED IN FINAL PRINTING.

(CCC, 2343).

the *Catechism* reminds us.

(CCC, 2347). Those who practice chastity become models for others of God's faithfulness and loving kindness (see CCC, 2346).

Learning to achieve that freedom through chastity will also mean learning what the Sixth and Ninth Commandments ask of us. They call people to choose sexual communion in a marriage, a marriage that unites a free and committed man and woman.

Our sexuality is a blessing from God. He created us as sexual beings and our fundamental vocation is to love him and others. By creating human beings in his image and likeness, God gave personal dignity to both genders. He crafted men and women with differences that complement each other and that orient them toward marriage and the growth of families.

In our very flesh we have a capacity for communion, generosity, and **fecundity**, or the bearing of children. Two people can come together in love and marriage to create a new life. God created us out of love. He created us to love one other, and our sexuality is one way for us to fulfill God's vision.

However, expressing our sexuality in the proper way requires maturity. We must understand and follow the idea of integrated sexuality. That is, we are to express ourselves sexually in ways that reflect our integrity as physical-spiritual beings made in God's image and likeness.

Qualities of Chastity

Jesus is the model of chastity. By being baptized into the life of Jesus, we are called to lead lives of chastity, whether we are single or married, laity or called to consecrated life as religious sisters, brothers, or priests. Here are qualities that are associated with this important virtue of chastity.

Self-mastery. The practice of chastity trains us to be truly free. We can either control our passions and find peace, or we can let our passions control us and become enslaved by them. We can give into our blind impulses, or we can consciously and freely choose what a conscience formed by Church teaching tells us is right and realize lives of harmony and holiness.

Good habits. To fulfill our baptismal promises and resist sexual temptation, we are encouraged to obey God's Commandments; exercise the virtues of prudence, justice, fortitude, and temperance; heed the teachings of the Church; and be attentive to the Holy Spirit in prayer.

Patience. The self-mastery involved in chastity is a lifelong endeavor. It requires discipline at all stages of life and a redoubling of effort at certain stages, particularly during adolescence.

Grace. Remember, chastity is a moral virtue. We acquire chastity, as all other mortal virtues, through education, deliberate actions, and perseverance. Grace purifies our efforts and heightens the virtue within us.

Define What is chastity?

Explain How did God design us to fulfill our sexuality?

Sins Against Chastity

Among the offenses against chastity as well as the Sixth and Ninth Commandments are lust, masturbation, fornication, pornography, prostitution, rape, and homosexual acts.

Lust and concupiscence are intense forms of human desire. Saint Paul identifies lust with the rebellion of the flesh against the spirit. Lust is a craving for sexual gratification without regard for boundaries, morality, or harm to others. Lust

GLOBAL PERSPECTIVES

Global sex trafficking experts estimate that millions of people—mostly girls and women—are trapped in the sex trafficking trade around the world. Trafficking is rampant in parts of Asia, including China, India, Thailand, and Cambodia. Eastern Europe is another area where trafficking is common. Young women from poor families or refugee camps are recruited with the promise of good jobs. Sometimes they are sold to sex trafficking "owners." Passports and money are taken away and the women are forced into prostitution.

In the United States, an estimated 100,000 girls are trafficked. Runaways and children who were sexually abused are more likely to be recruited.

There are a growing number of organizations working to free trafficking victims and stop this violation of the Sixth Commandment that condemns sexual abuse of people for profit. International organizations like Catholic Relief Services are working to provide employment alternatives to vulnerable populations and stop the trafficking.

- Research local organizations working to stop sex trafficking.
- Research the issue of sex trafficking and create "Did You Know?" posters with eight or more facts about sex trafficking and its consequences. Share your work with the rest of the class..

Global sex trafficking has put young women, often from poor families, at risk.

Go to the student site at **hs.osvcurriculum.com**

REFLECT

Entertainment today has a lot of sexual content.

- How has your religion helped you appreciate sexuality to a greater degree?
- What are some ways to integrate the virtue of chastity into your daily life?
- With the amount of sexual content in movies, TV, and other forms of entertainment, do you think society has become addicted to sexuality? Explain your answer.

Masturbation is the erotic, self-stimulation achieved by means other than sexual intercourse. As such, masturbation is an act that violates the intended purpose of God's gift of sexuality. Sexual pleasure is meant for marriage and for the expression of the mutual self-giving and procreation that are a vital part of marriage.

(CCC, 2352).

Fornication is sexual intercourse between an unmarried man and an unmarried woman. Once again, the gift of sexual union is meant for the benefit of the married couple and the generation of children.

(CCC, 2353).

Pornography is the display of erotic behavior in written or pictorial form for the purpose of sexual excitement. It violates chastity by perverting the gift of sexuality—the intimate giving of husband and wife to each other (see CCC, 2354). Pornography is an assault on human dignity. It demeans the dignity of everyone involved—the actors, the sellers, and the public—and thus constitutes a grave sin. The *Catechism* calls for government authorities to prevent its production and distribution.

Prostitution is the practice or the act of engaging in sexual relations for money or other forms of profit. Those who pay for sexual intercourse sin against God, the person prostituted, and themselves. Those who sell themselves violate their dignity by making themselves into mere objects of pleasure. As a people created by a loving God, we have reason to grieve as we see men, women, adolescents, and even children selling their bodies in order to make money or gain in other ways (see CCC, 2355).

disregards the principle that God intends sexual relationships for the procreation of children and the sharing of love within the union of marriage (see CCC, 2351). We offset the power of lust by aligning our minds and our wills to the pursuit of holiness, charity, and truth. We practice modesty by respecting our bodies, being patient in our relationships, clothing ourselves in a decent manner, and talking carefully about sexuality.

Rape is the forceful sexual violation of another person. It severely damages the respect, freedom, and physical and moral integrity to which everyone has a right, and it can cause damage that scars the victim. Rape

QUOTATION TO BE
INCLUDED IN FINAL PRINTING.

(CCC, 2356).

because they oppose natural law and

(CCC, 2357).
(CCC, 2359). The Church acknowledges the number of people who have homosexual tendencies, and teaches that they must be accepted with

(CCC, 2358). Unjust discrimination against homosexual people should be avoided.

Explain How do we practice modesty?

Consider What violation of chastity do you consider most destructive to society? Why?

Sexuality in Marriage

The Sacrament of Marriage symbolizes the loving union that Christ has for his Church. The Sacrament imparts to the husband and wife the grace to love each other with the depth of love with which Jesus loves the Church. Sexual intimacy becomes a sign and a pledge of the couple's spiritual covenant.

QUOTATION TO BE
INCLUDED IN FINAL PRINTING.

(CCC, 2361).

A husband and wife give themselves totally to each other. They are no longer two, but one. This freely chosen union forms a covenant that obligates the married couple to work to preserve their marriage as unique and unending. Marriage is a vocation, a calling to live life and to encounter God in a particular way. Through marriage a couple forms an

(CCC, 2364). Out of their commitment to each other comes the married couple's

(CCC, 2367).

QUOTATION TO BE
INCLUDED IN FINAL PRINTING.

—CCC, 2362

Violations of Marriage

Marriage is a total, lifelong, indissoluble, and exclusive commitment between a man and a woman. Marriage is naturally intended for the good of husbands and wives and for the procreation and education of children (see CCC, 1601). The following acts violate this understanding of marriage.

Adultery, expressly forbidden by the Sixth Commandment, violates the dignity of marriage. Adultery is

QUOTATION TO BE
INCLUDED IN FINAL PRINTING. (CCC, Glossary, p. 865). Adultery is an act of injustice against one's spouse and against the sanctity of marriage. Jesus did not mince words when speaking about adultery, condemning even the desire to commit adultery (see Matthew 5:27-28). Adultery compromises the well-being of children who need a stable parental relationship (see CCC, 2381).

GO TO THE SOURCE

After they are married, Tobias and Sarah pray to God.

Read Tobit 8:4-9.

- How committed are Tobias and Sarah?
- What does Tobias ask of God?
- What could couples today learn from this passage?

Divorce breaks the contract two people have asked God to join together and causes harm to spouses and to children, whose loyalty to both of their parents has been undermined, and toward the good ordering of society that is built on the stability of marriage and family.

QUOTATION TO BE
INCLUDED IN FINAL PRINTING.

(CCC, 2384). The *Catechism* teaches that divorce is immoral because it disturbs the order of the family and of society. Sometimes, one of the spouses tried to be faithful to the marriage.

QUOTATION TO BE
INCLUDED IN FINAL PRINTING.

—CCC, 2386

(CCC, 1665) violates the law and plan of God. Nonetheless, the Church still embraces those who are remarried; and even though they cannot receive the Eucharist, they are encouraged to lead Christian lives, to attend Mass, and to educate their children in the practice of the faith.

GO TO THE **SOURCE** 📖

We are often reminded in Scripture that Jesus told us not to judge each other.

Read John 8:2-11 and John 4:7-30.

- What can you learn from Jesus' treatment of the woman caught in adultery?
- What can you learn from Jesus' treatment of the woman at the well?
- What does Jesus say about the sins of these two women?
- How well have you modeled Jesus' approach to moral judgment? Explain.

Polygamy is having more than one spouse at the same time. It violates the dignity of marriage, which God intends to be an exclusive commitment between one man and one woman (see CCC, 2387). In the United States, polygamy is against civil law.

Incest is defined as sexual relations between people who are so closely related that the law forbids them to marry (see CCC, 2388). The practice of incest corrupts the values that strengthen families. An issue often related to incest is the sexual abuse of children and adolescents by adult relatives. This is an act that is both criminal and deeply evil. Such abuse causes inestimable damage to its victims, who are among the most vulnerable and innocent members of society.

Sometimes couples say they are living in a *free union* or are going to *live together* with the intention of marrying later. The Catholic Church teaches that both of these are wrong because both lack the covenant commitment to each other (see CCC, 2390).

(CCC, 2391). Sexuality is a part of our lives that draws us out of ourselves and urges us to seek union with others. As male and female, God intended us to be attracted to each other. This is part of our sexuality, which we must safeguard by showing prudence and practicing modesty. The Sixth and Ninth Commandments remind us to treat our sexuality with reverence and to express our sexuality in responsible ways.

The Ninth Commandment leads us to practice modesty and purity in our hearts, which directs our thoughts, words, action, and appearance. Purity of heart is essential because our heart is where evil thoughts form (see CCC, 2517). In one of the Beatitudes, the pure in heart are promised that they will see the face of God (see CCC, 2519).

The virtue of temperance leads to purity because purity of heart requires modesty.

(CCC, 2521). Purity of hearts remains difficult in today's society because of our social climate.

ADVANCE REVIEW COPY

NATURAL Family Planning

Natural Family Planning respects the gift of life when conception is possible in the sexual union of a married couple. Artificial means of birth control fail to respect the gift of life because they block or destroy this gift when conception is possible in the sexual union of a married couple. Natural Family Planning, when properly, used is very effective.

Many people think Natural Family Planning is the same as the old rhythm (or calendar) method that was developed in the 1930s. It is not. The rhythm method was based on the theory that the time of next ovulation could be determined by calculating previous menstrual cycles. This method often proved inaccurate because of the unique nature of each woman's menstrual cycle: some women have very irregular cycles and almost all women have a cycle of unusual length once in a while.

Natural Family Planning is an umbrella term for certain methods used to achieve and avoid pregnancies. These methods are based on the naturally occurring signs and symptoms of the fertile and infertile phases of a woman's menstrual cycle. Married couples using NFP to avoid pregnancy abstain from intercourse and genital contact during the fertile phase of the woman's cycle. No drugs, devices, or surgical procedures are used to avoid pregnancy. NFP reflects the dignity of the human person within the context of marriage and family life, promotes openness to life, and recognizes the value of the child.

NFP methods, take advantage of the changes associated with ovulation, treating each cycle as unique. It works with, rather than against, how God made us.

Natural Family Planning works with, rather than against, the way God made us.

How is Natural Family Planning different from the rhythm method?

Our attitude toward sexuality is greatly shaped by our culture.

- List five songs that have positive messages about different aspects of the moral life and the kind of topics we have discussed so far. Name each song and its message in your own words.

Christian purity requires that the media show respect and restraint, so when we achieve this kind of purity, we will be able to avoid and free ourselves from the eroticism and voyeurism that is widespread in our entertainment (see CCC, 2325).

QUOTATION TO BE
INCLUDED IN FINAL PRINTING.

—CCC, 2527

More Than Our Bodies

When it comes to describing what it means to be human, our language fails us. We may say, "I have a body" and "I have a soul." However, such language is just an attempt to capture in words the richness and the subtlety of the human condition. As we live our lives, we cannot divide ourselves into such clear-cut physical and spiritual dimensions as "body" and "soul." We can say we have human bodies because they are animated by our spiritual souls (see CCC, 364). Similarly, our sexuality should not be divided into "physical" and "spiritual" since it is intended to be both.

Sexuality . . . is by no means something purely biological, but concerns the innermost being of the human person as such.

—Pope John Paul II,
On the Family, number 11.

Sexuality is a way for us to create new life. It is a reflection of the creative power of the Holy Trinity. The love of the Father, the Son, and the Holy Spirit created Heaven and Earth. This act of creation was the first proclamation of God's (CCC, 315).

God gave us the gift of sexuality. With this gift, we share in God's creative love by forming bonds with other people. Reflecting the Creator, the gift of sexuality finds its fullest expression in the lifelong committed union of marriage from which comes the procreation of children.

There are legitimate reasons for a married couple to want to space out the births of their children. The Church allows "periodic continence" to regulate procreation. This is based on observing the signs of the woman's menstrual cycle to determine fertile and infertile times (see Expressions of Faith, p. 115). In contrast, any other method that attempts to make procreation impossible is (CCC, 2370).

Methods of artificial contraception—such as condoms, birth control pills, tubal ligations, and vasectomies—separate the sexual act from the act of procreation and thus are morally unacceptable. Artificial methods of birth control run counter to the nature of marriage in which sexuality must be open to both the sharing of mutual love and creating a family with children. God established the link between sexual activity, love, and childbearing. Human beings cannot break this link.

In calling a child a gift from God, the *Catechism* discusses the morality of research and techniques developed for sterility. This research must always be aimed at the service of the human person and his or her inalienable rights as well as the will of God (see CCC, 2375). Any techniques that separate the husband and wife and involve a third person are immoral.

QUOTATION TO BE
INCLUDED IN FINAL PRINTING.
(CCC, 2376).

Techniques that include just the married couple are still morally unacceptable when they involve separating the sexual act from procreation.

ADVANCE REVIEW COPY

What the Church is saying is that a child is not something owed to anyone. A child is a gift.

(CCC, 2378).

Define What is adultery?

Consider In what ways can sexuality exploit us where we are most vulnerable?

QUOTATION TO BE INCLUDED IN FINAL PRINTING.

—CCC, 2377

SECTION 3 REVIEW

QUICK REVIEW

1a. **Connect** What is the relationship between love, chastity, and freedom?

b. **List** What are the qualities of chastity?

c. **Consider** Why must we work actively to be chaste?

2a. **Apply** Why is marriage a vocation?

b. **Explain** How does divorce hurt society?

3a. **Explain** How is sexuality a way for us to create?

b. **Reflect** How does sexuality create bonds?

ACT

Write an essay about the ideal married couple.

• Describe their personalities and ways of showing love toward one another.

• Explain how this ideal could be better realized.

SELF-ASSESS

Which statement best reflects where you are now?

☐ I'm confident enough about the material in this section to be able to explain it to someone else.

☐ I have a good grasp of the material in this section, but I could use more review.

☐ I'm lost. I need help catching up before moving on.

Seventh and Tenth Commandments

KEY TERMS IN THIS SECTION

commutative justice an exchange between persons and institutions in accordance with a strict respect for their rights

distributive justice

QUOTATION TO BE INCLUDED IN FINAL PRINTING.

reparation making amends for harming another; returning stolen property

envy

(CCC, 2553)

avarice

(CCC, 2552)

greed the desire to amass limitless earthly goods

Violations of the Seventh and Tenth Commandments have led to war, death, imprisonment, breakdown within families, sadness, and tragedy. The simplest version of the Seventh Commandment is just four words: "You shall not steal." Part of our fallen nature, the Church has always taught, is a persistent selfishness, a clinging to what is "mine," and a longing for what is "yours." As the *Catechism* explains, the Seventh Commandment:

- forbids stealing someone's goods and wronging him in any way as to his possessions;
- commands justice and charity for all the resources of the Earth and the products we produce;
- requires respect for the distribution of products and for the right to private property;
-

(CCC, 2401).

Stealing and covetousness are personal matters with immense social consequences, as well as social matters with devastating personal consequences. The Seventh Commandment involves the many faces of stealing, the necessity of making amends for what we have stolen, our right to private property, the nature of "coveting," the importance of charity, justice as the moral character of society, and Catholic Social Teaching.

In the Book of Genesis, God's plan to provide for our living and our "daily bread" unfolds. God entrusted humankind with the Earth and its resources. The goods of creation are still intended for the whole human race. The universal destination of goods refers to this common and continuing stewardship that all people have for the planet's resources. We are all stewards of these goods or resources. But the enjoyment and use of resources is also intended for all.

The Seventh and Tenth Commandments give order to the world's goods and resources.

ADVANCE REVIEW COPY

QUOTATION TO BE
INCLUDED IN FINAL PRINTING.

—CCC, 2404

The Seventh Commandment commands the respect for the goods and money of others. In addition to theft, the Commandment forbids any unjust taking or keeping of property that belongs to others. It also prohibits paying unjust wages or taking advantage of the ignorance or hardship of others. Other sins against the Seventh Commandment include overcharging customers, keeping things loaned to you, or profiting through unethical means, such as business fraud. And the list continues with tax evasion, forging checks, and vandalism (see CCC, 2408-2409).

The Church also wants us to know that these Commandments prohibit "stealing" from others through contracts. In writing contracts and establishing agreements, the Church points to the standard of "commutative justice." **Commutative justice** refers to an exchange between "persons and institutions in accordance with a strict respect for their rights." **Distributive justice**

QUOTATION TO BE
INCLUDED IN FINAL PRINTING.

(CCC, 2411).

The Church's social doctrine, developed in the nineteenth century as a response to industrialization, brings Gospel values to the modern world of work and business. This social doctrine continually reminds industries, corporations, and governments that any economic system that is concerned only with profits is "morally unacceptable."

El Salvador's late Archbishop Oscar Romero criticized unjust economic systems in his country. During his life, he directed the world's attention to the plight of the poor in El Salvador. In 1978, he said, "When the church hears the cry of the oppressed it cannot but denounce the social structures that give rise to and perpetuate the misery from which the cry arises."

Love for the poor and love for justice are natural fruits for those who live in the spirit of the Seventh and Tenth Commandments. Blessed Mother Teresa of Calcutta knew that love was the great equalizer. "I try to give to poor people for love what the rich could get for money," she said. At another time, she asked: "I want you to be concerned about your next door neighbor. Do you know your next door neighbor?"

The right to private property, then, coincides with the responsibility to find ways to make our goods benefit others. In this regard, the following advice is given:

(CCC, 2405).

Explain How does the Seventh Commandment address salaries and wages?

Consider Why did Archbishop Oscar Romero say the Church must speak out against unjust economic systems?

Other Violations of the Seventh Commandment

We have talked about stealing, commutative justice, and distributive justice. The *Catechism* also teaches about keeping promises, reparation for injustice, gambling, enslavement of humans, and caring for creation and animals when discussing the Seventh Commandment.

Promises and contracts must be kept as long as they are morally just. The *Catechism* points out the importance of honoring contracts to the economic and social lives today.

(CCC, 2410).

Commutative justice requires that we make **reparation** whenever we have stolen property from another or used it in an unjust manner. The Seventh Commandment requires us to return stolen goods. If the stolen property has disappeared, we are to return the equivalent in kind or in money. If we have participated in stealing from another or have in some way benefited from a theft, we are obliged to make reparation in proportion to our responsibility and to the amount we have gained (see CCC, 2412).

Gambling or games of chance and betting are not necessarily morally wrong.

(CCC, 2413). The *Catechism* notes that gambling can become addictive. Unfair bets and cheating that results in significant loss are grave sins.

PRIMARY SOURCES

Catholic Social Teaching helps build a just society and shows how to live lives of holiness amidst the challenges of modern society. The wisdom of this tradition can be understood best through a direct reading of Church documents. Following is a synopsis of one of the seven key themes that are part of our Catholic social tradition. See all seven in an appendix at the back of the text.

Life and Dignity of the Human Person

"The Catholic Church proclaims that human life is sacred and that the dignity of the human person is the foundation of a moral vision for society. This belief is the foundation of all the principles of our social teaching. In our society, human life is under direct attack from abortion and euthanasia. The value of human life is being threatened by cloning, embryonic stem cell research, and the use of the death penalty. The intentional targeting of civilians in war or terrorist attacks is always wrong. Catholic teaching also calls on us to work to avoid war. Nations must protect the right to life by finding increasingly effective ways to prevent conflicts and resolve them by peaceful means. We believe that every person is precious, that people are more important than things, and that the measure of every institution is whether it threatens or enhances the life and dignity of the human person."

➔ Go to the student site at
hs.osvcurriculum.com

Give five examples of how these principles reflect the Commandments and the moral values of the Gospel.

Cardinal Timothy Dolan of New York helps with a Catholic Charities food drive.

especially of noble beings, and knowledge of happiness and misery in the next life

ADVANCE REVIEW COPY

Slavery of human beings is also forbidden by the Seventh Commandment. Buying, selling, or exchanging human beings as though they were pieces of merchandise is a grave sin against human dignity and fundamental rights. Saint Paul writes to Philemon for a Christian owner to treat his Christian slave "no longer as a slave but more than a slave, a beloved brother" (Philemon 16).

The Seventh Commandment also requires that we respect the integrity of creation and animals. For example, we should ask what is being "stolen" from the human race and from future generations when rain forests are destroyed or species are made extinct?

> QUOTATION TO BE
> INCLUDED IN FINAL PRINTING.
>
> —CCC, 2415

We must care for animals. We owe them kindness in the example of Saints Francis of Assisi and Philip Neri. It is legitimate too to use animals for food and clothing, for domestic work and for leisure. Medical and scientific experimentation on animals is morally acceptable if there are limits and the goal is caring for or saving human lives (see CCC, 2417).

> QUOTATION TO BE
> INCLUDED IN FINAL PRINTING.
>
> —CCC, 2418

Define What is the meaning of the term reparation?

Explain How does slavery violate the Seventh Commandment?

Economic Activity

Economies and work are meant to provide for the needs of people.

> QUOTATION TO BE
> INCLUDED IN FINAL PRINTING.
>
> (CCC, 2426). The

REFLECT

Discuss the moral implications of the following incidents. Suggest possible ways of making reparation appropriate for each incident.

- A group of kids walks through a park and purposely breaks playground equipment.
- A girl finds a wallet outside of a store and notices a license with a name and address in it. The wallet contains $50. She takes the money but leaves the wallet.
- You ask a friend to download a copyrighted movie for you.
- Driving home at night, you clip a neighbor's mailbox and break it.
- You buy some clothing item to wear to a party, then return it the next day and ask for a refund just as you had planned.

moral good limits economic activity to meet requirements for social justice and to correspond with God's plan for humankind.

Human work is the duty of every capable person because it honors God's gifts and the talents he has given each of us. Work is also a redemptive practice. Through work, we unite with Christ by picking up our crosses daily in the work we are called to do.

> QUOTATION TO BE
> INCLUDED IN FINAL PRINTING.
>
> (CCC, 2427).

While we are responsible to make legitimate use of our talents for the benefit of all, states and companies have responsibilities as well. The task of nations and states is to provide freedoms, a stable currency, and public services to allow those who work to enjoy the rewards of their labor as well as to feel encouraged to work. The state must oversee human rights in the marketplace, but that responsibility primarily lies with everyone that makes up society (see CCC, 2431).

Business enterprises, or companies, are responsible for the impacts of their operation. They are obligated to consider the fortunes of people and not just increases in profits. The *Catechism* notes, however, that profits are necessary to ensure the future of the company and its employees (see CCC, 2432). The *Catechism* also calls for access to employment for people without discrimination and a just wage for workers. Workers can strike to gain a reasonable benefit, but it is morally unacceptable to resort to violence or when the goals of a strike are not for the common good (see CCC, 2434-2435).

On a larger scale, the Catholic Church teaches that there must be solidarity among nations so that resources can be accessed more equally and so less advanced countries can develop.

QUOTATION TO BE
INCLUDED IN FINAL PRINTING.

—CCC, 2439

In order to reduce these inequalities, the Church teaches that responses include direct aid following catastrophes, reform of international economic and financial institutions, and increased knowledge of God among all peoples. It is the responsibility of lay Catholics to participate in political and social life to help these steps take place. They are to be the agents for peace and justice in the world.

QUOTATION TO BE
INCLUDED IN FINAL PRINTING.

—CCC, 2442

Thou Shall Not Covet

The Tenth Commandment makes it clear that our attitudes can be as destructive as our actions. Some people struggle with this Commandment and their criminal desires. Examples from the *Catechism* include merchants who want items to be scarce in order to drive up the price; doctors who want disease to spread; and attorneys who desire many important cases (see CCC, 2537).

LIST

- Read Luke 12:16-21. List three lessons that this parable teaches.
- Give examples of envy, avarice, and greed from recent news stories or from history.

The Commandment also forbids envy, avarice, and greed.

> You shall not covet . . . anything that belongs to your neighbor.
>
> —Exodus 20:17

- **Envy** eats away at the person who is envious as well as at the person's relationships. Envy can be sadness at the thought of another's good fortune. It also means perversely delighting in someone else's misfortune. A serious expression of envy is wishing grave harm to a person or people whom we envy and knowingly persist in the envy. This is a mortal sin.

We can want what other people have, but not through evil means.

(CCC, 2538). Envy can lead to worse actions that lead to crime.

- **Avarice** is an excessive and unquenchable desire for wealth, power, or other forms of gain. An example of avarice is Ebenezer Scrooge in Charles Dickens', *A Christmas Carol*. Like Scrooge, avaricious people become addicted to the object of desire. Avarice can consume people, making them blind to the demands of the Commandments and the needs of others. Instead of worshipping God, they worship money, power, or something they cannot get enough of (see CCC, 2536).

- **Greed** is a desire to amass more and more possessions. The Tenth Commandment forbids greed. It often expresses itself in oppressing and doing violence to others. A greedy person is liable to take advantage of others and trick them out of their belongings. Jesus warned: "'Be on your guard against all kinds of greed; for one's life does not consist in the abundance of possessions'" (Luke 12:15).

ADVANCE REVIEW COPY

Observing Detachment

The time to start fulfilling our desire for true happiness is always the present. Following God's Law and living a moral life is how we quench that desire. In this way, we will lessen our attachment to amassing possessions and find our fulfillment in the happiness of God. Saint Gregory of Nyssa said that the promise of seeing God exceeds all happiness. Scripture tells us that to see is to possess something. Saint Gregory summarized it this way:

(CCC, 2548).

God's Law and grace turn our hearts from such evils as avarice and envy, and teach us the desires of the Holy Spirit. The law, however, was never enough to justify us. There was always a gap between wanting to do what God's Law commands and actually doing it because we were also drawn to the captive law of sin. But the righteousness of God manifested itself apart from the law in the person of Christ.

(CCC, 2543).

We must free ourselves from earthly goods. This precept of detachment is the only path to spending eternal life with God in Heaven. Jesus told us to do this for his sake and for that of the Gospel (see CCC, 2544). Jesus rejoices in the poor and grieves for the wealthy. The Kingdom of God already belongs to the poor, but the rich find their consolation in gathering possessions. There is a practical reason to detach ourselves from things. We will worry less.

(CCC, 2547). We should also be happy for others.

QUOTATION TO BE
INCLUDED IN FINAL PRINTING.

—CCC, 2540

Detachment counteracts theft, envy, avarice, and greed because it reminds us that people are

The Holy Spirit gives us the grace to live a Christian moral life.

more important than things and that everything must be viewed in light of concern for others. Poverty of spirit invites us to trust in God and to become humble as Jesus was humble, "so that by his poverty you might become rich" (2 Corinthians 8:9b).

Analyze Why is observing detachment important?

Discuss How can envy ruin a close friendship?

REFLECT

Studies indicate that generous people tend to live longer. Why do you think this is?

- Is being generous beneficial for oneself as well as for others? Do you think that generous people are happier?

- Tell about a time when you were blessed by someone's generosity?

- If you could repay any person or group for the generosity you've been shown, who would it be?

QUICK REVIEW

1a. **Summarize** What does the Seventh Commandment forbid?

b. **Apply** Why is stewardship of the Earth protected by the Seventh Commandment?

2a. **Link** How is slavery a sin against the Seventh Commandment?

b. **Elaborate** How is reparation made for stealing?

3a. **Explain** When is envy a mortal sin?

b. **Link** How are avarice and greed related?

ACT

Design a project that is consistent with Catholic Social Teaching and will serve the people of your parish.

- Talk to parish staff members to determine your community's needs.

- Plan the project with those needs in mind.

- After completing the design, find a way to implement it. Be sure to evaluate your results.

Pray Compose a litany of saints asking for help in keeping the Ten Commandments.

SELF-ASSESS

Which statement best reflects where you are now?

☐ I'm confident enough about the material in this section to be able to explain it to someone else.

☐ I have a good grasp of the material in this section, but I could use more review.

☐ I'm lost. I need help catching up before moving on.

ADVANCE REVIEW COPY

PRAYER

Opening Prayer

We begin in the name of the Father, and of the Son, and of the Holy Spirit. Amen.
Lord God, I open my heart to you to assist me in the important mission of planning my future.

With your grace, if marriage is part of your plan for my life, may I decide wisely concerning the person who is to be my spouse through life.

I pray that this person is even now receiving the love and care needed in their home to hopefully reciprocate that with me. May this person be honest, devoted, and pure so that we both may strive to perfect ourselves with your help.

Dear Lord, make holy our friendship before marriage. May our shared love unite us and our future home may ever be a domestic Church to serve you.

Amen.

Closing Prayer

Prayer to Saint Joseph for Mothers and Fathers
Dear God, Father of us all, I thank you for my mother and father. In cooperation with your divine plan, they gave me the gift of life. Please take care of them now and be with them as you prepare them for the rewards of eternal life.

Through the changes in my life, help me to become more mature.

There is serenity, a feeling that I know I am secure in my knowing that my parents' love for me survives through everything we face.

May this great love that my mother and father share continue to bless them and our family.

Amen.

ADVANCE REVIEW COPY

TERMS

Use each of the following terms in a sentence that shows you know what the term means in the context of the chapter. You may include more than one term in a sentence.

abortion

euthanasia

capital punishment

scandal

chastity

fecundity

commutative justice

distributive justice

reparation

envy

avarice

greed

PEOPLE AND IDEAS

Identify the person who best fits each description./ Define each person or idea in the context of the chapter.

1. Cain

2. terrorism

3. *The Challenge of Peace*

4. *Roe v. Wade*

5. Theology of the Body

6. Archbishop Oscar Romero

7. detachment

8. Saint Francis of Assisi

9. Saint Vincent de Paul

UNDERSTANDING

Answer each question and complete each exercise

SECTION 1

1. **Explain** Why is murder a sin?
2. **Expand** List the range of offenses that the Fifth Commandment includes.

SECTION 2

3. **Link** Explain the two options for peace: resisting bearing arms and bearing arms.
4. **Discuss** Why is allowing death to occur not the same as killing?

SECTION 3

5. **Reflect** Why is chastity so difficult to achieve?
6. **Recall** What does the Sacrament of Marriage symbolize?
7. **Link** How does artificial contraception undermine marriage?
8. **Explain** How is sexuality a psychological, spiritual, and physical reality?

ADVANCE REVIEW COPY

9. **Reflect** Why is obeying the Seventh Commandment more complex than it first appears?

10. **Differentiate** What is the difference between being an owner and a steward?

11. **Recall** How do we observe the Seventh and Tenth Commandments?

12. **Define** What is the point of Catholic Social Teaching?

CONNECTING

Visual This photo shows a young Catholic couple entering the Sacrament of Marriage.

What symbols in the picture show that a Sacrament is taking place? How can living chaste lives help strengthen this marriage?

Challenge You are driving your sister and her friend to the mall, when her friend says, "Sometimes I think about taking clothes into the dressing room, and then just wearing them out of the store under my real clothes." Your sister says she hears about people doing that all the time. How do you respond? Be sure to use information from the chapter.

Imagine A friend comes to you and tells you she's pregnant. She says the father, her parents, and some of her other friends want her to get an abortion, but she doesn't. How do you support her? Use information from the chapter.

SELF-ASSESS

On Your Own Make a list of the most important things you learned from this chapter. Select three things that represent your growth in understanding as you worked through this chapter. Write a paragraph explaining your choices.

With a Partner List what you found most helpful or interesting in this chapter as well as any other questions that have surfaced.

CHAPTER 5

- How can we know if something is the truth?
- What responsibility do we have when we step up to one of these?

Truth and the New Covenant

Go to the student site at
hs.osvcurriculum.com

ADVANCE REVIEW COPY

YOU WILL

- Apply the Eighth Commandment to your life.

- Discover what Jesus said about truth and lies.

- Identify how media and art relate to the Eighth Commandment.

- Develop a way for pursuing the truth.

- Evaluate the sinful nature of racism and prejudice.

- Analyze the two Great Commandments given to us by Jesus.

- Connect the Great Commandments with the Decalogue and Beatitudes.

- Explore alternatives to violence.

- Apply the real meaning of charity and love.

ADVANCE REVIEW COPY

The Eighth Commandment

KEY TERMS IN THIS SECTION

lying QUOTATION TO BE INCLUDED IN FINAL PRINTING.

calumny telling lies that injure someone's character

detraction revealing derogatory information about a person's faults or weaknesses without just cause

rash judgment presuming as true the worst about a person without sufficient information

S aint Edith Stein (1891–1942) died in a Nazi concentration camp. At her canonization on October 11, 1998, Blessed Pope John Paul II noted that she had found the deeper truth that Christ taught. "She discovered that truth had a name: Jesus Christ. From that moment on, the incarnate Word was her One and All." She once wrote that whether we know it or not, if we seek truth, then we are seeking God. Pope John Paul II added: "At the end of a long journey she came to the surprising realization: *only those who commit themselves to the love of Christ become truly free.*"

CONNECT

Saint Edith Stein wrote that if we seek truth, then we are seeking God, whether we know it or not.

- How is this possible? What are the reasons she would say this?

The Eighth Commandment is about seeking truth. The Commandment says: "You shall not bear false witness against your neighbor" (Exodus 20:16). Referring to Saint Thomas Aquinas, the *Catechism of the Catholic Church* makes the point that we could not live with one another without mutual confidence that we are being truthful to each other. Truthfulness involves honesty and discretion by balancing what ought to be said with what ought to be kept secret (see CCC, 2469).

Those who are true in their actions and truthful in their words are living by this virtue of truth. They demonstrate truthfulness, sincerity, and candor in their lives while avoiding dishonesty, deceit, and hypocrisy (see CCC, 579 and 2468). Disciples of Christ have the perfect example of truth. We respond to Christ's invitation by abiding in his truth. In this way, our lives are illuminated by his truth.

> God is light and in him there is no darkness at all. If we say that we have fellowship with him while we are walking in darkness, we lie and do not do what is true.
>
> —1 John 1:5-6

The Eighth Commandment is important for all of our relationships.

ADVANCE REVIEW COPY

Those who are close to God and growing in relationship with him are those who practice the virtue of truth.

> O LORD, who may abide in your tent?
>   Who may dwell on your holy hill?
> Those who walk blamelessly, and do what
>   is right,
>   and speak the truth from their heart;
> who do not slander with their tongue.
>
> —Psalm 15:1-3a

A line from the Book of Zechariah echoes this message. "These are the things that you shall do: Speak the truth to one another, render in your gates judgments that are true and make for peace" (Zechariah 8:16). All the prophets of the Old Testament knew that their difficult calling and their divinely given role was to tell God's truth. He identified his ministry and himself with truth as he says to Pilate: "'For this I was born, and for this I came into the world, to testify to the truth. Everyone who belongs to the truth listens to my voice'" (John 18:37).

It is our duty as Catholics to take part in the Church's life and to be witnesses to the Gospel. Our faith must be seen in our words and behavior.

QUOTATION TO BE
INCLUDED IN FINAL PRINTING.

—CCC, 2472

Some have been witnesses to the faith to the point of giving up their lives.

(CCC, 2473). The word "martyr" itself means witness. Early Christians who recognized Christ's truth refused to deny him. As a result many were killed, proclaiming a message of truth with their very blood. Over the centuries, the Church collected records of these supreme witnesses who never stopped acting or speaking in faith. Saint Polycarp was one such witness who died in the middle of the second century:

RECALL

- Describe a time when you have spoken the truth at a cost to you? What truth were you naming and what was the cost?

- Describe a time when someone courageously spoke the truth to you? What was it about and how did you hear it?

- Describe two of the most truthful people you know and what makes you say that about them. When was the last time you told them so?

- Make a summary statement about truth telling based on your experience.

QUOTATION TO BE
INCLUDED IN FINAL PRINTING.

—CCC, 2474

Define What is a Christian martyr? How does it describe Jesus?

Explain How can we use the Eighth Commandment to reveal the power of the Holy Spirit?

Offenses Against Truth

Living in darkness for our entire lives would be unbearable. As humans, we long for the light. When we act falsely or don't speak in truth, we contribute to the darkness, fostering an atmosphere of uncertainty and mistrust.

> 'For all who do evil hate the light and do not come
> to the light, so that their deeds may not be exposed.
> But those who do what is true come to the light,
> so that it may be clearly seen that their deeds have
> been done in God.'
>
> —John 3:20-21

Disciples of Christ are called to live in such a way that their lives reflect their being made in the image and likeness of God. That means

Margaret Hassan, an Irish aid worker, was abducted while serving in Iraq. She was murdered by her kidnappers in 2004.

Respect for the truth requires us to make judgments about what to do with the many truths that we discover. Respect for the truth does not give us permission to be brutally honest.

Lying

(CCC, 2483). More than once, Jesus bluntly addressed leaders in terms of their dishonest hearts and motives. In the Gospel according to John (see John 8:44), he told them,

QUOTATION TO BE
INCLUDED IN FINAL PRINTING.

(CCC, 2482).

The Church reminds us, however, that some lies are more serious, more sinful than others.

QUOTATION TO BE
INCLUDED IN FINAL PRINTING.

—CCC, 2484

In the Gospel according to John, we find one of the most hopeful testimonials for searching for the truth. "Then Jesus said to the Jews who believed in him, 'If you continue in my word, you are truly my disciples; and you will know the truth, and the truth will make you free'" (John 8:31-32).

There are a number of additional sins against truth to avoid. **Calumny** means telling lies about someone in a way that injures his or her reputation and provides the opportunity for others to make false judgments about the person. **Detraction** refers to revealing derogatory information about a person without just cause. Revealing information about someone is wrong if our intention is to dishonor or make fun of the person. QUOTATION TO BE INCLUDED IN FINAL PRINTING.

(CCC, 2479).

Rash judgment means presuming the worst about another without sufficient information to support our judgment. To avoid rash judgment, we need to interpret the actions, thoughts, and words of others in the most favorable way (see CCC, 2478). Gossip is also an offense against truth.

living with true righteousness and holiness.
QUOTATION TO BE
INCLUDED IN FINAL PRINTING.
(CCC, 2475).

Lying is when we communicate a falsehood in order to mislead someone. By misleading others or leading them into error, we do not respect their human dignity.

Outright lying is not the only way to offend against the Eighth Commandment. We can violate the Commandment even by telling the truth when we should keep silent. For example, if a close friend tells us something deeply personal about himself and asks us to keep it a secret, we are duty bound to avoid telling anyone else. If we find out information about someone that could be damaging, we are to keep this information to ourselves. If we hear a rumor about someone without knowing whether there's any truth to it, we are not to pass it on.

Knowledge about others is precious. We need
QUOTATION TO BE
INCLUDED IN FINAL PRINTING.
(CCC, 2488). We must also be reminded that,
QUOTATION TO BE
INCLUDED IN FINAL PRINTING. (CCC, 2492).
At the same time, we must be judicious about keeping secrets. Certainly the secrets confessed in the Sacrament of Reconciliation cannot be revealed. And when confidences that may harm others are entrusted to us, we are responsible not to divulge them to others.

ADVANCE REVIEW COPY

CONFRONTING
When Necessary

> "If another member of the church sins against you, go and point out the fault when the two of you are alone. If the member listens to you, you have regained that one. But if you are not listened to, take one or two others along with you, so that every word may be confirmed by the evidence of two or three witnesses."
>
> —Matthew 18:15-16

God expects us to address someone's harmful behavior if possible. This is what God asked the prophets to do throughout Scripture. Jesus taught the Apostles to confront when necessary, and they taught the first Christians to do the same.

Confronting takes courage for sure, but it also requires empathy. Your empathy for someone wronged moves you to confront—but you also should have empathy for the person or group you are confronting.

And it takes skill. Confronting should not rob someone of his or her dignity, nor should it water down the issue that needs to be addressed. When you engage in the practice of confronting keep in mind the verbal, non-verbal, and interpersonal dynamics:

Verbal: Choose your words carefully whether face-to-face, online, or texting. Address a behavior that is a problem—not a person or a group. For example, "Cheating is like stealing" instead of "You cheated yesterday."

Use "I" instead of "You" if you can, such as: "I feel hurt when I hear things like that" instead of "You hurt me when you said that."

Always be specific. "Rumors hurt. Kelly was crying over the false rumor about her." Instead of saying "Poor attitude hurts the team." Describe exact action or words. Speak clearly and calmly. Avoid yelling, cursing, and arguing.

Non-verbal: When confronting face to face, sit or stand at eye level instead of standing over the other person. And look at the person you are confronting. Pay attention to your body language. Try not to cross your arms or clench your fist.

Interpersonal: The practice of confronting requires both courage and kindness. Consider the intentions and feelings of the one(s) you are about to confront. Try to do it one on one like the Scripture above says. Avoid shaming or embarrassing the one(s) you are confronting.

Pray for the Holy Spirit's guidance as you prepare to confront, and take time to listen for it. Pray also for the Holy Spirit's presence when you actually do confront, and look for it while confronting.

> Recall a time when you practiced confronting in the right way and for the right reasons. What made it successful: the verbal, non-verbal, or interpersonal dynamics?
>
> When have you had a negative experience of confronting? What made it so bad and what might have made it better?

Calumny, detraction, and rash judgment are each slightly different form each other.

- Which of these three seem to be most common in your world? Explain.
- Is one of these most common online and another more common in school? Explain.

These offenses are assaults on human dignity since they involve humiliating someone. Belittling remarks about another person can spread very quickly. Therefore, the offender is not just the person speaking, but also the person who seeks out and readily accepts the comments. In other words, if we harbor a desire to hear about someone's faults then we are fostering an atmosphere simmering with gossip and rash judgment. Such an atmosphere creates a culture of mistrust.

One venue ripe for gossip and rash judgment is the Internet. People can feel comfortable spreading stories about others in Internet exchanges that they wouldn't say about them in person. However, despite the impersonal nature of the Internet, peoples' good names can be injured just as badly. Sharing derogatory stories over the Internet can increase the audience and the potential harm.

> The Church's call and God's commandment to reverence the truth teach us that without truth there can be no trust, and without trust there can be no true community. . . .

—Cardinal Donald W. Wuerl, *The Catholic Way* (New York: Doubleday, 2001), p. 339

The most public form of bearing false witness is perjury. Someone commits perjury who lies under oath, such as in a court of law. Perjury is a punishable crime because the judicial system depends upon a witness telling the truth (see the Second Commandment).

QUOTATION TO BE
INCLUDED IN FINAL PRINTING
(CCC, 2476).

Further sins against the Eighth Commandment include boasting, bragging, and making fun of others. These distort the truth, especially when done to gain advantage over others. Bragging only honors an individual and reduces others (see CCC, 2481). Catholic teaching also condemns flattery and adulation of others when it encourages their sins.

(CCC, 2480). It is a venial sin when the purpose is to be agreeable, to avoid evil, to meet a legitimate need, or to get a legitimate advantage.

These offenses against the Eighth Commandment damage our ability to know what is true and what is false and that impacts our moral decision-making. Lying and these other sins sew discord and discontent that can lead to evil. They hurt friendships and families. They undermine the trust vital to our communities. We have seen that even revealing factual information can be destructive.

It is also important to realize that we can show disrespect for truth through our silence. Love and respect for truth should govern our every response to information. The *Catechism* says we have sufficient reason to remain silent when there is concern for the safety of others, for the respect for privacy, and for the common good.

QUOTATION TO BE
INCLUDED IN FINAL PRINTING.

—CCC, 2489

APPLY

- Give an example of what bearing false witness could mean in your community?
- How can you apply what Jesus said about "the truth" and about "lies?"

COMPARE

Think about an actual experience of distorting the truth, as described in this section: lying, bragging, perjury, irresponsible silence, calumny, detraction, rash judgment, gossip.

- Write three realistic ways these distortions could have been avoided.

There are also times when we are called upon to make our voices heard, such as when we see bullying taking place or when rash judgments hurt teachers, strangers, or public figures. Instead we need to tell the truth in love. Standing up for ourselves and others is hard. Asserting ourselves, even in the cause of truth, can be very difficult. Still, when we do, we are using the Holy Spirit's gift of courage and aligning ourselves with God, who is truth.

All these sins against justice and truth oblige us to make amends, even if we have been forgiven. This reparation should be public if possible, but if not, then in private. It should be done out of love. We may need to repair someone's reputation, but whatever the reparation, it should equal the damage done through our sinful actions (see CCC, 2487).

Explain Why is it difficult to restore a person's reputation once it has been unfairly damaged?

Recall Why is boasting or bragging considered a sin?

SECTION 1 REVIEW

QUICK REVIEW

1a. Link How is Jesus' ministry linked to the truth?
 b. Recall How is the seriousness of a lie measured?

2a. Connect How can being truthful exact a heavy price?
 b. Reflect Why is perjury a crime as well as a sin?
 c. Explain How does gossip violate the Eighth Commandment?

Discuss When have you seen lies or gossip or one of the other offenses against the Eighth Commandment hurt people?

Pray Compose a short prayer asking God to help you share the truth.

SELF-ASSESS

Which statement best reflects where you are now?

☐ I'm confident enough about the material in this section to be able to explain it to someone else.

☐ I have a good grasp of the material in this section, but I could use more review.

☐ I'm lost. I need help catching up before moving on.

Pursuing the Truth

KEY TERMS IN THIS SECTION

discrimination a situation in which people suffer disadvantages simply because they are members of a particular group

The Eighth Commandment calls for the pursuit of truth. Civic leaders have a special responsibility to uphold the truth. Sometimes, however, politicians try to get elected by attacking one another not on issues but on personal integrity. Such exchanges feed into the mentality that "all politicians are corrupt." While we need to be cautious of statements made by political leaders, we also need to be cautious about harboring expectations of deception on their part. That is, rash judgment of public figures contributes to a culture of mistrust.

Television and the Internet have become the primary mediums through which we receive news of current events. Both mediums lend themselves to a particular approach to reporting the news—brief sound bites of information. What we often hear from interest groups is their own version, or spin, on events. "Spinning" is a relatively new term and has come to mean manipulation of the truth intended to deceive. "Spin doctors" are political commentators or spokespersons who present information in such a way that aspects of the story unfavorable to their view are left out.

QUOTATION TO BE
INCLUDED IN FINAL PRINTING.

—CCC, 2512

The media must be true and complete in its reporting.

ADVANCE REVIEW COPY

We are to form

(CCC, 2496). A well-formed conscience is truthful in that it makes judgments using sound reason, the wisdom of Church teachings, the advice of wise and holy people, and the Gifts of the Holy Spirit. With the help of a well-formed conscience, we are more capable of sifting through the media's spin and sound bites. Our conscience can lead us to an understanding of what is true and what is false in the world around us.

Sources of information available to us have multiplied exponentially. News programs are under pressure to be both entertaining and informative. Many news shows spend more time discussing celebrities than events that genuinely impact the lives of viewers. Sometimes, actual news is reduced to a brief segment. Extensive coverage of an issue often takes place only during major crises. The truth can become blurred or lost, even though we encounter an overwhelming number of images from the media.

According to the *Catechism*, information from the media should be true and complete, as well as communicated honestly and properly (see CCC, 2494). A quick factual statement may be true but not complete. As mentioned in relation to spinning, true statements can be less than honest if only partial or slanted information is given.

Like the media, works of art also have responsibility to the truth. Michelangelo's "Pietà" portrays the Blessed Mother holding her son, Jesus, right after he was taken down from the Cross. The sculpture captures the human experience of death and grieving in a powerful way. Under its discussion of the Eighth Commandment, the *Catechism* examines the role of such pieces of art in human life.

QUOTATION TO BE
INCLUDED IN FINAL PRINTING.

(CCC, 2500).

COMPARE

Check off any of the following statements that are true about your reaction to media information:

___I don't believe most of what I hear on the news.

___I tend to believe that most of what is being reported is accurate.

___When politicians make their case, I try to find out the truth.

___When politicians make their case, I tune out.

___ I try to get accurate information about issues.

___ I can tell when a reporter or a public figure is telling the truth about a situation.

___ I don't think you can tell when people involved in a situation are being truthful.

___ I am slow to trust that people involved in a situation are telling the truth.

___ I pretty much take people at their word and assume they are telling the truth.

___ I'm tend to make rash judgments.

___ I'm slow to make any judgment until I get more information.

The beauty of a work of art reveals an otherwise hidden truth and sheds new light on it. Works of art should

(CCC, 2501). Artistic creation is a particular activity since human beings are created in the image of God. Great works of art unveil the beauty of truth in ways that we would otherwise miss. This is why the Church urges the promotion of sacred art in our places of worship or the removal of those pieces that don't conform to the truth of faith (see CCC, 2503).

Explain How should we approach social media, according to the *Catechism*?

Analyze How can a well-formed conscience help us make sense of the world around us?

Robert Bolt's *A Man for All Seasons* tells the story of Saint Thomas More's fight for his beliefs. It was first produced as a play and later adapted as a film, which won six Oscars, including Best Picture. In one of the film's most dramatic scenes, More confronts his accusers at a public trial. Richard Rich, an ambitious former student of More's, is called to testify against him. The king's allies had promised to appoint Rich as Chancellor of Wales if he incriminates More, so Rich lies and tells the court More once denied the king's authority over the Church. Based on that false testimony, More is convicted of treason. As Rich is leaving the witness stand, More says to him, "Why Richard, it profits a man nothing to give his soul for the whole world . . . but for Wales?"

Before he was beheaded on July 6, 1535, More said, "I am the king's good servant, but God's first." Saint Thomas More was canonized in 1935. His feast day is June 22.

- How would Saint Thomas More be a good model for modern politicians?

Paul Scofield portrays Saint Thomas More in *A Man for All Seasons.*

Faith & Culture

↗ Go to the student site at
hs.osvcurriculum.com

Respect for Truth

We mentioned earlier that Scripture refers to Satan as "'the father of lies'" and "deceiver" (John 8:44, Revelation 12:9). In other words, evil is particularly sinister when it passes itself off as the truth. We accept many falsehoods because they are ingrained in our cultural consciousness. We can miss seeing evils around us because they appear to be true or because we have been numbed to them through frequent use.

People in our world and even in our communities are hurting in ways that we are barely aware of. Respect for truth includes bringing to light ways that people are hurting in our society and seeking ways to help the people of the world who are suffering from **discrimination**. Certain perspectives on people are deeply entrenched in the group consciousness of our society. Sometimes we overlook the truth because we don't look behind stereotypes.

GO TO THE SOURCE

Jesus has some sobering words for his listeners.

Read John 8:42-47.

- Summarize how Jesus describes the devil's relationship with truth.
- What would it be like to hear Jesus say we do not hear him because we are not from God?
- How can we attempt to make sure that never happens?

Every form of social or cultural discrimination in fundamental personal rights on the grounds of sex, race, color, social conditions, language, or religion must be curbed and eradicated as incompatible with God's design.

—*Gaudium et Spes*, #29 § 2.

ADVANCE REVIEW COPY

God has created us in his image and likeness and looks upon each of us as a person of dignity. We are called to respect that dignity by considering everyone as "another self." We are called to do what we can to   that undermine the dignity of God's children (CCC, 1947).

Discrimination exists when people suffer disadvantages simply because they are members of a particular group—for example, because they belong to a certain socioeconomic class, or to a particular race, gender, or age.

SECTION **2 REVIEW**

QUICK REVIEW

1a. Summarize How can media outlets promote truth?

b. Connect How does art help us discover the truth?

2. Reflect How do stereotypes keep us from seeing the truth?

ACT

With a small group of classmates, discuss works of art that you feel have taught you about the truth.

- You need not confine your discussion to religious art.

- Access photographs or reproductions of the artworks you are interested in.

- After your discussion, write a short paragraph summarizing what your group members shared about the art.

Pray Compose a short prayer asking for guidance in avoiding sins against the Eighth Commandment.

SELF-ASSESS

Which statement best reflects where you are now?

☐ I'm confident enough about the material in this section to be able to explain it to someone else.

☐ I have a good grasp of the material in this section, but I could use more review.

☐ I'm lost. I need help catching up before moving on.

New Covenant Asks More

This twentieth-century painting shows Jesus teaching a gathering of people.

The Old Law, including the Ten Commandments, is fulfilled, refined, and perfected in the New Law, the Law of the Gospel, and the New Covenant of Jesus. We see this reflected in Jesus' answer to a question from a Pharisee. "'Teacher, which commandment in the law is the greatest?'" (Matthew 22:36). He replied that loving God above all is the first and greatest commandment, and the second is the love of neighbor as oneself. The Ten Commandments QUOTATION TO BE INCLUDED IN FINAL PRINTING. (CCC, 2055).

> "'You shall love the Lord your God with all your heart, and with all your soul, and with all your mind. This is the greatest and first commandment.' And a second is like it: 'You shall love your neighbor as yourself.' On these two commandments hang all the law and the prophets."
>
> —Matthew 22:37-40

These two Great Commandments come from the Old Testament (see Deuteronomy 6:5 and Leviticus 19:18). The Ten Commandments must be interpreted through the Great Commandments' twofold yet singular commandment of love (see CCC, 2055). They give us very specific responses to God's love, which we are called to give to God (see CCC, 2083). God loved us first. We are called to respond to that love.

As the Son of God, Jesus initiated the New Law, a New Covenant. This new relationship, according to the *Catechism*, QUOTATION TO BE INCLUDED IN FINAL PRINTING. (CCC, 1972). The New Covenant would not abolish the Old Covenant. The New Covenant would represent a new kind of relationship between God and his people. It would fulfill the Old Covenant and would be established in love and in the hearts of the faithful.

ADVANCE REVIEW COPY

QUOTATION TO BE
INCLUDED IN FINAL PRINTING.

APPLY

- What truth was Saint Thomas Aquinas pointing to after he stopped writing?

- Would you say you are more like him as he wrote—or more like him after he stopped writing? Explain.

—CCC, 1965

The New Law and Covenant was to be a very intimate one. Jesus wanted God's people to follow the Law written in their hearts. Following this Law of the heart would not exclude adhering to the Commandments written on stone tablets. But, it would ask more.

as the *Catechism* explains. It also quotes Saint Irenaeus, an early Church Father,

(CCC, 1964).

In the thirteenth century, there were few people who knew more about Scripture than Saint Thomas Aquinas, a brilliant Italian Dominican priest. Aquinas was acknowledged in his own lifetime as one of the most important theologians of the Church. But even this Doctor of the Church learned what God wanted most of all wasn't his scholarship—but what was written in his heart.

Thomas Aquinas had been a clumsy, shy boy. Born to a wealthy family, he had the best education available. He chose to enter the Dominican order and began a career as a priest and scholar. One of his most important contributions was the *Summa Theologiae* (*Summary of Theology*). He intended this large work to be a theological manual for those who were new to the faith but also serve as a summation of the main theological teachings of the Church.

In early December 1273, the friends of then-Father Thomas were surprised to hear that he had decided to quit writing the third part of the *Summa*. He laid aside his pen—for good. On December 6, the feast of Saint Nicholas, Father Thomas was celebrating Mass and encountered Jesus in a deep and powerful way. Thomas told a

fellow priest that Jesus revealed even more about the immense love of God.

"All that I have written seems like straw to me," explained the man considered by some as the greatest theologian of the Church. Thomas Aquinas died three months later on March 7, 1274. The great scholar had learned the most important lesson of the New Covenant. "To love God is something greater than to know Him," he wrote. He knew that this is what Jesus meant when he answered that question about the greatest Commandment.

Recall What is the title of Saint Thomas Aquinas' theological manual?

Compare What do you think Jesus meant by saying the second Great Commandment was like the first?

The Two Great Commandments

To love God with everything we have, echoes the Old Testament call from God that he told Moses to teach the Israelites.

> Hear, O Israel: The LORD is our God, the LORD alone. You shall love the LORD your God with all your heart, and with all your soul, and with all your might.
>
> —Deuteronomy 6:4-5

God wants us to keep these words in our hearts, to share them with others. "Bind them as a sign on your hand, fix them as an emblem on your forehead, and write them on the doorposts of your house and on your gates" (Deuteronomy 6:8-9).

The first Great Commandment of Jesus is reported in Matthew 23:37 and also in Mark 12:30. It demands a complete investment, a total commitment from anyone who wants to live as a disciple. The first Great Commandment relates to the first three Commandments of the Decalogue.

- I am the Lord your God: you shall not have strange gods before me.

- You shall not take the name of the Lord your God in vain.

- Remember to keep holy the Lord's Day.

The first Great Commandment did not delete these specific expectations. Instead, Jesus incorporates them and challenges us to live out our love for God even more deeply. We must not only avoid worshipping false gods. We must put the one true God at the center of our lives. We must do more than avoid using God's name in vain. We're commissioned to share his sacred name and the life it gives with others. We must go further than keeping the Lord's Day holy. Our love of God should lead us to celebrate God's holiness and his creation every day.

In the same way, Jesus' second Great Commandment echoes Leviticus 19:18. The Commandment to love our neighbors as ourselves incorporates the seven remaining Commandments (see Mark 12:31):

- Honor your father and your mother.

- You shall not kill.

- You shall not commit adultery.

- You shall not steal.

- You shall not bear false witness against your neighbor.

- You shall not covet your neighbor's wife.

- You shall not covet your neighbor's goods.

A person who loves and has respect for him or herself as a son or daughter of God is a person animated by the Holy Spirit.

(CCC, 1966). When that person loves others as he loves himself in the light of Christ, he will adhere to these seven Commandments.

GO TO THE SOURCE 📖

Each of us receives grace from the Holy Spirit for the common good of the Church.

Read 1 Corinthians 12:4-11.

- Which of these gifts have you noticed in your church community?

- Which of these gifts are particularly strong in you?

- Which of these do you wish you could develop?

QUOTATION TO BE INCLUDED IN FINAL PRINTING.

—CCC, 2054

The Holy Spirit empowers the Catholic Church to collaborate in the work of salvation through grace. QUOTATION TO BE INCLUDED IN FINAL PRINTING. (CCC, 2003). That grace fills the Body of Christ with gifts to do three things:

- to connect us with the work of the Holy Spirit

- to allow our collaboration in the salvation of others

- to allow our collaboration in growing the Body of Christ, the Church

These are specific gifts of grace that we receive during the various Sacraments. Plus, there are other special graces called charisms. Some are extraordinary spiritual gifts such as working miracles or prophecy. They are different gifts from the same Spirit meant to make us holy and contribute to the good of the Church. They help us serve our call to love others, which builds up the Church (see CCC, 2003).

Recall Which of the Ten Commandments are referenced in Jesus' first Great Commandment?

Define What are charisms?

Guiding Principle of Love

Jesus embodied love—through his presence, his healing touch, his words of comfort to the sorrowing, his words of challenge to the comfortable, and through the ultimate expression of love by offering himself on the Cross for our salvation.

Throughout his public life Jesus went to great pains to show us how much God loves us. "In this is love, not that we loved God but that he loved us and sent his Son to be the atoning sacrifice for our sins. Beloved, since God loved us so much, we also ought to love one another" (1 John 4:10-11).

Clearly, love is the guiding principle of Christian morality. Jesus revealed the centrality of love when he was tested by a group of religious leaders of his day. He responded to their questioning about commandments by proposing his own commandment—love.

Guidelines for True Happiness

Happiness is a natural desire, and love is the foundation of that emotion. Living in a loving community is what makes us alive and happy. When we live according to the New Law and New Covenant, as the Church teaches, life really works.
QUOTATION TO BE
INCLUDED IN FINAL PRINTING.

(CCC, 1967).

The New Law works through love and does the following:

- fulfills the divine promises of the Old Law by "elevating and orienting" them to the Kingdom of Heaven (CCC, 1967)

- fulfills the commandments of the Old Law releasing their hidden potential. New demands arise from them (see CCC, 1968)

- practices the acts of religion, including almsgiving, prayer, and fasting.
(CCC, 1969)

- is summed up in the Golden Rule to treat others as you would want to be treated.
QUOTATION TO BE
INCLUDED IN FINAL PRINTING.

Guiding Principles for a Christian Moral Life

All love comes from God
Love on our part is a response to and a participation in God's love
Love others as we love ourselves, that is, with our whole being
Love of others and love of God are inseparable

QUOTATION TO BE
INCLUDED IN FINAL PRINTING.

(CCC, 1970)

Saint Augustine noted that we all want to live a happy life. "In the whole human race there is no one who does not assent to this proposition, even before it is articulated" (*De moribus eccl.* 1,3,4:PL 32,1312).

He went on to explain that as human beings learn more about true happiness, they see that any successful search for happiness eventually leads them to God. Augustine, a man who spent his early adulthood desperately trying to find happiness in easy living, ultimately concluded that, "God alone satisfies."

At the age of thirty-three, Augustine could see that only the Gospel of Jesus, the Beatitudes, and the Church would lead him to true happiness. Along with his son, Adeodatus, he was baptized on Easter in A.D. 387.

QUOTATION TO BE
INCLUDED IN FINAL PRINTING.

(CCC, 1718).

APPLY

In 1 Corinthians 13, Saint Paul writes a passage dedicated to love.

- Read the passage, then choose one of the characteristics and illustrate it with a collage, photograph, drawing, or poem.

RELIEF FOR Suffering People

Catholic Relief Services works all over the world following the Great Commandments to love God and neighbor. One of its toughest challenges in recent years has been providing support for the people of Sudan and the newly formed country of South Sudan in Africa.

CRS has been working in Sudan since 1972. At first, efforts to help focused on resettling displaced people in Khartoum, Sudan's capital. But, in 1984, CRS operations moved to the Darfur region in the western part of the country. In Darfur, genocidal war continued for more than a decade. An estimated 2.5 million people were displaced; between 200,000 and 400,000 people have been killed.

Peace is still not firmly established in Sudan and South Sudan, but CRS works in both countries, distributing food, building and equipping health care clinics, building roads and power plants to generate electricity.

Together, Sudan, with 43 million people, and South Sudan, with about 8.5 million people, are bordered by Egypt, the Red Sea, Ethiopia, the Central African Republic, Chad and Libya. The Nile River runs north and south through these two countries and has profoundly shaped their history. After two long, civil wars, South Sudan, with a significant Christian population, separated from Islamic Sudan in 2011.

War, religious differences and poverty have characterized life in these two countries for decades. Many people in these regions farm at the subsistence level. Hunger, malnutrition, and disease are ever-present in the region where the average annual income of individual citizens is only $1,546.

How do you think the needs of the people may have changed over the years?

Research the annual income of ten North African nations. Create a map of North African countries and compare these statistics.

How does the work of CRS give us a model for the two Great Commandments?

ADVANCE REVIEW COPY

QUOTATION TO BE
INCLUDED IN FINAL PRINTING.

—CCC, 1716

Recall that both the Gospel according to Matthew (see Matthew 5:3-11) and the Gospel according to Luke (see Luke 6:20-22) include versions of the Beatitudes delivered by Jesus. The Beatitudes give us a picture of Christ's charity, and they:

- give us our vocation connected with Christ's Paschal Mystery

- show us how we are to act and think as Christians

- are promises from Christ that give us hope during life's difficult times

- announce the blessings and rewards already won for those with faith in Christ

- are modeled in the lives of the Virgin Mary and the saints (see CCC, 1717)

The goal of human existence is revealed in the Beatitudes in that God calls us to his own happiness.

The New Testament uses several expressions to characterize the beatitude:

- the coming of the Kingdom of God

GO TO THE SOURCE

Compare the two accounts of the Beatitudes in the Sermon on the Mount and the Sermon on the Plain.

Read Matthew 5:1-12 and Luke 6:20-26.

- Summarize the differences and similarities of the two accounts.

- Which of the Beatitudes are easiest to understand? Which are more difficult?

DISCUSS

- Choose two Beatitudes and rephrase them using contemporary language. Begin each statement with: "Blessed are the persons. . . ."

- the vision of God: Blessed are the pure in heart, for they shall see God

- entering into the joy of the Lord

- entering into God's rest (see CCC, 1720)

Recall What is the guiding principal of Christian morality?

Explain What did Saint Augustine spend much of his early life searching for? Where did he ultimately find it?

The Person of Jesus

Through his example, Jesus shows us his morality as he encounters people who are being hurt and people who are hurting others. We discover Jesus' New Law through accounts of him and by him as well as through the specific moral pronouncements that he makes. The Sermon on the Mount contains key moral teachings of Jesus' New Law, which works through charity. The New Law uses the Sermon on the Mount to teach what we must do to lead a moral life and the Sacraments to give us the grace to do it (see CCC, 1966).

The happiness Jesus promises through the Beatitudes is the goal of our moral life. "God alone satisfies," Saint Thomas Aquinas told us. The eight pathways that we know as the Beatitudes each contain a divine reward. We will inherit the Kingdom of God; we will receive consolation from God; we will receive his mercy; we will see God; we will become his children; we will find justice.

QUOTATION TO BE
INCLUDED IN FINAL PRINTING.

—CCC, 1726

Let's look separately at each of the pathways to happiness outlined by Jesus in the Beatitudes.

GO TO THE SOURCE

The Sermon on the Mount contains many pronouncements about morality. However, a parable such as the Good Samaritan also contains moral implications.

Read the following passages: Matthew 13:24-30; Matthew 13:44-50; Mark 10:2-12; Luke 6:32-36; Luke 10:38-42; Luke 12:1-3; Luke 19:11-27; or John 8:1-11.

- State the moral messages that they contain and share it with the class.
- Apply the messages to situations that exist today.

The poor in spirit. Blessed Pope John Paul said this goes back to the beginning of Jesus' ministry when he reads the scroll: "'The Spirit of the Lord is upon me, because he has anointed me to bring good news to the poor'" (Luke 4:18). This does not mean just the materially poor, but everyone who is open to God's truth and grace. The poor in spirit are "detached from material things and are willing to use and share them with others according to the demands of justice and charity," Pope John Paul II wrote.

Those who mourn. These include people experience feelings of grief and sorrow. The Beatitude promises God's comfort and consolation, assuring grieving people that victory of Christ will be theirs. This Beatitude also includes those who mourn over the power of sin in the world and in

their lives. Through the gift of the Holy Spirit, they are aware of this sin and the need for God's grace in overcoming it. They know they cannot do this themselves. They, as all of us, rely on God's plan for salvation to reach the happiness of Heaven.

The meek. These people have rejected the power of the world, and in fact, they have little power in this life. They put their trust in God even if, like Jesus, they are mocked for it. They are seen as weak on Earth, but will one day inherit it.

The merciful. These are people who respect and forgive others. They reject the notion that no one else matters but himself or herself. They don't spend time building up their egos or thinking only of themselves. They do acts of mercy, the spiritual and the corporal. They recognize the dignity of the poor among us. They visit the prisoners and the people that no one else wants to be around.

Those who hunger and thirst for righteousness. These are people who long for God and take Jesus seriously when he says to be perfect as his heavenly Father is perfect. They live in imitation of Jesus. They embrace absolute truth and justice rather than see right and wrong as merely a point of view.

The pure of heart. These are people governed by sincerely good intentions who pursue what is right. They reject the glamour of deviance and see chastity as a virtue and marriage as an enduring lifelong Sacrament. They realize that Original Sin has left us with impure hearts, but also know that the heart is where the Lord looks rather than our appearance or achievements. They know God wants us to be like his Son through the gift of the Holy Spirit.

The peacemakers. These are people who love others because God created us all in his image and likeness. They strive for peace for themselves and share the gift of peace with others. They recognize the dignity in every person and reject the evils of the arms trade and the damage done through war. They will do whatever they can to reach peaceful resolutions. They try to imitate the Lord's love for people.

Tabgha, Israel, located on a hill on the north side of the Sea of Galilee, is where scholars say Jesus preached the Sermon on the Mount.

QUOTATION TO BE
INCLUDED IN FINAL PRINTING.

(CCC, 2307).

Those persecuted for righteousness sake. These are people who see suffering for their faith in Christ as a blessing. They have done nothing wrong other than trying to live as a disciple of Christ, which has placed a mark on them. In some places in the world, this might result in ridicule or oppression, but in many places, it also includes persecution and martyrdom.

The Beatitudes are a path to eternal life and the entrance into the glory and joy of Trinitarian life with God. This kind of happiness is not understandable for us. Instead, it is a gift from God.

The Beatitudes give us specific moral choices. Each one QUOTATION TO BE INCLUDED IN FINAL PRINTING. (CCC, 1723). As wonderful as human achievements can be, God alone is the source of all good and all love.

The late Archbishop Fulton Sheen was declared blessed by Pope Benedict XVI in 2012. He described the Beatitudes not as ideals or things that can be taken separately. "They are hard facts and realities inseparable from the Cross of Calvary," Archbishop Sheen said.

The Beatitudes direct us to love those who don't love us back; to do whatever it takes to avoid sinning; to be pure rather than follow our passions to sin; to forgive people who want to hurt us; to face evil with good. We are called, he said, "to live in the world and still keep oneself unpolluted from it; to deny ourselves sometimes legitimate pleasures in order to . . . crucify our egotism." The Beatitudes lead to happiness because they change and renew us.

SECTION 3 REVIEW

QUICK REVIEW

1a. Compare What is the relationship between the two Great Commandments?

b. Reflect What does it mean to say that the law of God is written on our hearts?

c. Summarize Why did Thomas Aquinas abandon work on the *Summa Theologiae*?

2a. Explain Tell the relationship between the two Great Commandments and the Decalogue.

b. Link How does receiving the Sacraments help us fulfill the New Law?

3. Connect How are the Beatitudes the heart of Jesus' teachings?

ACT

With a partner, page through one of the Gospels.

• Look for instances where Jesus' actions showed us how to live.

• Make a list of the incidents and discuss what lessons you can learn from them.

SELF-ASSESS

Which statement best reflects where you are now?

☐ I'm confident enough about the material in this section to be able to explain it to someone else.

☐ I have a good grasp of the material in this section, but I could use more review.

☐ I'm lost. I need help catching up before moving on.

Loving One's Enemies

KEY TERMS IN THIS SECTION

nonviolence conflict-resolving techniques that do not rely on physical or psychological injury of an opponent

As Catholics, we are to safeguard peace. The Fifth Commandment and Jesus' admonition to love our enemies call us to tamper our anger and avoid hatred. In the Sermon on the Mount, Jesus tells us that anyone who is angry with another is subject to judgment (see Matthew 5:22). Hatred and anger that grow into a desire to kill or seriously hurt others is a mortal sin.

'You have heard that it was said, "You shall love your neighbor and hate your enemy." But I say to you, Love your enemies and pray for those who persecute you, so that you may be children of your Father in heaven.'

—Matthew 5:43-45a

Peace does not only mean the absence of war. It can only be attained when there is respect for the development of human life. Good actions by people, free communication, respect for the dignity of others, and the practice of building relationships with others must be safeguarded (see CCC, 2304).

On the subject of peace, Church teaching says that the state can impose obligations for defending a nation. We can opt out in conscience, but we are still obliged to do some other service (see CCC, 2310-2311).

When war does break out, it doesn't mean that moral law is discarded and everything becomes licit. For example, innocent people, wounded soldiers, and prisoners must be treated humanely. Weapons with the intent to destroy who areas or cities are a crime against God (see CCC, 2312-2314).

There are also strong moral reservations about accumulating arms as a deterrent to war. An arms race does not ensure peace, the *Catechism* teaches. The production and sale of weapons also must be regulated so that they don't promote violence and conflict among nations (see CCC, 2315-2316). The Church also urges nations to avoid disorders that build up war instead of peace, such as QUOTATION TO BE INCLUDED IN FINAL PRINTING. (CCC, 2317).

The Old Testament sometimes speaks of retribution against enemies. Many of the Psalms appeal for God's help in defeating a foe. Others thank the Lord for an enemy's destruction. "My eyes have seen the downfall of my enemies; my ears have heard the evil of my assailants," the Psalmist wrote (Psalm 92:11).

Disciples of Christ serve one another in many ways. That could mean providing basic needs as well as friendship or encouragement, working to support peace, or being present for those who mourn.

ADVANCE REVIEW COPY

PRIMARY SOURCES

Saint Thérèse de Lisieux, the Doctor of the Church known as the "Little Flower," was a cloistered Carmelite nun. She has been admired for generation for her "little way" of loving God and loving others. The Great Commandments drove her to find simple, constant ways to love the Lord and those around her. She only lived to the age of 24. Her compelling message of love applies today more than ever.

Here are some quotations from Saint Thérèse that show her respect for Jesus' two Great Commandments.

"May today there be peace within.
May you trust God that you are exactly where you are meant to be.
May you not forget the infinite possibilities that are born of faith.
May you use those gifts that you have received, and pass on the love that has been given to you.
May you be content knowing you are a child of God.
Let this presence settle into your bones, and allow your soul the freedom to sing, dance, praise and love.
It is there for each and every one of us."

"Without love, deeds, even the most brilliant, count as nothing."

"Miss no single opportunity of making some small sacrifice, here by a smiling look, there by a kindly word; always doing the smallest right and doing it all for love."

"I know now that true charity consists in bearing all our neighbors' defects—not being surprised at their weakness, but edified at their smallest virtues."

"O my God! I offer Thee all my actions of this day for the intentions and for the glory of the Sacred Heart of Jesus. I desire to sanctify every beat of my heart, my every thought, my simplest works, by uniting them to Its infinite merits; and I wish to make reparation for my sins by casting them into the furnace of Its Merciful Love.
"O my God! I ask of Thee for myself and for those whom I hold dear, the grace to fulfill perfectly Thy Holy Will, to accept for love of Thee the joys and sorrows of this passing life, so that we may one day be united together in heaven for all Eternity."

> Go to the student site at
> **hs.osvcurriculum.com**

How can you tell from these quotations that Saint Thérèse de Lisieux lived the two Great Commandments?

What in her words resonated with you?

How do her words help you understand the meaning of the word "love"?

ADVANCE REVIEW COPY

GO TO THE SOURCE 📖

Here are two Gospel passages that exemplify values and priorities that build up peace.

Read Mark 10:42-44 and Luke 6:28-31.

- Think about the leaders you know. How did they serve you as well as lead?
- How is the passage from Luke contrary to what society would say?
- Explain the Golden Rule with an example from your life.

Jesus recited the Psalms by heart. He knew the Old Testament. Nonetheless, he knew that the New Covenant would establish a higher standard for those who live under it. Christians would have to be different in the way they lived and loved. Loving enemies was a hallmark of Kingdom living. "'For if you love those who love you, what reward do you have?'" he pointed out. "'Do not the tax collectors do the same? And if you greet only your brothers and sisters, what more are you doing than others? Do not even the Gentiles do the same?'" (Matthew 5:46-47).

The mandate to love and forgive enemies would set Christians apart. The *Catechism* explains that Christian prayer includes the forgiveness of enemies. This conforms us to our Savior:

QUOTATION TO BE
INCLUDED IN FINAL PRINTING.

—CCC, 2844

Alternatives to Violence

We must live the Beatitudes with absolute trust in God. He makes the sun shine on the evil and the good. He provides nourishment for us. Jesus taught us trust the Father and to pray, "Give us this day our daily bread" (see CCC, 2861).

QUOTATION TO BE
INCLUDED IN FINAL PRINTING.

(CCC, 2828).

For centuries, Christians have been learning to trust in the Father's providence and the power of reconciliation. They have modeled their lives after Jesus, who forgave his enemies from the Cross.

The Lord's Prayer, the prayer that Jesus taught us, played a part in the recovery of a Catholic woman named Immaculée Ilibagiza. During the Rwandan genocide in 1994, she and seven other women spent more than ninety days huddled in the cramped bathroom of a local pastor's house. She had been a 115-pound university student with a loving family, but she emerged from that bathroom weighing just sixty-five pounds. Most of her family had been murdered.

Before she went into hiding, her devout Catholic father gave her a set of rosary beads. When anger and resentment over what had happened to her threatened to destroy her and her faith, she was able to turn to praying the Rosary. She began to pray daily from morning to night, and eventually, she found it possible to forgive her tormentors and those who killed her family. She later met the man who murdered her mother and brother. She said to him: "I forgive you."

Immaculée discovered that the Holy Spirit helps us to forgive when our own human emotions and experiences would seem to make it impossible. Forgiving enemies has been a Christian story repeated in each century. The deacon, Saint Stephen, died from stoning outside of Jerusalem, saying, "Lord, do not hold this sin against them." (Acts 7: 60). Blessed Jerzy Popieluszko (1947–1984) of Poland is a man who preached forgiveness and a modern martyr. Father Jerzy joined

CONNECT

- Name three ways that you personally could place God first in your life.
- If you truly did these things, would your life be easier or more difficult? Explain your answer.

the Solidarity movement while Poland was still a Communist nation. He was kidnapped, tortured, and murdered on October 19, 1984, by three Polish government agents.

He was aware before his death that he would be a target for Communist reprisal. He warned striking Catholic Polish laborers not to retaliate. "Do not struggle with violence. Violence is a sign of weakness. All those who cannot win through the heart try to conquer through violence."

The Church does remind us, however, that people do have the right to defend their own lives or the lives of others. This applies to ordinary citizens as well as to those in law enforcement or in military service. In these situations, any violence used to truly defend life doesn't intend the injury or death of an aggressor.

QUOTATION TO BE
INCLUDED IN FINAL PRINTING.

—CCC, 2265

Jesus teaches and exemplifies the truth that unjust violence is a contradiction of our faith in God, the Creator of all people, who cares for all of his children. Such violence runs counter to our faith in Jesus, who teaches **nonviolence**: "'if anyone strikes you on the right cheek, turn the other also'" (Matthew 5:39). Unjust violence, then, con-

RECALL

- Write an essay recalling a personal experience of forgiveness. Revisit the circumstances, conflict, your feelings and actions at the time, etc. Tell how the conflict was resolved or why it wasn't.

REFLECT

Unjust violence violates the teaching of the Church and our faith in God.

- Give two examples when nonviolence would require courage.

- Both violence and nonviolence can result in suffering. Is there a difference in the suffering that each entails? Explain.

tradicts the teaching of the Church and is contradictory to our faith in God (see CCC, 2306).

Charity to Others and Avoiding Hypocrisy

Charity is the cornerstone of all virtues. Every other virtue that we might practice represents some dimension of Christian love. Love, like hope, can be misunderstood. The theological virtue of love does not mirror the romantic love that is often referred to in the media. As with hope, sometimes we consider love to be only a passive quality. Also, people sometimes suggest that selfish and possessive behaviors are motivated by love. In fact, selfish love is a contradiction in terms. The *Catechism* defines love in the words of the Saint Thomas Aquinas:

(CCC, 1766).

Charity is the virtue that places concern for God, manifest especially through concern for others, above everything else.

On one occasion, when Jesus went ashore at a deserted place, a great crowd from the town came to him. He showed compassion to them and healed the sick. The disciples came to Jesus as evening approached and suggested that the crowd be dismissed to get something to eat. There were thousands of tired, hungry people who would have to return to their villages on foot and on empty stomachs. Jesus instead told the disciples to feed the people with the five loaves and two fished that he blessed.

The Feeding of the Five Thousand found in Matthew Chapter 14 is a compassionate miracle exemplifying Jesus' divine power and great love.

Saint Benedict the Moor

(1526–1589)

Saint Benedict the Moor was the son of African slaves brought to Messina, Sicily. Like his parents, who had converted to Catholicism, Benedict worked hard at farming. Because of his parents' loyal service, Benedict was granted his freedom at eighteen. Though he made very little money, he often gave to the local people living in poverty. He saved the little money he had left and bought a pair of oxen to help his parents plow their fields.

As a young black man in a white culture and community, he was often subjected to vicious racial slurs and prejudice. He displayed great patience in the face of these insults. His self-control and courage caught the eye of the leader of a local community of hermits named Lanza. These hermits followed the Franciscan rule.

There was something strong and Christ-like in the young man's loving eyes and spirit. Benedict was invited to join the community of hermits at Monte Pellegrino, and shortly after, he gave away his few belongings and joined this community. Later, when this group disbanded, Benedict joined the Franciscans in Palermo.

Born and raised as a slave, Benedict had never attended school or learned to read. At the Franciscan friary, he was

ADVANCE REVIEW COPY

Saint Benedict the Moor served with the Franciscans in Palermo, Italy, on the island of Sicily.

a lay brother and cook. However, his fellow friars could see that Benedict easily grasped theological principles as well as the deepest truths of Scripture. Benedict became known for gifts of healing and spiritual direction, and his fellow friars chose him as guardian of the friary. Later, he was selected as novice master. Lay people from all over Sicily and all walks of life came to visit and ask Brother Benedict for his spiritual advice.

Franciscan superiors were not usually lay brothers like Benedict, but he guided his brothers with humility, sound judgment, and love. Once, after correcting a novice and assigning him a penance, he discovered that the young man was actually not guilty of the offense. Benedict immediately went to the novice, knelt down before him, and prayerfully asked for forgiveness.

Benedict's reputation as a holy man continued to grow. He often met and prayed with visitors. He wanted everyone to know that what God wanted from them wasn't complicated. The two Great Commandments to love God and neighbor governed his life. The monastery friars believed

that Benedict had been faithfully fulfilling those commandments every day of his life. He was unselfish, and even referred to his own personal possessions as "ours," not "mine." He fasted frequently and allowed himself only a few hours of sleep each night.

After a difficult illness, Benedict died in 1589. He was canonized in 1807, and has become a particularly beloved saint for African-Americans because of the strong but peaceful way he handled racial prejudice. Seven U.S. Catholic parishes are named for him as St. Benedict the Black or St. Benedict the Moor.

> **Think About It** Why do you think the poor were drawn to Saint Benedict? What part of Saint Benedict's life could you do better in your own life?

➚ Go to the student site at
hs.osvcurriculum.com

ADVANCE REVIEW COPY

When asked what it means to be a good person, some would answer along the lines of "do no harm." To be a good person also includes "do good."

- Which of these is a passive approach to being a good person and which is active?
- Name the virtue(s) involved in each approach.
- Which approach one is more challenging?

QUOTATION TO BE
INCLUDED IN FINAL PRINTING.

—CCC, 1823

When someone has a need, those who want to be disciples of Christ should try to answer it. The need could be food, clothing, or shelter. The need could be friendship or encouragement. Catholics must respond to the needs and suffering of the world out of love.

Jesus not only fed thousands of people, he provided leftovers. As Matthew noted: "and they took up what was left over of the broken pieces, twelve baskets full" (Matthew 14:20). The charity (love) of Jesus and his Father, God, was overflowing.

Nothing would be more important than charity in the New Covenant, wrote Saint Paul, the theologian of the New Testament, echoing the words of Jesus.

QUOTATION TO BE
INCLUDED IN FINAL PRINTING.

—CCC, 1826

The most devoted followers of Jesus throughout the Christian centuries have learned this Gospel message well. Charity comes first. "If we pray, we will believe. If we believe, we will love. If we love, we will serve," wrote Blessed Mother Teresa of Calcutta, one of the most famous and inspirational humanitarians of modern times. In fact, Mother Teresa first learned about the joyful obligations of charity from her parents in Albania.

Agnes Bojaxhiu (Mother Teresa) was the youngest of the three children of Kole and Drana Bojaxhiu. Kole was a successful businessman in Skopje, Albania, and provided his family with a comfortable lifestyle. Kole was also generous with his wealth. He was constantly taking his children along when he delivered food and clothing to the less fortunate.

After his sudden death in 1919 when Agnes was only nine, Drana was left to raise and support their children. Though Kole's business partners abandoned her, Drana eventually regained her balance and began making a good living again. Like her husband, she was committed to charity but offered help discreetly with no fanfare.

Many years later, Mother Teresa wrote: "Many of the poor in and around Skopje knew our house, and none left it empty-handed. We had guests at table every day. At first I used to ask, 'Who are they?', and Mother would answer: 'Some are relatives, but all of them are our people.' When I was older, I realized that the strangers were poor people who had nothing and whom my mother was feeding."

- Give three examples of misusing or misinterpreting the concept of love.
- Describe three specific situations when the *Catechism's* description of love—to will the good of another—might be a real challenge for those involved.

My Faith

➚ Go to the student site at **hs.osvcurriculum.com**

To Be With Jesus

In Matthew Chapters 14 and 15, you read of thousands of people gathering to be with Jesus. Among the thousands that gathered to hear Jesus, some must have been seeking truth, others seeking healing. Some must have gathered because they had been in his presence earlier and knew it touched them spiritually, others might have heard about Jesus from a friend or relative, others may simply been curious as to what was going on.

People wanted to be with Jesus for different reasons.

What interest do you have in Jesus? (check all that apply)

__ Need some Healing

__ Curious

__ Seeking something for my soul

__ Want Truth

__ Felt his presence before

__ Longing for spiritual strength

__ Like being with others who believe

__ Agree with his directions for living

__ He's the Son of God and our Savior

Some people brought loaves and some brought fish. What do you bring?

__ an open mind

__ a sincere heart

__ two hands

__ questions

__ honesty

__ desire to get better

__ my future

__ love for God

__ compassion

You can use anything from this My Faith as part of the report you turn in at the end of the class.

Discipleship ... within the Body of Christ ... for the glory of God and the good of the world.

CONNECT

Listen as one student reads aloud 1 Corinthians 13. Share these questions and reactions to the reading.

- What lines about love really resonate for you?
- What line or lines would you choose to memorize?
- What can people learn from the passage about love?
- What's the most important thing Paul says about love?

Those early examples of helping others and finding strangers at the family dinner table deeply affected Mother Teresa. There, in Skopje, she received her first lessons in charity. Those lessons were put to good use later in India and other places.

It is charity, the *Catechism*, reminds us, that

QUOTATION TO BE
INCLUDED IN FINAL PRINTING.

(CCC, 1827).

Consider How can you address the virtue of charity in your own community?

Explain How did Mother Teresa's childhood teach her about Christian charity?

SECTION **4 REVIEW**

QUICK REVIEW

1a. Reflect Why are some of Jesus' teachings hard to obey?

b. Recall What reward awaits those who follow Jesus?

2. Clarify When is defense of someone else a duty? Who might have this duty?

3. Consider Why is nonviolence often neglected as a strategy for change?

4a. Explain How is love an active virtue?

b. Summarize How did Mother Teresa live out the Gospel message of love?

ACT

With a group of classmates, go through several issues of newspapers and magazines.

- Look for articles about people who are pursuing nonviolence as a means to change.
- Outline how the nonviolent campaigns are progressing.
- Follow these stories in newspapers or on the Internet for a few weeks.
- Discuss the place of nonviolence in today's world.

Pray Compose a short prayer asking God to help the world find peaceful means to bring about God's kingdom.

SELF-ASSESS

Which statement best reflects where you are now?

☐ I'm confident enough about the material in this section to be able to explain it to someone else.

☐ I have a good grasp of the material in this section, but I could use more review.

☐ I'm lost. I need help catching up before moving on.

ADVANCE REVIEW COPY

PRAYER

Opening Prayer

We begin in the name of the Father and the Son and Holy Spirit.
Living Word of God, live in me today so that others may read my life and be led to you.

Lord Jesus Christ, give me courage this day to witness to you through my life.

Give to us Lord God, eyes to see and hearts to apprehend all we do not now see. Keep revealing it until we understand.

O God, open my lips and my mouth will proclaim your praise.

Send me Lord and I will go. Give me words and I will speak.

Amen.

Closing Prayer

Prayer of reflection on the divinity of Christ
When we have an expectation of our strength, we fall short,
When we hope to stand alone without Christ, we fall,
When we trust too much in our knowledge, we show our ignorance.

Teach us to be humble,
Give us your strength, give us, and give us your knowledge.

We may not be the light, but we can help your light shine to others,
We may not be the shepherds, but we can tend your sheep,
We may not hate others, but help us to show your love.

Help us to discern our weaknesses so we can realize strength,
Teach us to substitute our pride with humility,
Our work is to serve you by serving all others in need.

Amen.

ADVANCE REVIEW COPY

TERMS

Use each of the following terms in a sentence that shows you know what the term means in the context of the chapter. You may include more than one term in a sentence.

lying   rash judgment

calumny   discrimination

detraction   nonviolence

PEOPLE AND IDEAS

Define each person or idea in the context of the chapter.

1. gossip

2. Greatest Commandment

3. New Covenant

4. *Summa Theologiae*

5. Saint Stephen

6. Blessed Jerzy Popieluszko

7. Blessed Mother Teresa

UNDERSTANDING

Answer each question and complete each exercise.

SECTION 1

1. **Recall** Why is it important to build relationships on the truth?

2. **Evaluate** Does the Eighth Commandment always require that we be brutally honest? Why or why not?

3. **Summarize** What should we expect of news reporters?

SECTION 2

4. **Apply** How do we show respect for truth?

5. **Explain** How was Jesus' life based on truth?

SECTION 3

6. **Reflect** Why was it possible for Jesus to initiate the New Covenant?

7. **Connect** How is obeying the Commandments a response to God's love?

8. **Define** What is the role of the Holy Spirit in helping us obey the commandments?

SECTION 4

9. **Relate** What standard does the New Covenant set for our behavior?

10. **Tell** Why is the story of Jerzy Popieluszko significant?

11. **Apply** Why should we prefer nonviolence over violence?

12. **Reflect** Why is charity central to all other virtues?

ADVANCE REVIEW COPY

CONNECTING

Visual This sign raised during a peaceful protest says something about the people in this community.

What does it say? How does this represent the Beatitude that it expresses? What other signs of the Beatitudes have you seen in your community?

Challenge A friend tells you that a student you both know named Andrea was caught cheating. Your friend didn't see it happen, but heard it from another mutual friend, Ellen. You are surprised Andrea was caught cheating, so you have doubts about this story. Based on the material in this chapter, what moral principle do you need to apply here? What do you say to your friend?

Question After working through this chapter and the two Great Commandments, what advice would you give someone who thinks that revenge is justified by the Bible?

Imagine You are a news producer and you want to do a series of stories on people whose lives reflect the Beatitudes.

- Make a list of the people you would interview from each of the eight Beatitudes, where would you look for them, and what you would ask them.

SELF-ASSESS

On Your Own Make a list of the most important things you learned from this chapter.

Select three things that represent your growth in understanding as you worked through this chapter. Write a paragraph explaining your choices.

With a Partner List what you found most helpful or interesting in this chapter as well as any other questions that have surfaced.

CHAPTER 6

- Where were you when Pope Francis was elected?
- What is the Pope's role as teacher and leader of the Catholic Church?

The Church, Our Teacher

Go to the student site at
hs.osvcurriculum.com

ADVANCE REVIEW COPY

Pope Francis, Cardinal Jorge Mario Bergoglio, 76, of Buenos Aires, Argentina, steps onto the balcony of Saint Peter Basilica after his election March 13, 2013. Pope Francis is the first Jesuit and the first Latin American to ever be elected Pope. He also is the first successor of Saint Peter to choose the name Francis, after Saint Francis of Assisi.

YOU WILL

- Examine how the Church serves as a moral guide.

- Explore the teaching office of the Catholic Church.

- Discuss the four distinct expressions of law.

- See how the New Law is the perfection of natural and revealed law.

- Discover how Canon Law connects us to Christ.

- Identify the obligations of Catholics and the Precepts of the Church.

- Investigate the principles of living morally and how a conscience is informed.

- Examine how a well-formed conscience determines the morality of an act.

ADVANCE REVIEW COPY

The Church as Moral Guide

KEY TERMS IN THIS SECTION

Magisterium the living, official teaching office of the Church, consisting of the Pope and the bishops acting in union with him. The office interprets Scripture and Tradition and ensures faithfulness to the teachings of the Apostles.

QUOTATION TO BE
INCLUDED IN FINAL PRINTING.

—CCC, 2031

Jesus Christ is the supreme teacher of Christian morality, and it is in his Church that Christians fulfill their vocations in union with everyone who has been baptized. Our communion with all the baptized is important because as Saint Paul's points out, we are all parts of one Body (see 1 Corinthians 12:12-14). In order to truly be one Body, we must receive the grace of the Holy Spirit through the Sacraments and know the laws of Christ, and for that we have the Catholic Church.

The Christian moral life is spiritual worship that

(*Catechism of the Catholic Church*, 2031).

Members of the Magisterium gather at the Vatican.

We receive continuing guidance in morality through the Church because she is the Body of Christ. Jesus commanded the Apostles to teach his truth. It is the Catholic Church under the leadership of the Apostle's successors—the Pope and bishops in union with him—that ensures faithfulness to Christ's teachings that he gave to the Apostles. In their role as teachers, the Pope and the bishops share the faith that relates to our moral lives. As leaders, they study moral questions involving natural law and reason that arise in this swiftly changing world and provide us guidance for our moral decision-making.

The teaching mission of the Church has its beginnings in the ministry of Jesus. During the three years of his active ministry, Jesus was often called "Rabbi," which means "Teacher." A rabbi at the time was a Jewish scholar or teacher, especially one who studied or taught Jewish law. Jesus, as the son of Joseph, was trained and worked as a carpenter. But he was also well educated in the Scriptures and Jewish law.

Jesus spent much of his time teaching about his Father's plan for salvation and the Kingdom of God that he was bringing into the world. "Jesus went through Galilee, teaching in their synagogues, and proclaiming the good news of the kingdom, and curing every disease and every sickness among the people" (Matthew 4:23).

DISCUSS

- What have you already learned about bishops and the role they play in the Church?
- Identify a moral issue the U.S. Bishops have recently addressed, and explain their teaching around that issue.

ADVANCE REVIEW COPY

Jesus traveled to Capernaum early in his ministry.

Read Luke 4:31-37.

- What did Jesus say to the unclean spirit?
- What did the people think of Jesus' actions?
- Did people understand who Jesus was? Explain.

Jesus our Redeemer taught people a new way of life in the Holy Spirit, who conforms our deepest desires to the Lord. The *Catechism* points out that QUOTATION TO BE INCLUDED IN FINAL PRINTING. (CCC, 2764). Before his Ascension to Heaven, Jesus commissioned his Apostles to continue his work—including teaching:

> 'Go therefore and make disciples of all nations, baptizing them in the name of the Father and of the Son and of the Holy Spirit, and teaching them to obey everything that I have commanded you.'
>
> —Matthew 28:19-20a

He also promised that he would be with them always, "'to the end of the age'" (Matthew 28:20b).

Not long after that, at Pentecost, the Apostles of Jesus were empowered and transformed by the Holy Spirit. These chosen men began to baptize, heal the sick, and teach the Good News about Jesus. On Pentecost, according to the Acts of the Apostles, Saint Peter taught with new courage and wisdom.

Then Peter stood up with all the Apostles, raised his voice, and proclaimed to them, "'Men of Judea and all who live in Jerusalem, let this be known to you, and listen to what I say.'" (Acts 2:14).

Saint Peter then shared the story of salvation history, explaining that Jesus was the promised Messiah, and that his Death and Resurrection fulfilled all Old Testament prophecies. Three thousand people accepted his message about Jesus and were baptized (see Acts 2:41).

The Catholic Church has taught the Word of God since that day when Peter, as the first Pope, began to evangelize. The Church baptizes those who accept the message and commit themselves to live the Catholic way of life. During every century, there have been exceptional Popes, bishops, priests and religious who were gifted and inspired teachers. The Church has also had many inspired lay teachers of the faith.

The *Catechism* says the Church QUOTATION TO BE INCLUDED IN FINAL PRINTING. (CCC, 2032). It is the Church's right and responsibility to announce moral truths and to make judgments on human events that protect fundamental human rights and for the salvation of souls.

The Catholic Church has always held up the example and the faith witness of Mary, the Mother of Jesus, and other Christian saints. In the lives of Mary and the Saints, a member of the Catholic Church finds QUOTATION TO BE INCLUDED IN FINAL PRINTING. (CCC, 2030).

The Church has also taught about salvation history and the life of Christ through the cycles of the liturgical year. Throughout Advent, Christmas, Lent, and Easter, we celebrate and deepen our understanding of the holiest mysteries: the Incarnation, Redemption, and the Paschal Mystery remembered during the Triduum—from Holy Thursday to Easter.

Identify What is the source and summit of the Christian moral life?

Describe How does the account of Peter on the Day of Pentecost encourage you?

Teaching Office of the Church

The living, official teaching office of the Catholic Church is known as the **Magisterium**. It consists of the Pope and the bishops acting in union with him. Guided by the Holy Spirit, the role of the Church's Magisterium is to give whether in its written (Sacred Scripture) or in the form of Sacred Tradition (CCC, 85). Scripture and Tradition are two distinct modes of transmitting Divine Revelation. The Magisterium looks to them as forming the single deposit of truth— the Word of God—to formulate teaching in matters of faith and morals.

GO TO THE SOURCE 📖

Saint Francis of Assisi (1118–1226) was inspired to live a life of poverty after reflecting on the Gospel account in Matthew 10:9.

Read Matthew 10:5-10.

- What is Jesus asking the Apostles to do in this passage?
- What kind of commitment are they making?
- What kind of commitment are you being asked to make for your faith?

To preserve the faith handed on by the Apostles, Christ gave the Church a share in his own infallibility. This is how the Body of Christ, guided by the Magisterium,

(CCC, 889). The *Catechism* describes the Magisterium's responsibility as keeping the People of God linked with the covenant founded by God with his People through Jesus.

QUOTATION TO BE
INCLUDED IN FINAL PRINTING.

—CCC, 890

The Magisterium also makes it possible, in fact guarantees, that the Church professes the true faith without error. The Pope can proclaim a teaching of faith or morals as infallible, either acting alone, speaking "from the chair of Peter" or by speaking together with the body of bishops.

QUOTATION TO BE
INCLUDED IN FINAL PRINTING.

(CCC, 891). These teachings are to be held with the obedience of faith.

The Magisterium also teaches with divine assistance even on doctrines that have not been declared infallible. The faithful are to abide by these ordinary teachings because the bishops and Pope are witnesses of divine and catholic truth (see *Lumen Gentium*, 25).

Name What is the role of the Magisterium?

Connect Why is the Magisterium important to the moral life of Catholics?

Moral Matters

Our moral life is connected to our spiritual worship. When we gather as the Body of Christ for Mass and to celebrate the Sacraments, the grace of Christ informs and feeds our moral life and actions.

QUOTATION TO BE
INCLUDED IN FINAL PRINTING.

(CCC, 2031).

The Magisterium's instruction on moral matters is ordinarily taught through preaching and catechesis (religious education) by priests, parents, and catechists. The Magisterium is also assisted in this effort by theologians and spiritual writers. This "deposit of Christian moral teaching" taught by the Magisterium has been transmitted to each succeeding generation. Moral teaching consists of rules, commandments, and virtues that proceed from our faith in Christ. They are driven by love.

QUOTATION TO BE
INCLUDED IN FINAL PRINTING.

(CCC, 2033).

What the Church teaches to the faithful is a way to promote life and truth (see CCC, 2037). These teachings help us with our moral judgments and God gives us the grace to heal any errors in our human way of reasoning. We have an obligation, then, to follow the authority of the Church. In order to teach Christian morality and have it bear fruit in the world, the Church must have the cooperation of all Christians and people of good will (see CCC, 2038). As we put the Gospel into practice, we will experience Christ and we will grow in our ability to make moral judgments and decisions based on God's divine plan.

IDENTIFY

- What teacher has taught you a concept in a very effective way? Explain what you learned.

ADVANCE REVIEW COPY

PRIMARY SOURCES

The ecumenical Council of Trent brought the Church's Magisterium together over three separate periods: 1545-1547, 1551-1552, and 1562-1563. Many issues and teachings were discussed during that time under the guidance of the Holy Spirit, including the Seven Sacraments and their role in God's plan of salvation. The Council decided, for example, that the teaching on transubstantiation and the doctrine of the real presence of Jesus in the Eucharist would be upheld. Following are two excerpts concerning the Holy Eucharist made by the Council of Trent.

Thirteenth Session (11 October 1551)

Decree Concerning the Most Holy Sacrament of the Eucharist

CHAPTER I. On the real presence of our Lord Jesus Christ in the most holy sacrament of the Eucharist.

First of all, the holy council teaches and openly and plainly professes that after the consecration of bread and wine, our Lord Jesus Christ, true God and true man, is truly, really and substantially contained in the august sacrament of the Holy Eucharist under the appearance of those sensible things. . . .

CHAPTER II. On the reason of the Institution of this most holy Sacrament.

Therefore, our Savior, when about to depart from this world to the Father, instituted this sacrament, in which He poured forth, as it were, the riches of His divine love towards men, making a remembrance of his wonderful works,[18] and commanded us in the participation of it to reverence His memory and to show forth his death until he comes[19] to judge the world. But He wished that this sacrament should be received as the spiritual food of souls,[20] whereby they may be nourished and strengthened, living by the life of Him who said: He that eateth me, the same also shall live by me,[21] and as an antidote whereby we may be freed from daily faults and be preserved from mortal sins.

➜ Go to the student site at
hs.osvcurriculum.com

How was the Magisterium performing its role at the Council of Trent?

What role did Sacred Tradition play in the Magisterium's teaching as seen here?

What does the excerpt teach about the connection between the Eucharist and mortal sin?

The Catholic Cathedral in Trent, Italy, is seen near the Piazza Duomo.

QUOTATION TO BE
INCLUDED IN FINAL PRINTING.

—CCC, 2038

To grow in moral awareness and respond faithfully to God's moral code, we must be open to the Holy Spirit, follow the teachings of the Church, and make decisions that go beyond only our personal needs. We need a servant attitude. Our moral judgments should consider, as much as possible, the good of everybody.

QUOTATION TO BE
INCLUDED IN FINAL PRINTING.
(CCC, 2039).

In this way, we grow as sons and daughters of the Church as an extension of the grace we receive at Baptism. Forming an informed conscience is part of the vocation we were given by our Baptism. The Church is to model the mercy of God. This is most apparent in the Sacrament of Reconciliation. In the same way, the Church also nourishes us within the liturgy where we receive the Word and Eucharist of our Lord (see CCC, 2040).

Describe How does the Magisterium's teaching get to the members of the Church?

Apply How do you cooperate with the Church in its teaching on Christian morality?

SECTION 1 REVIEW

QUICK REVIEW

1a. Trace Where did the authority of the Catholic Church as a moral guide originate?

b. Explain Why did Jesus deserve the title of "rabbi"?

c. Compare How did Pentecost change Saint Peter?

d. Reflect Why is setting a good example a strong teacher?

2a. Recall Which two sources of truth does the Magisterium use to formulate matters of morals?

b. List What are the responsibilities of the Magisterium?

3a. Reflect Why are the Creed, the Our Father, and the Decalogue the basis of Church teachings?

b. Explain Why should moral judgments consider the good of everyone?

4. Consider How does the life of Blessed Pope John XXIII serve as a model for teachers?

ACT

Read about some recent Popes and how they influenced the way that the Catholic Church teaches.

- Meet with a group of classmates and discuss what you found.

- Summarize what you learned and share the summary with the class.

Pray Compose a short prayer asking God to guide the Church as it teaches its members.

SELF-ASSESS

Which statement best reflects where you are now?

☐ I'm confident enough about the material in this section to be able to explain it to someone else.

☐ I have a good grasp of the material in this section, but I could use more review.

☐ I'm lost. I need help catching up before moving on.

ADVANCE REVIEW COPY

Moral Law

KEY TERMS IN THIS SECTION

Old Law the Law of Moses and the Ten Commandments; the law of the Old Testament

New Law the Law of the Gospels or the New Testament presented by Jesus

When we talk about moral law, there are four distinct, but related, expressions of law:

- eternal law, the source, in God, of all law

- natural law, the law of reason

- revealed law, comprised of the **Old Law** and the **New Law** (Law of the Gospel)

- civil and ecclesiastical laws (see CCC, 1952)

These expressions of law are all united through Christ, who is the way of perfection. Only Jesus teaches and delivers the justice of God. "For Christ is the end of the law so that there may be righteousness for everyone who believes" (Romans 10:4).

Moral law points out how to act in ways that lead to God's promised happiness, and it condemns the ways of evil that turn us away from the love of God.

(CCC, 1950).

The rule of law comes from competent authority and works for the common good. All law finds its ultimate truth in the eternal law of God. Moral law is inscribed on the human heart and is known as reason. It is based on the rational order of things. Humans are the only earthly creatures worthy enough to be given law because we have been elevated to a supernatural level through sanctifying grace and, because of our rational ability, humankind is

QUOTATION TO BE INCLUDED IN FINAL PRINTING.

(CCC, 1951).

The words "authority" and "author" come from the same root meaning. They have a Latin root in the word "auctoritas" which means one who creates or invents. The author of a book, of course, creates the book. An author knows everything about his or her book. The author knows better than anyone else how that book was put together and what makes it unique.

God is our author. He created us in his own image and likeness. And because he is our author, God knows how we are made and what we need for happiness. God's *authority* is properly expressed in his Law.

Moral law, then, is part of God's instruction given for the common good. It is the work of divine wisdom that guides God's sons and daughters generation after generation.

The natural moral law remains always written on the heart of each of us.

Natural Moral Law

The original moral sense given to all people is reflected in the natural moral law. Saint Leo XIII described this interior sense of the moral law as   of each human being. It is written in our souls because God is its author (CCC, 1954).

QUOTATION TO BE
INCLUDED IN FINAL PRINTING.

(CCC, 1955). The Ten Commandments express natural law's principal precepts. They are the first and essential principles that govern a moral life.

There are other things that are important to know about natural law. This law, for example, is never outdated or irrelevant—in any culture or era. It is how we determine our fundamental rights and duties (see CCC, 1956). The natural law is unchanging over time as ideas and customs fluctuate.

QUOTATION TO BE
INCLUDED IN FINAL PRINTING.

—CCC, 1958

Added to that, natural moral law serves as a foundation for building a structure of moral rules and as a foundation for the human community. This natural law is reflected in the Old Law, meaning the Law of Moses and the Commandments. It is also expressed in the New Law or the Law of the Gospel, which fulfills the Old Law. Finding the correct path hinges on two things: our longing for God and seeing one another other as equals. Saint Thomas Aquinas describes it as the light of understanding placed in us by God from the moment of creation.

The way we apply natural law can vary greatly, especially when the setting, the time, and the circumstances are applied. Still, the natural law unites all of us as a rule and, despite our differences, it gives us common principles (see CCC, 1957). It is the foundation on which we build our moral guidelines as individuals and on which societies base their laws.

APPLY

Some groups apply laws in ways that seem to violate natural moral law. Give two examples of this from current events today.

The common principles of natural law, while natural, are not necessarily clear to everyone. We still need grace and revelation because of our fallen nature. God's grace and revelation through Sacred Scripture and Sacred Tradition allow each of us to know the truth with a sense of certainty.

List What are the four expressions of moral law and how are they united?

Explain What does natural moral law hinge upon?

The Old Law

The first stage of revealed Law is the Old Law, meaning God first revealed his Law to the Chosen People of Israel. This prepared the world for the coming of Jesus by connecting salvation with the truths that come to us naturally through reason. The moral prescriptions of the Old Law are summed up in the Ten Commandments.

QUOTATION TO BE
INCLUDED IN FINAL PRINTING.

(CCC, 1962).

Our Christian Tradition has always found the Old Law to be imperfect because, while it tells us what to do, it does not give us the grace of the Holy Spirit to fulfill it. Sin still binds the Old Law. Nevertheless, it is the first stage on our way to the Kingdom of Heaven. It prepares us for the Gospel, like a prophecy if what will come (see CCC, 1963). Again it is Saint Thomas Aquinas who points out that there were people under the Old Covenant who possessed the love and grace of the Holy Spirit, just as there are people under the New Covenant who remain far from the perfection of the New Law.

ADVANCE REVIEW COPY

The watercolor by Canziani Estella (1887-1964) depicts the tongues of fire descending on the Apostles and Mary at Pentecost.

QUOTATION TO BE
INCLUDED IN FINAL PRINTING.

—CCC, 1964

QUOTATION TO BE
INCLUDED IN FINAL PRINTING.

—CCC, 1968

The New Law

The New Law is the work of Christ. It is also the work of the Holy Spirit, through whom it becomes the law of love, grace, and freedom written in our hearts. Love is the key. Jesus gives us the Beatitudes as an answer to the question of happiness and as a model of the Christian moral life. He also instituted the Sacraments to give us the necessary grace to carry it out.

The Beatitudes take the Old Law and direct us toward the Kingdom of Heaven. They are given to those most open to accepting their surprising and hopeful message, namely the poor, the humble, the afflicted, the pure of heart, and those persecuted because of Christ. The Sermon on the Mount shines on the Old Law and reveals the hidden potential of the Ten Commandments. We are called to a new level of holiness, a greater fulfillment of God's original design for humanity.

We act in accordance with the New Law through almsgiving, prayer, and fasting, but we do these things not to call attention to ourselves, but to

GO TO THE SOURCE

In the following readings, we find some of the moral teachings of the Apostles.

Read one of the following, Romans 12–15; 1 Corinthians 12–13; Colossians 3–4; or Ephesians 4–5.

- What teachings can you discern from your reading?
- How is love represented in the reading?
- How is the New Law put into practice in your reading?
- How can you implement what you've learned into your own life?

honor God's commands. The prayer of the Law of the Gospel is the Our Father. As we have said, love is the basis for the New Law.

After Pentecost, the Apostles put the New Law into action, especially by teaching the virtues that flow from faith in Christ and from the love that he taught. Love is the supreme gift that we receive from the Holy Spirit.

The New Law has three other names:

- the *law of love* because we act out of love given to us by the Holy Spirit rather that out of fear

- the *law of grace* because through faith and the Sacraments, the New Law gives us grace to act with virtue

- the *law of freedom* because it frees us from the ritual and the judgments that came from the Old Law. Love prompts us to act more spontaneously, and we move from a servant who doesn't know what the master is doing to a friend a Christ, who makes everything known to us (see CCC, 1972).

REFLECT

Describe your experience with the New Law in the three ways that it is expressed.

- Law of love: When did you do the right thing out of love rather than fear?

- Law of grace: When have you felt the Holy Spirit prompt you to do a good thing that you normally might not have?

- Law of freedom: Describe a time you did something that was a positive break from old habits or old attitudes.

The New Law also includes the evangelical counsels found in the Gospel according to Matthew. These are intended to remove anything that that is incompatible with charity or that might get in the way of the development of charity. For example, Jesus says to the rich young man, "If you wish to be perfect, go, sell your possessions, and give the money to the poor, and you will have treasure in heaven" (Matthew 19:21).

Identify What is the first stage of God's revealed law?

Define What is the New Law, also known as the Law of the Gospel?

SECTION 2 REVIEW

QUICK REVIEW

1a. Reflect Why is moral authority an important element to society?

b. Consider What breeds distrust in authority?

c. Recall What is the function of moral law?

d. List What are the four expressions of the moral law?

2. Explain How does natural moral law unite all people?

3a. Recall Why is the Old Law the first level on our way to heaven?

b. Link How does the New Law use the Beatitudes and Sacraments?

c. Explain Why does the New Law give hope?

d. Connect What does the Holy Spirit have to do with the New Law?

e. List What are additional names for the New Law, and why are these names appropriate?

ACT

Find two expressions of moral law from art or sketch one yourself. Share your examples with the rest of the class.

SELF-ASSESS

Which statement best reflects where you are now?

☐ I'm confident enough about the material in this section to be able to explain it to someone else.

☐ I have a good grasp of the material in this section, but I could use more review.

☐ I'm lost. I need help catching up before moving on.

Canon Law

ADVANCE REVIEW COPY

KEY TERMS IN THIS SECTION

Canon Law

QUOTATION TO BE INCLUDED IN FINAL PRINTING.

(CCC, Glossary, p. 869)

precepts general rules, directions, or commandments intended to regulate behavior or thought

Canon Law is a body of laws and rules created or borrowed and adopted for use by the Catholic Church that establish

(CCC, Glossary, p. 869). The Code (or Collection) of Catholic Canon Law was last revised in 1983. Canon laws guide the Church in many different areas of Church life. Here are a few examples:

- **Canon Law 767-2:** "A homily must be given at all Masses on Sunday and holy days of obligation which are celebrated with a congregation, and it cannot be omitted except for a serious reason."

- **Canon Law 802-1:** "If schools which offer an education imbued with a Christian spirit are not available, it is for the diocesan bishop to take care that they are established."

- **Canon Law 842-1:** "A person who has not received baptism cannot be admitted validly to the other sacraments."

Canon Law connects us to Christ and the Catholic Church. Here is how Pope Benedict XVI addressed this connection on the twenty-fifth anniversary of the Canon Law revision:

> "Church law is first and foremost *lex libertatis:* a law that sets us free to adhere to Jesus. It is therefore necessary to be able to present to the People of God, to the new generations and to all who are called to make canon law respected, its concrete bond with the life of the Church.

—Pope Benedict XVI

It is the Holy Spirit who makes this connection. Saint Basil tells us that the Holy Spirit restores us to paradise, leads us to the Kingdom of Heaven, and adopts us as sons and daughters who grow confident enough to refer to God as Father. Through the Holy Spirit, we receive Christ's grace and are

(CCC, 736).

The Holy Spirit, here depicted in a tapestry, connects us to the Christ and his Church through Canon Law.

Church leaders are to carry out their ministries in compliance with Canon Law.

Canon lawyers are trained in the legal system of the Catholic Church to help maintain order and secure individual rights within the Church all around the world. Church leaders are obligated to carry out their ministries in compliance with Canon Law. These laws provide rules and regulations for almost every part of Church life. When any Catholic believes his or her rights or interests are being ignored or abused, a canon lawyer can be consulted. The case can be heard in an ecclesiastical court. Once, canon lawyers were almost always priests who studied theology before studying Canon Law. Now, more and more lay canon lawyers are also serving Catholics. Concerns brought to canon lawyers deal with such issues as marriage annulments, a school's religious educational policies, the role of a parish council, and the rights of a parish employee. Like their civil law counterparts, ecclesiastical or church lawyers help protect rights—the rights of Catholics. In 1983, a revised Code of Canon Law was released for the Church. It contains 1,752 canons or laws, and replaced the 1917 Code.

Faith & Culture

➚ Go to the student site at **hs.osvcurriculum.com**

QUOTATION TO BE
INCLUDED IN FINAL PRINTING.

—CCC, 736

QUOTATION TO BE
INCLUDED IN FINAL PRINTING. (CCC, 737). We call the Church the Body of Christ and the Temple of the Holy Spirit. The work of Christ and the Holy Spirit, then, brings us into communion with the Father. The Holy Spirit prepares us for intimacy with Christ. It is the Holy Spirit that makes present the Risen Jesus to us, reminds us of Jesus' words, and opens our minds to understanding the Paschal Mystery.

QUOTATION TO BE
INCLUDED IN FINAL PRINTING.

(CCC, 737).

The Church's work is not separate or in addition to that of Christ and the Holy Spirit. Instead, she is its Sacrament in who she is and in her members. QUOTATION TO BE
INCLUDED IN FINAL PRINTING. (CCC, 738). The Holy Spirit lives in us, and we live in Christ as one Body. Saint Cyril of Alexandria describes it this way:

ADVANCE REVIEW COPY

QUOTATION TO BE
INCLUDED IN FINAL PRINTING.

—CCC, 738

Name What does Canon Law establish for the Catholic Church?

Connect How and why does the Holy Spirit make the mystery of Christ present?

Precepts of the Church

In addition to Canon Law, the teaching mission of the Church is reflected in the Precepts of the Church. The Precepts are positive laws of the Church intended to oblige Catholics to perform the minimum prayer and moral action, so they can grow in their love of God and neighbor.

These five **precepts** present us with the minimum requirements for prayer and moral obligation that help us grow in love for God and each other.

The precepts call for Catholics to:

- attend Mass on Sundays and holy days of obligation and rest from work. We sanctify Sunday that commemorates the Resurrection of Christ. We also participate in the main feasts that mark the mysteries of Christ, the Blessed Virgin Mary, and the saints. We take part in the Eucharist and avoid work and activities that could block that participation (see CCC, 2041)

- confess our sins at least once a year, which prepares us for Eucharist through the Sacrament of Reconciliation. This extends the work of conversion and forgiveness

from the Sacrament of Baptism (see CCC, 2042)

- receive Holy Communion at least during the Easter Season. This ensures a minimum reception of the Body and Blood of Christ (see CCC, 2042)

- keep the days of fasting and abstinence set by the Church. This ensures the self-discipline and penance that prepares us for liturgical feasts and holds us accountable for our instincts and freedom (see CCC, 2043)

- help provide for the material needs of the Church, according to each person's ability (see CCC, 2043)

In a sense, these specific actions define the ordinary, baseline obligations of a Catholic. They are to be observed for the good of the Church, for the individual's spiritual benefit, and to help our neighbor. As Catholics, we are nourished by the liturgy, the public worship of the Church.

APPLY

The Precepts of the Church spell out the minimum necessary for our moral and liturgical life, but out of love for God and his Church, we should do more than just the minimum.

- What other practices would you include to energize and strengthen you moral/liturgical life?

Pope John XXIII and Education

(1881–1963)

Angelo Giuseppe Roncalli was born to poor, but warm and loving parents in November 1881. He was the first boy for the Roncallis. Like many people in Lombardy in northern Italy, the Roncallis were sharecropping farmers. Strong boys would be needed to help in the fields. Eventually, there were thirteen Roncalli children to help their parents make a living.

Angelo was smart, loving, and funny. He was also determined, and would walk to school barefoot, carrying his shoes to save the leather soles from wearing out too quickly. The Roncallis' oldest boy was also reflective and concerned about life's most important questions. As a teenager, he began to keep a spiritual diary. Many years later, the diary was published and titled, *Journal of a Soul*. Soon, the young man knew that he wanted to be a priest.

After ordination, Father Roncalli became secretary and assistant to the bishop of Bergamo. The young priest learned a great deal about the way a bishop must care for a particular Church. When World War I began, Roncalli was drafted into the Italian Army. As a sergeant, he was a stretcher-bearer and chaplain. He witnessed pain and cruel death during the war. More than ever, he saw what a beautiful grace it was to help people pray. After the war, the priest's special gifts as

ADVANCE REVIEW COPY

a scholar, seminary teacher—and his simple holiness—were even more obvious to leaders of the Church—including the Pope.

Father Roncalli became a bishop and was named as Apostolic Visitor to Bulgaria. Later, in the 1930s and during the rise of Nazi Germany, he became the Pope's representative to Greece and Turkey. Because of his political connections, Bishop Roncalli was able to shelter and save thousands of Jews. Before World War II ended, he was named Apostolic Nuncio to France. It was a key diplomatic post. Back in Italy, Roncalli became the bishop of Venice and was soon named a cardinal.

When Pope Pius XII died in 1958 after almost twenty years as Pope, Cardinal Roncalli of Venice was already 77. Because of his age, he thought there would be no chance that he would be elected pope. But he was chosen by his brother cardinals, and the new Pope chose the papal name of John to honor his father and his parish church in Bergamo. The world quickly saw that Pope John XXIII was approachable and fun-loving. People felt comfortable talking with the Vicar of Christ, the Bishop of Rome. Late at night, he would often "escape" from the Vatican and walk through Rome's neighborhoods, meeting people and talking about their families and their jobs.

Just a few months after becoming Pope, John XXIII announced that he was convening a new Church council—the first since 1870. The world was fascinated with this Pope. *Time* Magazine named him "Man of the Year" in 1962. Informally, the Pope shared his view that it was time to open the windows of the Church and let in fresh air.

As bishops from all around the world gathered for the Second Vatican Council, they called on the Holy Spirit to guide the Council Fathers.

Pope John XXIII did not live to see the results of the council he called. He developed cancer of the stomach and died on June 3, 1962, at the age of 81. Shortly before his death, he told people, "My bags are packed and I am ready, very ready to go." The world mourned the man who had been the Pope for only four years. In 2000, Pope John Paul II beatified John XXIII. Blessed John XXIII's feast day is October 11.

> **Think About It** What role did the Holy Spirit play in the life of Blessed Pope John XXIII? Why did Pope John XXIII want to call the Second Vatican Council?

Go to the student site at
hs.osvcurriculum.com

ADVANCE REVIEW COPY

Church and Natural Law

We discussed natural moral law earlier. The Magisterium's authority extends to specific precepts of the natural law that must be observed for salvation. The Magisterium has the responsibility to remind people who they are and who they should be before God (see CCC, 2036).

In making statements about morality, the Magisterium and other Church leaders constantly look to the life and message of Jesus for guidance. Then, they seek to provide teachings that address the very real problems facing people in current historical situations and in diverse cultures. To help apply Sacred Scripture and Tradition to current moral issues, the Church teaches us about natural law, an approach to moral reasoning that has guided Christian thinkers since the early centuries of the Church.

QUOTATION TO BE INCLUDED IN FINAL PRINTING.

—CCC, 2037

As the People of God, we have the responsibility to observe the teaching and doctrine given by the authority of the Church. Even in disciplinary matters, as faithful Catholics, we are to accept what the Church prescribes (see CCC, 2037).

Natural law is foundational to the Church's teaching on morality. It is inscribed in our hearts, for God has placed the essential principles of the natural law within us. We can access them by using the reason God gave us. As we

GLOBAL PERSPECTIVES

The Vatican Apostolic Library, usually known as the "Vatican Library" is one of the oldest and most valuable libraries in the world. It is still housed in an ornate building Pope Sixtus V had built around 1587. In fact, the library—at first just collections of ancient Greek, Latin and Hebrew manuscripts—had been established more than a century earlier, in 1448. Over the centuries, the monarchs of Europe often donated precious manuscripts they had acquired through wars or as gifts. In the early centuries of the library—before printed books were widely available—manuscripts were placed open and chained to reading benches. Then, as now, only scholars doing research were permitted to use the library. Today, the library has 75,000 manuscripts and more than one million printed books. Among its most valuable holdings is the so-called *Codex Vaticanus*, a fourth-century Bible with the Old and New Testaments written in Greek. It was written on 759 pages of vellum—calf skin processed and prepared for writing. The Vatican Library obtained this treasured and ancient edition of the Bible in the fifteenth century.

Aerial view of the Vatican where the Vatican Library and its historic collection are located.

- What does the existence and maintenance of such a library say about the Catholic Church?
- Religious writings, works of art, and artifacts all point to what truth?

Go to the student site at **hs.osvcurriculum.com**

ADVANCE REVIEW COPY

mentioned earlier, one expression of these principles of natural law is the Ten Commandments. And since every human has the natural law engraved on his or her heart by God, natural law has served served societies throughout history as a basis for moral rules and civil law (see CCC, 1979).

List Name the five Precepts of the Church?

Apply Why do members of the Church have the right to be instructed in the divine saving precepts?

DISCUSS

Natural law refers to principles that are so natural to our human condition that they are "engraved on our hearts." Imagine that you are a member of a commission established to formulate a declaration of universal moral principles—that is, a list of principles that would apply to everyone everywhere simply because they are human.

- Create this list of such principles as universal pronouncements about how people should or should not act.

SECTION **3 REVIEW**

QUICK REVIEW

1a. Connect Why is Canon Law needed?

b. Define What is the role of the Holy Spirit in relation to law?

2. List What are the Precepts of the Church?

3a. Clarify How do the Magisterium and other Church leaders arrive at decisions on morality?

b. Recall Why is natural law included in the Church's moral teaching?

c. Link How does natural law unite people?

Listen and Discuss Meet with a small group of classmates and discuss the types of careers in the Church that would lend themselves to teaching others about morality.

- Possibilities include teachers, priests, canon lawyers, and others.
- Discuss the rewards and drawbacks of any of these careers.
- Present your group's thoughts to the class.

Pray Compose a short prayer asking God to guide Church leaders in interpreting and sharing moral principles.

SELF-ASSESS

Which statement best reflects where you are now?

☐ I'm confident enough about the material in this section to be able to explain it to someone else.

☐ I have a good grasp of the material in this section, but I could use more review.

☐ I'm lost. I need help catching up before moving on.

Living Morally

Second Corinthians describes how we become new persons in Christ. "So if anyone is in Christ, there is a new creation: everything old has passed away; see, everything has become new!" (2 Corinthians 5:17).

The Church teaches that this reconstruction of our lives must begin with the proper formation of the person's moral conscience. Cardinal John Henry Newman described the conscience as the "law of the mind." It is a messenger of God, who through nature and grace, communicates with us. Conscience is using reason to recognize the moral quality of what we are about to do, what we are doing at the time, or what we have already done.

QUOTATION TO BE INCLUDED IN FINAL PRINTING.

(CCC, 1778).

Church teaching informs our conscience, which is the voice that, at the right moment, is always calling us to love and to do what is right and avoid evil.

QUOTATION TO BE INCLUDED IN FINAL PRINTING.

(CCC, 1776). We must be attentive to that "voice" within.

QUOTATION TO BE INCLUDED IN FINAL PRINTING.

—CCC, 1779

The moral life is strengthened by prayer and adoration as well as nourished by the Eucharist, the source and summit of all Christian life.

Saint Augustine challenges us get to know our conscience. "Turn inward . . . and in everything you do, see God as your witness" (Saint Augustine, *In ep Jo.* 8, 9: PL 35, 2041). By turning inward and becoming familiar with our conscience, we will understand the principles of morality, how they are applied in various situations, and what judgments we can make about actions we might take and about things we've already done. We practice the virtue of prudence when we choose to conform with these judgments (see CCC, 1780).

A well-formed and active conscience also helps us to accept responsibility for what we do. Even if we commit a sin, the verdict of our conscience tells us what we should have done. The judgment gives us information in order to make things right and hope to not commit the same sin in the future.

QUOTATION TO BE INCLUDED IN FINAL PRINTING.

(CCC, 1781).

ADVANCE REVIEW COPY

CHOOSING A Papal Name

Once a person accepts the office of Pope, he states the name by which he will be known. In March 2013, Cardinal Jorge Mario Bergoglio spoke about the moment when he was elected to succeed Pope Benedict XVI as the Bishop of Rome. The new Pope said as the votes were counted and it was obvious that he would be the new Pope, Brazilian Cardinal Claudio Hummes hugged him and said, "Don't forget the poor." That's when Pope Francis thought about the Saint from Assisi. Pope Francis is the first successor of Saint Peter to take the name Francis.

At his inauguration Mass, Pope Francis spoke about Saint Joseph's role as a protector. In his homily that day, he said being a protector also means protecting all creation as taught in the Book of Genesis and as Saint Francis of Assisi demonstrated for us all. It means protecting people, especially children and those in need, he said. "In the end, everything has been entrusted to our protection, and all of us are responsible for it. Be protectors of God's gifts!"

At his first Angelus, Pope Francis said he chose the name of the Patron of Italy because it strengthened his spiritual ties with Italy, which is where his family originated. He added, however, that Jesus calls us to belong to a new family—the Church, the family of God, "walking together on the path of the Gospel."

Then in a meeting with journalists, Pope Francis explained that he took the words of Cardinal Hummes to heart. In choosing the name of Saint Francis of Assisi, he chose the example of "the man of poverty, the man of peace, the man who loves and protects creation," Pope Francis said. "How I would like a Church that is poor and that is for the poor."

Pope Francis chose his name from the example of Saint Francis of Assisi.

How does Pope Francis live up to his name choice?

How are you a protector of God's gifts?

Determining Good and Evil Acts

Once our conscience is well-formed, it can more accurately reflect on the moral goodness or evil of any action. The morality of an action depends on the object or nature of the action, the intention or end, and the circumstances (see CCC, 1757).

The **object** of the action refers to the judgment of the will (see CCC, 1751). If an action is good, the "object" is the good toward which a person's will directs him or her. For example, a person could choose to fast and pray. These are spiritual disciplines promoted in the Gospel and modeled by Jesus himself. However, even though these acts are good in themselves, the intentions attached to them could be evil, selfish, or corrupt. A person could decide to pray and fast simply to appear holy to others.

QUOTATION TO BE
INCLUDED IN FINAL PRINTING.

(CCC, 1755).

The **intention** belongs to the person performing the action. It indicates the purpose of the action or its end. It is the goal of the activity, and the intention may not direct just one action. Instead, it can guide several actions to the same purpose. In some cases, the intention can direct a person's whole life. Doing something for a neighbor may have the intention of helping the neighbor. On the other hand, the intention could be to obtain a favor or to be able to boast about doing it (see CCC, 1752).

The **circumstances** of an action include the environment or social pressure. The circumstance could also be that someone is under duress or in an emergency. The circumstances also include consequences of an action. Compared with the object and intention, these are secondary elements of a moral act. They can in fact increase or lessen the goodness or evil of an act. For example, stealing a dollar from someone is different than scamming them out of their life savings. Circumstances can also add or subtract from the person's responsibility, such as an action taken out of fear of death. Circumstances by themselves QUOTATION TO BE INCLUDED IN FINAL PRINTING.

DISCUSS

In teaching about the importance of reflecting on our moral lives, Saint Augustine, the fourth-century Doctor of the Church, wrote: "Turn inward, brethren, and in everything you do, see God as your witness."

- How do you "turn inward" to find space for personal reflection?
- Write a letter addressed to someone who helped you understand what it means to be a moral person. Then, consider sending the letter.

(CCC, 1754).

It is an error to judge the moral goodness of an act from just the intention or the circumstances. There are acts, such as fornication, that are always gravely wrong because of their object. These also include blasphemy, perjury, murder,

(CCC, 1756).

Knowing and understanding how our conscience works is essential to living the Christian moral life. With knowledge and honest reflection, we can become truly free to act. That freedom reflects the true and innate dignity of the human person. People have the right to act in conscience and in freedom to make moral decisions.

QUOTATION TO BE
INCLUDED IN FINAL PRINTING.

(CCC, 1782).

Explain Why must we be attentive to the voice of our conscience?

Elaborate Explain how to determine the morality of an action.

The Splendor of Truth

In 1993, Blessed Pope John Paul II wrote an encyclical called, *Veritatis Splendor*, "The Splendor of Truth." In the document, he offers his thoughts on morality and moral decision-making. He reaffirmed what the bishops of the Second Vatican Council said about conscience.

My Faith

➚ Go to the student site at **hs.osvcurriculum.com**

Renewal of Your Mind

Do not be conformed to this world, but be transformed by the renewing of your minds, so that you may discern what is the will of God—what is good and acceptable and perfect.
—Romans 12:2

Saint Paul's Letter to the Romans gives us three strong statements to think about:

- *Do not be conformed to this world.*

Today's moral standards may not be in line with the moral standards of Christ.

- *Be transformed by the renewing of your minds.*

New insights, information, and experiences can open your mind, change your attitudes, and change the way you live.

- *Discern what is the will of God, what is good, acceptable, perfect.*

We are expected to figure out how God wants us to live. Form an informed conscience.

Which of these statements do you think the Holy Spirit is asking you to address now?

Which have you already started addressing during this course?

Make some notes about how you can pursue these statements.

You may choose to include some of your reflections as part of the report you turn in at the end of this course.

Discipleship ... within the Body of Christ ... for the glory of God and the good of the world.

DISCUSS

DISCUSS

Veritatis Splendor describes developing an informed conscience and living a moral life as "heroic."

- What's heroic about forming an informed conscience?

- What's heroic about living a moral life based on an informed conscience?

- Name someone you know who lives a moral life based on an informed conscience. Explain how you know this about that person.

He also expressed great misgivings about the way many modern people interpret their responsibility to follow their conscience. In our strongly individualistic climate, many people view "follow your conscience" as an invitation to do "whatever I want to do." Pope John Paul II pointed out that for Christians, following conscience means properly forming their conscience and doing what Jesus would want them to do.

According to Pope John Paul II, striving to form a correct conscience involves intense, honest searching for the truth and then living in line with the dictates of that truth. Some people hear "follow your conscience" and believe it lets them off the hook. In fact, forming a correct conscience often requires self-denial. In short, conscientious living requires great heroism—a word used frequently in the Pope's encyclical.

Pope John Paul II offered the following points for a more accurate and challenging understanding of conscience:

- Conscience can never be divorced from Jesus, who is truth.

- Our seeking to be true to conscience is not the same as an individualistic conscience. An individualistic conscience disregards the will of Jesus, Church teaching, and the wisdom and concerns of the broader community. Therefore, an individualistic conscience is not really conscience at all.

- The teaching of the Magisterium holds a privileged place as a source of moral guidance. That is, Jesus appointed the Apostles to teach in his name. The Magisterium—the Pope and the bishops as the successors of the Apostles—continues to teach in his name.

SECTION 4 REVIEW

QUICK REVIEW

1a. **Reflect** Why is it important to form a correct conscience?

b. **Explain** How does our conscience assess actions?

c. **Reflect** How does developing a well-formed correct conscience result in freedom?

2a. **Recall** What does a morally good act require?

b. **List** Name three acts that are always gravely wrong because of their object?

3a. **Explain** How can a conscientious person judge wrongly?

b. **Link** How does striving to live in accordance with the dictates of a correct conscience call forth heroism?

Discuss Write down a moral decision you made and then list its object, intention, and circumstances.

Pray Compose a short prayer asking the Holy Spirit to help you form a good and correct conscience.

SELF-ASSESS

Which statement best reflects where you are now?

☐ I'm confident enough about the material in this section to be able to explain it to someone else.

☐ I have a good grasp of the material in this section, but I could use more review.

☐ I'm lost. I need help catching up before moving on.

ADVANCE REVIEW COPY

PRAYER

Opening Prayer

Open our eyes, Lord.
With the gift of your Revelation, help our human eyes to
recognize you.

Appear before us in your time in your glory.

Help us to proclaim to a world in despair that we have seen
the Risen Lord.

Stay with us in every part of our journey.

In the good times, help us rejoice.

In the bad times, helps us have unwavering hope.

In all your beauty, providence and power be with us today,
tomorrow, and forever.

Amen.

ADVANCE REVIEW COPY

VOCABULARY TERMS

Use each of the following terms in a sentence that shows you know what the term means in the context of the chapter. You may include more than one term in a sentence.

Magisterium   Canon Law

Old Law   precept

New Law

PEOPLE AND IDEAS

Identify the person who best fits each description. Define each person or idea in the context of the chapter.

1. Pentecost

2. Peter

3. infallibility

4. Blessed Pope John XXIII

5. natural moral law

6. eternal law

7. natural law

8. revealed law

9. civil law

10. Canon Law

11. Thomas Aquinas

12. Cyril of Alexandria

13. object

14. intention

15. circumstances

16. *Veritatis Splendor*

UNDERSTANDING

Answer each question and complete each exercise

SECTION **1**

1. **Explain** Why was Pentecost a pivotal event for the Church?
2. **Reflect** How does the Church teach us?
3. **Clarify** Explain why the Magisterium can teach with infallibility.
4. **Recall** How did Blessed Pope John XXIII minister to the need to update the teachings of the Church?
5. **Connect** How does *Mater et Magistra* link morality with social concerns?

SECTION **2**

6. **Connect** Why must the rule of law come from a competent authority?
7. **Connect** How do grace and revelation help us clarify natural law?
8. **Explain** Why is the Old Law imperfect?
9. **Extend** Why is the New Law the perfection of divine law?

SECTION **3**

10. **Reflect** Why are canon lawyers necessary?
11. **Consider** How do the Precepts of the Church help to clarify our role as Catholics?
12. **Trace** What factors influence Church statements on morality?
13. **Apply** What does natural law suggest about people?

ADVANCE REVIEW COPY

14. **Evaluate** What is the role of the conscience *after* a bad moral decision?
15. **Explain** Why must object, intention, and circumstances be considered in evaluating moral decisions?
16. **Define** What does it mean to be *conscientious*?

CONNECTING

Visual This painting by contemporary Italian artist Alberto Ruggieri is called "Man with Moral Compass in Head."

Do you feel that it is an appropriate interpretation of the function of a moral compass? What effect does the compass have on the man? How does he seem to feel about it? What other titles could be given to the painting? Is this a good depiction of how to use our conscience? Explain.

Challenge You and some friends are eating at a restaurant after a game. You start debating something that one of your other classmates did online. One of your friends at the table says, "That's just wrong." Another replies, "Don't judge people. We don't know the whole story."

• How do you explain way object, intention and circumstance apply here?

Question After working through this chapter, what advice would you give someone who wonders why a conscience is important and says that as long as no one gets hurt, then anything should be permitted?

Imagine You are in charge of compiling a list of quotations about a topic related to this chapter. An example would be Saint John Bosco's saying, "God does not pay us for results, but for effort." Possible topics include conscience, natural law, and learning about good and evil.

• Do an Internet search or use a book of popular quotations to find appropriate quotations. With a group of classmates, select a few that could serve as mottos.

• Devise ways of presenting the quotations artfully, with typefaces or colors that reflect their sentiments.

• Post the art in your classroom or meeting space.

SELF-ASSESS

On Your Own Make a list of the most important things you learned from this chapter.

Select three things that represent your growth in understanding as you worked through this chapter. Write a paragraph explaining your choices.

With a Partner List what you found most helpful or interesting in this chapter as well as any other questions that have surfaced.

CHAPTER 7

- What book is the deacon holding aloft?
- What does it mean to live the Gospel message?

Living the Gospel Message

 Go to the student site at
hs.osvcurriculum.com

ADVANCE REVIEW COPY

- Explore the role of God's grace in our lives.
- Define the different types of grace.
- Examine how you, your generation, and others love and serve each other.
- Identify how saints, clergy, religious, and laity answer the call to discipleship.
- Discern your call to discipleship.
- Connect the Law of the Gospel to Christian moral life.
- Become familiar with Catholic movements and lay organizations.
- Take a closer look at the meaning of grace through the hymn, *Amazing Grace*.
- Contrast virtues and vices and how they impact the moral life.

ADVANCE REVIEW COPY

Call to Discipleship

KEY TERMS IN THIS SECTION

grace the gift of the Holy Spirit; it is QUOTATION TO BE INCLUDED IN FINAL PRINTING. (CCC, Glossary, p. 881)

justice the virtue stating that we are to give God his due and that all people have rights and should have their basic needs (CCC, 1836)

vocation calling or destiny to love and serve God and our neighbor in this life which prepares us for eternal happiness in Heaven

laity all the faithful who are members of the Catholic Church through Baptism except ordained men and those in consecrated life. The laity share in the priestly, prophetic, and kingly office of Christ and have their own role in the mission of the whole Christian people in the Church and in the world (see CCC, 897)

The results of Original Sin can be seen all around us. People are addicted to power, wealth, and material goods. We kill, steal, and hurt one another. There is unjust oppression and even genocide in many parts of the world. People suffer from physical and psychological illness. And yet, the world contains goodness, and with Jesus Christ, we have hope.

The Catholic Church reaches out to people all over the world to fight illness, poverty, and oppression.

QUOTATION TO BE INCLUDED IN FINAL PRINTING.

—*Catechism of the Catholic Church*, 2448

Following Jesus' example, the Catholic Church gives particular care to those oppressed by poverty. The Church has always worked for the relief, defense, and freedom of the oppressed through acts of charity. Catholics are doing great work in missionary areas and in parishes and surrounding communities. Catholic Relief Services and Caritas Internationalis fight poverty, oppression, and disease in many countries. Catholic hospitals serve millions each year. The morally good actions in our world come from people responding to God's **grace**.

Grace allows us to act out of love, and all the good things about us are based on the charity of Christ. When we overcome our human tendency to sin, we can recognize that the foundation for Catholic morality is grace from living in Jesus Christ and following the Gospel message of love.

QUOTATION TO BE INCLUDED IN FINAL PRINTING.

—CCC, 2011

The more open we are to God's grace in our lives, the more our actions will be driven by Christ's love rather than our own efforts, which

ADVANCE REVIEW COPY

- Make note of the ways you see students in your school living the Gospel message to serve and love others.
- How are you living this message?
- How do you recognize God's grace in these actions?

often fall short. Our merits, the goodness that we possess, and the times when we act out of love are possible because of God's grace and our response to it. Saints like Thérèse of Lisieux had a keen awareness that their goodness was based on the grace of Christ. "I want to work for your *love alone*," Saint Thérèse wrote. She said she didn't want to gather good deeds for Heaven. Instead she wanted to go before God with empty hands.

QUOTATION TO BE INCLUDED IN FINAL PRINTING.

(CCC, 2011).

We can recognize God's grace and be more open to it through prayer. The graces needed for our sanctification, as well as spiritual and temporal goods, such as health and friendship, are the object of Christian prayer (see CCC, 2010). Without prayer making us more aware and open to the action of grace in our lives, we will not achieve the moral goodness we desire.

Grace enables us to live in Christ. We are connected to the Son of God because he united himself to each of us through the Incarnation, when he took on our human nature. That is why the image of the Body of Christ is more than an inspiring metaphor.

(CCC, 521).

This is also why Jesus gave us the two Great Commandments: to love God with all we are and to love our neighbor as ourselves. Saint Paul reminds us:

(CCC, 2196). When we act morally toward others, we do not commit adultery, we do not kill, we do not steal or covet.

(CCC, 2196).

It was also Saint Paul who used the image of the Body of Christ to show how we are interrelated. No one part of the Body can function on its own.

God arranged the members in the body, each one of them, as he chose. If all were a single member, where would the body be? As it is, there are many members, yet one body.

—1 Corinthians 12:18-20

Communion with Jesus and with his Church—the Body of Christ—is fundamental to moral living.

Jesus described himself as the vine, and we are the branches. He used this common image from his time to communicate how our relationship with him and the Church would work. Jesus also instituted a deeper and mysterious communion through the Eucharist. "'Those who eat my flesh and drink my blood abide in me, and I in them'" (John 6:56).

Jesus is the vine, and we are the branches. When branches separate from the vine, they soon die. They no longer connect to the source of life that nourishes, supplies water, and enables growth. Jesus constantly helped those who were alienated, hungry, or dying. His Church and her members—the Body of Christ—do the same.

CONNECT

Jesus said he is the vine and we are the branches.

- What is the relationship between the vine and its branches?
- What exactly is Jesus telling us about how we are to be in relationship with him? List two aspects of this relationship.

He also states clearly the power of Eucharist.

- What do his words regarding the Eucharist tell us about our communion with him?
- What does it say about going to Mass?

GO TO THE SOURCE 📖

We are called to use our abilities to enhance our own lives and the lives of those around us, just like the servants who are given talents (a sum of money) in the following parable told by Jesus.

Read Matthew 25:14-30.

- What does the parable say about fear?
- How have you increased the talents and gifts that have been given to you by God?

God's Co-workers

Vocation means calling. The way we live out our vocation as disciples differs from person to person, but everyone's vocation is to serve God, to honor him with love, and to love our neighbor. Jesus spent the years of his earthly ministry calling people to turn their lives around. Today, Christ still calls people to holiness.

The English word "talent" comes from the word used in the Gospel parable about the servants who are given talents by their master. In the story, the talent refers to a unit of money in use at the time; but it later came to designate all the natural endowments with which we are born.

All of us have been given talents. Our vocation is to make something beautiful out of the talents that God has given us. He has created us to show forth his truth, goodness, and beauty. Whenever we live his truth, share his goodness, and help to fashion the world to be the way he intends it to be, we are using our talents well. The *Catechism* calls for the creative use of our talents in these simple words: QUOTATION TO BE INCLUDED IN FINAL PRINTING. (CCC, 1721).

We are created in God's image and likeness. Therefore, we have a vocation to be co-workers with God in the continuing story of creation. Humans are co-workers when they help transform the world and the human community into what God intends them to be. Our aim should be to (CCC, 307).

We can practice Catholic moral decision-making in all our attempts to love God and others and to promote human welfare. We do not make decisions in isolation, but within a community. Catholics are members of the worldwide Church founded by Christ to be a source of salvation for the world. Catholics are called to respond to God's grace and be faithful to him. We are invited to live out our vocation so that our moral decisions embody the Holy Spirit at work in us and in the world.

Jesus is the perfect example for us as disciples. "For I have set you an example, that you also should do as I have done to you" (John 13:15). We have a lifetime to answer Christ's invitation to follow him. It is difficult to meet the radical demands of the Gospel. This requires prayer. That's where Christ's example comes in. He has taught us how to pray by praying himself. By humbling himself and by his poverty, he taught us to accept the challenges that will come our way if we follow him (see CCC, 520).

> May the God of steadfastness and encouragement grant you to live in harmony with one another, in accordance with Christ Jesus.
>
> —Romans 15:5

IDENTIFY

Violence, drug abuse, homelessness, eating disorders—the list of societal problems is long.

- Identify three critical social problems that currently exist in your community.
- For each problem, describe the damage caused, the grace needed, and the potential results of responding to grace.

What do you envision that God has done with you, is doing with you, or will do with you?

If we follow Jesus' way, we live in him and he in us. Saint John Eudes said we have to beg Jesus to perfect his life and his mysteries with our lives.

QUOTATION TO BE
INCLUDED IN FINAL PRINTING.

(CCC, 521).

Explain Can vocation be used as another term for Catholic morality? Explain your answer.

Apply What does it mean to be a co-worker with God?

Examples of Discipleship

All of us are called to discipleship in Christ. Discipleship is more than just believing. It means being a student. Being a disciple of Christ means studying his teachings and living by them. We have always recognized the saints as examples to follow as they have answered the call to discipleship. Saint Justin, for example, was a wealthy, brilliant pagan with a restless mind. He was disappointed when none of the Greek philosophers could satisfy his questions about God. Then, an elderly Christian man explained the Old Testament prophecies and how Jesus fulfilled them. Saint Justin believed

and became one of the great Christian teachers of the second century.

Much later, Sudanese Saint Josephine Bakhita was kidnapped as a child by slave traders around 1876. Sold and resold, she was harshly treated, branded, and forced to convert to Islam. In Venice, Italy, she met Canossian sisters and was struck by their kindness and their stories about Jesus. After several years, she decided to become Catholic. Then, in 1893, she joined the Canossian order.

Saints Justin and Josephine are examples of disciples who embraced and assisted the spreading of the Gospel message. These disciples of Jesus certainly contributed to the Kingdom of God on Earth through their heroic witness, their writings, and their ministries. No matter what nation or century, those who follow Jesus Christ recognized that they have to model their lives after his. This is what Jesus asked of his first followers and the rest of us.

Every follower of Christ has a vocation, a universal call to holiness as his disciple. Most members of the Body of Christ are part of the **laity**—members of the Church who are not ordained as bishops, priests, or deacons, and have not joined a religious order as a religious brother or sister. As the *Catechism* says, lay men and women can follow Jesus just as they are—as husbands and wives, mothers and fathers, students, workers in an office or factory, etc.

GO TO THE SOURCE

Jesus told us to love one another as he has loved us.

Read John 13:31-35.

- To what degree is your generation following this New Commandment?
- How easy or difficult is it to follow this New Commandment?

QUOTATION TO BE
INCLUDED IN FINAL PRINTING.

—CCC, 901

These spiritual sacrifices can be offered to God during the celebration of the Eucharist. The *Catechism* then makes this connection: that these spiritual sacrifices become a way of worshipping all over the world, so that the laity consecrates the world to God through their holy actions (see CCC, 901). Also, parents share in these holy actions by being examples of Christian life as well as ensuring a Christian education for their children (see CCC, 902). Lay people with the necessary qualifications can be accepted for the ministries of lector and acolyte. They can also read and serve at Mass, preside over liturgical prayers, confer Baptisms, and distribute the Eucharist in accordance with the Church's law.

Through Baptism, Christians are

QUOTATION TO BE
INCLUDED IN FINAL PRINTING.

(CCC, 897). The laity engages in the temporal affairs in the world. Lay Christians direct their work toward God's will. In a special way, lay people

QUOTATION TO BE
INCLUDED IN FINAL PRINTING.

(CCC, 898).

Pope Pius XII said

(CCC, 899). In a talk given on February 20, 1946, the Holy Father said that the laity should "have an ever-clearer consciousness

Lay Catholics involved in serving others impact Church life and the wider community.

CONNECT

- Interview a lay member of the Catholic Church and ask how he or she lives out the Christian vocation.

- Or, research the life of a saint canonized in the last twenty-five years and answer: How did this person live out their calling as a Christian disciple?

not only of belonging to the Church but of being the Church." The *Catechism* adds:

QUOTATION TO BE
INCLUDED IN FINAL PRINTING.

—CCC, 900

Christ gives us the grace of his Word to spread our faith.   QUOTATION TO BE INCLUDED IN FINAL PRINTING. (CCC, 904). In this way, we help to fulfill Christ's prophetic mission. In fact, lay people may have the right and responsibility to let their pastors and other Christian faithful know their opinion on matters that concern the good of the Church. This must be done in a faithful and reverent way that respects the pastors and considers the common good and dignity of others (see CCC, 907).

Jesus gave us a perfect example of obediently following the will of the Father even unto death. Following Christ's example, we will overcome the weight of sin in our lives. In this way, the *Catechism* teaches, we share in Christ's kingly office. We will not let ourselves be governed by sin or take part in evil. In this way, we will infuse

(CCC, 909).

Many of us are also called to serve our parish communities and to help our parish priests in their ministry. Lay people can serve on pastoral councils and diocesan assemblies called synods and councils. They can also help in the pastoral care of parishes, work on finance councils, or participate in Church courts called tribunals. The *Catechism* urges lay people to weigh their responsibilities to the Church with those of their daily life.

ADVANCE REVIEW COPY

GLOBAL PERSPECTIVES

The *Catechism* explains that Jesus taught about unity with many different images. Many of the people Jesus addressed were farmers. He knew that they grew barley to make their own bread but also lentils and a wide variety of fruits and vegetables. Many also cultivated grape vines that were fragile looking but incredibly strong. Some of these vines had been producing impressive crops of delicious grapes for many decades. Some productive grape vines live more than one hundred years; at least one has lived for more than four hundred years. Grape vines are one of the earliest wild plants cultivated by humans. There are about fifty species of grape vines.

- How do the properties of grape vines fit into the teaching of Jesus?

↗ Go to the student site at **hs.osvcurriculum.com**

QUOTATION TO BE
INCLUDED IN FINAL PRINTING.

—CCC, 913

High school students can also serve as disciples for Jesus. As the Second Vatican Council reminded us, Christians are incorporated into Christ and into the People of God through Baptism. The Second Vatican Council document *Lumen Gentium*, or "Light of the Nations," notes that all of us are disciples-in-the-making from the day of our Baptisms.

Recall What did Jesus ask of his first disciples that he still asks us today?

Describe What is a spiritual sacrifice?

Married and Single Lay Catholics

The call to love shapes who we are and what we do professionally and personally, whether we are single, married, or in the religious life. Single or married lay Catholics are called to live their faith through just and loving relationships.

The Catholic Church teaches that the single life is a calling and a state of life, just as marriage and religious life are. Today, more people are choosing to remain single than ever before, yet many still struggle with the notion that single life can be a calling from God. Some are single by choice, others by circumstances. Some have always been single; others are single again due to death or the annulment of their marriage.

The single life can provide someone with more time and space to pray, reflect, and serve. The freedom and flexibility of the single life can become a vocational gift. Some careers, for example, may be more compatible with the single life because of constant travel or very long hours.

All vocations come with challenges and the single lay vocation is no exception. While single people often have more freedom to integrate prayer and charity into their lives, they also can become consumed by the pursuit of work,

DISCUSS

- What constitutes a good personal relationship? Look up the definition of good and think about how it applies to human relationships. Discuss your ideas about what makes a relationship good. Afterward, turn to the opposite question.

- What kinds of relationships are not good?

- Brainstorm a few examples, then discuss: What are the underlying causes of relationships that are not good?

- How can peer pressure affect a young person's decision to perform or avoid certain actions? Give examples.

- Since the family is a domestic Church, what does this say about how we are to treat our parents and siblings?
- What does it say about the need to pray together at home or encourage family members to read the Bible?

pleasure, and self-centeredness since they do not have the daily demands of marriage and parenting. There is also the increased risk of loneliness and economic stress. Being alone and lonely, however, are not the same thing. While married couples can experience loneliness, a single person who does not actively maintain a network of friends can end up feeling lonely rather quickly.

Each of us is called to practice chastity according to our status in life.

(CCC, 2349). In so doing, they give themselves completely to God. Other single people practice chastity. Married people are called to live according to the moral law by being faithful to their spouses.

Within the calling of the laity, there is also a particular call to married life. According to the *Catechism*, marriage is

QUOTATION TO BE
INCLUDED IN FINAL PRINTING.

(CCC, Glossary, p. 887). The Sacrament of Marriage helps couples grow stronger in their spiritual relationship with God as they grow in their physical, mental, and emotional relationship with each other.

The faithfulness required by marriage and raising children mirrors the faithfulness and love Christ has for the Church. Psychologists, sociologists, and theologians agree that the family is the most basic unit of society. The Church calls a family the domestic Church, meaning that it is the first place where we learn about God and where our discipleship is nurtured by those who love us. A loving Christian family contributes significantly to the Church and to the whole human community.

Saying yes to the vocation of marriage means taking seriously the lifelong commitment that marriage entails. The choice of a spouse is a serious matter, to be made in light of one's Christian vocation. Parishes and dioceses around the country routinely require those who plan to marry to participate in marriage preparation, often called "Pre-Cana," referring to the wedding in Cana where Jesus performed his first miracle. It is important that couples discern in depth their desire to marry each other before they plan their wedding. Marriage preparation helps couples deeply examine their relationship.

Christian marriage is ordered to God's plan in creation, and reflects the natural law. Marriage is not simply what we make of it, but has a special character sanctified by Christ himself. Christian marriage is the covenant, the permanent and lifelong spiritual bond, on which family life is built. It mirrors the covenant God made with us and the covenant between Christ and his Church.

Marriage and family life embody challenges and struggles as well. As the story of Adam and Eve in the Garden of Eden shows, sin entered into the world and into the relationship between man and woman early in human history. The story of Cain and Abel points out the early presence of jealousy and violence within the family. Sin remains a force to be overcome. Still, God's grace and presence can lift us above any sin. We can never forget that Jesus died for our sins and redeemed us, and especially that he has promised to be with us always through the love of the Holy Spirit and in the Sacraments. This is our hope, and this is the Good News.

Identify What challenges come with the vocation of the single life?

Connect Why does the Church call the family the domestic Church?

- When you think about the Christian vocation of marriage, who or what couples come to mind as exemplary models?
- What qualities or characteristics do these marriages have that make them stand out for you?

ADVANCE REVIEW COPY

QUICK REVIEW

1a. List What are some Church organizations that do God's work?

b. Tell What makes possible our merits and the goodness we possess?

c. Recall What makes us open to God's grace?

d. Explain Why is the image of the vine and branches an appropriate metaphor for the relationship between Jesus and the Church?

2a. Identify What vocation does everyone share?

b. Reflect How do humans show that they are co-workers with God?

3a. Describe How are lay people to share their thoughts on issues that affect the Church?

b. Contrast How are the challenges of married life different from the challenges of single life?

Listen and Discuss With a group of classmates, discuss what helps young people in discerning whether they are best suited for married or single life?

Pray Compose a short prayer asking for guidance in discerning your vocation.

SELF-ASSESS

Which statement best reflects where you are now?

☐ I'm confident enough about the material in this section to be able to explain it to someone else.

☐ I have a good grasp of the material in this section, but I could use more review.

☐ I'm lost. I need help catching up before moving on.

Life in the Spirit

KEY TERMS IN THIS SECTION

evangelical counsels teachings of the New Law that have as their aim QUOTATION TO BE INCLUDED IN FINAL PRINTING. (CCC, 1973). These are embodied especially in the vows of poverty, chastity, and obedience. They lead to the perfection of Christian life

consecrated life refers to (CCC, Glossary p. 872) in which a person is set aside and totally devoted to God's work and the pursuit of Christian perfection. For example, religious order brothers and sisters, consecrated virgins, and hermits

According to the Gospels, on the night before Jesus was crucified, he shared his Last Supper with his closest friends. At that first Eucharist, Jesus tied a towel around his waist, got on his knees, and washed his Apostles' feet.

The Apostle Peter at first objected to Jesus washing his feet. But Jesus told him: "'Unless I wash you, you have no share with me'" (John 13:8). Peter immediately consented. Jesus sent a clear message about the type of behavior he expected of his disciples (see John 13:15).

At one point, Jesus gathers together his Apostles and tells them, "'Whoever wants to be first must be last of all and servant of all'" (Mark 9:35). The message is clear: Christians are commissioned by Jesus to serve one another and those who are hurting in their midst.

QUOTATION TO BE
INCLUDED IN FINAL PRINTING.

—CCC, 1962

If we look at the incidents when law is mentioned in the Gospels, we discover that often Jesus' actions were misunderstood as being in conflict with the Law. He was confronted for violating Sabbath law—for healing on the Sabbath and for allowing his disciples to pick grain on the Sabbath. He was challenged by advocates of the Law to name the greatest Commandments and to pronounce judgment on difficult legal matters. He was baffling to many because he frequently spent time with people who did not keep the Law and who were officially the "outlaws" of his society, such as tax collectors and prostitutes.

The Law of the Gospel

Jesus tells his followers, "'Do not think that I have come to abolish the law or the prophets; I have come not to abolish but to fulfill'" (Matthew 5:17). The Old Law is good and holy but still imperfect. It shows the way to do good and avoid evil, but QUOTATION TO BE INCLUDED IN FINAL PRINTING. (CCC, 1963). It remains a law of bondage, which it cannot remove. It prepares us for

GO TO THE SOURCE

When Jesus cures a blind beggar, the man's immediate response shows his conversion.

Read Luke 18:35-43.

- What did Jesus say that saved the man?
- What was the man's immediate reaction?
- Describe your reaction for what God has done in your life?

ADVANCE REVIEW COPY

- Based on what you have read, heard, or studied in the past, how would you describe Jesus' approach to the Law?

- How would you describe the Law of the Gospel?

perfect the Christian life and found in the **consecrated life**. The evangelical counsels bring about the fullness of charity, which can never be satisfied. Charity always wants to give more. The perfection of the New Law is the love of God and neighbor. The evangelical counsels offer ways to do this (see CCC, 916).

the Gospel. Jesus fulfills the Old Law by atoning for our sins and giving us the grace of the Holy Spirit, which we receive by having faith in Jesus, being people of charity, and receiving the Sacraments. Jesus communicated God's love for us. For our part, he calls for a change of heart, a conversion in response to our experience of God's love.

Jesus gives us the Law of the Gospel. It does not abolish the Old Law, but builds on it by calling us to change our hearts and give ourselves into God's loving care. Jesus' teachings describe what happens when we change our hearts. For example, we have already examined the Beatitudes. In them, Jesus reaches out to those who are open to his New Law of love: the poor in spirit, the gentle, those who are persecuted for their beliefs, those who mourn, justice seekers, the merciful, the pure in heart, and peacemakers. Elsewhere he reminds us to "'change and become like children'" (Matthew 18:3) and to "'sell your possessions, and give alms'" (Luke 12:33). Statements such as these are not laws, but rather are descriptions of the behavior of people changed by the experience of God's love.

The Gospels' message of love, contained in the New Law, perfects the Law of Moses and the Old Testament. Jesus taught his disciples the New Law, which leads to the perfection of Christian life. The practical guidance that Jesus proposes is called the **evangelical counsels**. They focus on whatever is compatible with love, or charity (see CCC, 1973).

QUOTATION TO BE INCLUDED IN FINAL PRINTING.

(CCC, Glossary, p. 877).

The evangelical counsels are embodied in the vows of poverty, chastity, and obedience that

QUOTATION TO BE INCLUDED IN FINAL PRINTING.

—CCC, 1974

Jesus washes the disciples feet in this Laura James painting from 2000.

Expressing AFFECTION

A junior girl tutors a guy in English class in order to raise his test scores. It works. Afterwards, he sends flowers to her house with a note "I got the score I needed. You're the best."

A college student calls home every Sunday to talk to mom. "Text me," Mom says as they are about to hang up. "It's not the same as hearing your voice mom. I love you."

After the last game of the season, a coach sends each player a note describing why it was so much fun having that individual on the team. Each card is laminated in plastic and ends with "I will always remember the effort you gave to our team. Coach Lucas."

Expressing affection lifts hearts. It can be done with words, gestures, objects, and facial expressions. Recall that Jesus told the Apostles: "'By this everyone will know that you are my disciples, if you have love for one another'" (John 13:35).

As much as expressing and getting affection can lift our spirit—it can also be done poorly.

Remember how awkward it was to do so when you were in junior high? Sometimes people express affection in a manipulative way. Affection doesn't seem genuine when it feels like the other person is only trying to get something from you.

The practice of expressing affection has been around as long as humans have existed. If you learn how to do it right, you will have a gift that will be a blessing to others and to yourself. Here's some things to keep in mind when expressing affection:

- Think of others as a son or daughter of God. Show affection one soul to another.

- Take the time and make the effort.

- Respect boundaries. Simple is fine. Over the top is awkward.

- Expect nothing in return.

- If your expression is coming from gratitude, admiration, or joy—then that works. If it's really about self-promotion, flirtation, or lust—then it's manipulation.

What have been some of the appropriate expressions of affection that you still remember receiving? What made it so memorable and how did it affect you?

How often and how well do you express affection?

Who might you need to express affection to these days—and how will you do so?

ADVANCE REVIEW COPY

Ever since the founding of the Church, there have been men and women who have committed to following Christ more closely through practicing the evangelical counsels. They dedicated their lives to God. The Church, in particular the Vatican, accepts and approves these forms of consecrated life, including the following:

- *Erimitic life*, also called hermits, are Catholics who demonstrate personal intimacy with Christ through separation from the world, and who live lives of solitude, prayer, and penance. Hermits devote themselves to God and the salvation of the world. (see CCC, 920-921)

- *Consecrated virgins and widows*, who through prayer, penance, and service have decided, with Church approval,

(CCC, 922)

- *Religious life*, those who as priests, brothers, and sisters live in institutes, profess the evangelical counsels publicly, live in fraternal life in community, and give witness to the union of Christ and his Church. They

(CCC, 926). They have played an important role in the spreading of the Catholic faith (see CCC, 927).

- *Secular institutes* are institutes of consecrated life comprised of people living in the world who work to perfect charity and the sanctification of the world.

QUOTATION TO BE
INCLUDED IN FINAL PRINTING.

(CCC, 929).

- *Societies of apostolic life* are Catholics who don't take religious vows, and still work toward an apostolic purpose. They live in

common as brothers and sisters following a particular way of life and strive for the perfection of charity through observing the constitutions of the group. Some of these brothers and sisters embrace the evangelical counsels (see CCC, 930).

Explain Why did Jesus wash the feet of the Apostles?

List What embodies the evangelical counsels?

New Movements and Third Orders

There are also particular movements or groups of people that include the laity. People in these movements consecrate themselves to God in a special way striving to imitate God as his sons and daughters (see CCC, 1694). We are already dedicated to God through our Baptism, but this consecration to God focuses on a particular theme or charism. It helps to manifest Christ to the world and shows the working of the Holy Spirit in the movement and the Church (see CCC, 931).

Some of these new movements approved by the Church include:

- *Cursillo* This movement tries to enliven the Christian life through the uniqueness and creativity of each person to proclaim that God, in Christ, loves us.

- *Focolare Movement* Begun in 1943 in Northern Italy, this movement center on the unity of the followers of Christ.

- *Communion and Liberation* Begun in 1954 in Italy, the movement is concerned with education in the faith and collaboration with the mission of the Church in contemporary life.

- *Schönstatt Movement* People in this movement are looking for a home, for renewed strength, and the spirit to live their faith in everyday life as a way for brining the love of Christ to the world.

- *Couples for Christ* Begun in Manila, the Philippines, in 1981, this movement is intended for the renewal and strengthening of Christian family life.

DISCUSS

- What implications does the fact that all Christians are called to chastity have for young people who date?

Living the Gospel Message **199**

- *Jesus Youth* This youth movement reaches out to other young people to form lives centered on Jesus Christ and nourished by prayer, Scripture, the Sacraments, and community.

- *Catholic Charismatic Renewal* This movement seeks to experience the Holy Spirit to open a life-changing relationship with Jesus Christ and the love of God the Father.

- *Sant'Egidio* This movement was started by a high school student in Rome in 1968 and is now in twenty countries. Young adults meet in small communities and focus on serving the poor and sick.

Those in consecrated life, moved by the Holy Spirit, propose to give themselves more fully to God. From the very beginning of her life, there have been men and women who have led lives more dedicated to God. There is also a unity in the Body of Christ of all disciples—those in and outside of the consecrated life. All of us are disciples of Jesus.

Some religious communities have lay affiliates or members who belong to a Third Order. These are lay people who share in the spirituality of the religious community, and may take part in their service projects and mission. They make promises to live as witnesses to the Gospel and to be true to the charisms of the founder, but they do not take vows. They can be married or single. The term Third Order comes from the custom of calling men's communities a First Order, nun's communities a Second Order and lay members a Third Order. Third Orders are approved by the Church. Members are attracted to an order's charism, rule and way of life, and

REFLECT

Religious have dedicated their lives to imitate God.

- In what way have you dedicated your life to Christ and his teachings?
- When have you felt yourself doing it well?
- What would you say is the key for doing it well and consistently?

they seek to grow in the spirituality that the order embodies.

An example would be the Third Order Regulars and Seculars of Saint Dominic. The Regulars take vows and the Seculars make a solemn promise. The object of the Third Order Dominicans is to bring part of the religious spirit of cloistered life into the world. They also strive to be holy in union with the fathers and nuns of the first and second orders. Secular members bring this added dimension to their regular lives doing ordinary work. They can be married or single.

The gifts and purposes of religious life are many. They put into practice the words from the Letter to the Ephesians: "Therefore be imitators of God, as beloved children, and live in love, as Christ loved us and gave himself up for us, a fragrant offering and sacrifice to God" (Ephesians 5:1-2). Religious life is a witness, an example of discipleship, a wellspring of prayer, a source of help for those in need, and an expression of God's grace for the Church and the surrounding world.

DISCUSS

- As a class, visit pre-selected websites of three or four religious institutes or communities to learn more about their ministries? Later, discuss how these orders were different.

QUOTATION TO BE
INCLUDED IN FINAL PRINTING.

—CCC, 825

Recall Name three new movements approved by the Church and describe what they do?

Describe What is a Third Order?

FOCOLARE
Movement

Focolare is a worldwide, non-denominational Gospel-based movement that fosters peace and unity among all people. Active now in 182 countries, it began in the heart of one young Catholic woman during a bombing raid in Trento, Italy, during World War II.

Silvia Lubich (1920–2008) was a young elementary school teacher in Trento which was being destroyed in Allied bombing raids. During a 1942 air raid, Lubich had a life-changing experience and heard God's call. She saw that in the midst of a violent war, only one thing made sense and offered hope—God is love! The words of Jesus resonated with her as they never had before: "'That they may all be one,'" Jesus prayed, "'as you, Father, are in me and I in you'" (John 17:21).

Silvia shared this hopeful insight with her young friends, and soon this inspired group began to visit and comfort the poor and the suffering of their terrified city. The lay group she founded began to be called "Focolare," an Italian word that means family fireside or hearth.

After the war, Focolare, now a society of apostolic life, spread throughout Europe and beyond. Focolare helps people to overcome prejudice and see that God is the loving Father of all. More than five million Catholics around the world are members of this movement.

At his general audience on September 5, 2012, Pope Benedict XVI welcomed a group of young people from the Focolare Movement. "Dear young people, you have taken to heart Christ's call to promote unity in the human family by courageously building bridges. I therefore encourage you: be strong in your Catholic faith; and let the simple joy, the pure love, and the profound peace that come from the encounter with Jesus Christ make you radiant witnesses of the Good News before the young people of your own lands. God bless all of you abundantly!"

The Focolare Movement is active in 182 nations.

How could the Focolare message help build bridges between people of different political, ethnic and religious backgrounds?

Discuss initiatives to welcome new students in your school or new families in your parish or neighborhood. Take one or two of the ideas to your principal, pastor or family to see if it can be implemented.

QUICK REVIEW

1a. Recall What is the message behind the washing of the feet on the first Holy Thursday?

b. Explain How did Jesus fulfill the Old Law?

c. Tell What does the Law of the Gospel compel us to do?

d. Link How does the consecrated life make the person living it closer to God?

2a. Summarize Retell the story of the founding of the Focolare movement.

b. Expand What are the purposes and gifts of religious life?

3a. Evaluate What actions set Saint Catherine of Siena apart from others?

b. List What changes did Saint Catherine of Siena bring about in her world?

Listen and Discuss Finish the following sentences after thinking about the difficulties we all experience in living out our baptismal call to holiness as well as the times when you were gifted by God's grace.

- We all struggle with . . .

- I've experienced a moment of grace when . . .

Pray Compose a short prayer for courage to fulfill your vocation.

SELF-ASSESS

Which statement best reflects where you are now?

☐ I'm confident enough about the material in this section to be able to explain it to someone else.

☐ I have a good grasp of the material in this section, but I could use more review.

☐ I'm lost. I need help catching up before moving on.

ADVANCE REVIEW COPY

God's Gift of Grace

KEY TERMS IN THIS SECTION

sanctifying grace a share in God's life; a gift from God that enables the soul to live with him and respond to his friendship. It is a habitual, stable, and supernatural disposition

actual grace the help God gives us for a particular need to help us conform our lives to his will

Grace is a pure gift. God justifies us, that is, he freely and graciously gives us the grace of the Holy Spirit that cleanses us from sin in Baptism. This justification was won for us by the Passion of Jesus, who offered himself as the spotless victim for our sins. It is a gift because nothing we do could possibly earn God's grace.

QUOTATION TO BE
INCLUDED IN FINAL PRINTING.

—CCC, 1997

The grace of the Holy Spirit allows us to share in the Father's holiness or righteousness. Grace unites us by faith and Baptism to the Paschal Mystery—Jesus' Passion, Death, Resurrection, and Ascension, and grace moves us toward God and away from sin. It helps us accept his forgiveness and justification. Justification includes the remission of sins and the sanctification and renewal of the inner person (see CCC, 1989).

Grace gives us the capacity to engage in the moral life. We are God's sons and daughters. Whenever we do good things, it is because of the grace of the Holy Spirit within us. Through grace our moral life grows and matures. The fulfillment of our moral life will be in the glory of Heaven.

GO TO THE SOURCE

To fathom the mystery of grace means that we humbly realize who we are in relationship to God.

Read Ephesians 2:1-10.

- After reading this passage, describe the role of grace in our lives.

- What do you think when Saint Paul writes that we were created for good works?

- What good works have you done with the grace of God this week?

- What does it mean that we are God's "handiwork"?

- What does the passage say about God's expectations for us?

A priest anoints the hands of a person during the Sacrament of Anointing of the Sick.

Saint Catherine of Siena
(1347–1380)

Saint Catherine of Siena and her twin sister, who did not long survive were the twenty-third and twenty-fourth children born to Giacomo and Lapa Benincasa. Catherine was so cheerful as a child that she was nicknamed "Euphrosyne" (Greek for "Joy"). It was customary for families with some financial stability to plan marriages for their children. Catherine continued to say "No" to any marriage. Catherine remembered the visions of Christ and his Blessed Mother she had as a tiny girl. She knew that her vocation was to devote her life completely to the Lord. At the age of 7, she had decided not to marry.

When Catherine attempted to become a Dominican tertiary or Third Order member, she found resistance from the local association. Typically, only widows became Third Order members. Catherine persisted, however, and was soon wearing the black and white Dominican habit while continuing to live in her own home.

When Catherine was nineteen, her spiritual life deepened even further. She wrote about an experience in which Christ told her to begin serving the sick and the poor. Her spiritual training was completed, and her journey as an active disciple and Gospel witness was beginning. Soon, all of Siena noticed that Catherine was always visiting hospitals

ADVANCE REVIEW COPY

The countryside around Siena, Italy, where Saint Catherine grew up.

and homes. Whenever someone was in need of food, care, or prayer, Catherine would be there. A group of supporters and followers began to join her in ministry. She became a teacher and spiritual leader for a band of devoted followers of both men and women, lay and religious. "Nothing great is ever achieved without much enduring," Catherine advised her followers.

Catherine's ministry grew, and she and her followers began to travel throughout Italy. She spoke to Church leaders about the needs for reform. Catherine also met with many lay people, assuring them that they could return to God through repentance and a renewed love for him and the Church. "Be who God meant you to be and you will set the world on fire," she told those seeking spiritual encouragement. In 1376, she began writing a mystical work called "The Dialogues."

Catherine also began to dictate and send hundreds of letters that are said to be literary masterpieces. They were written with a purpose, however, to political and Church leaders. She begged them to work for peace and for the return of the Pope to Rome. Catherine, an independent but undeniably Spirit-filled woman in her 20s, also wrote often to Pope Gregory XI who was then living in Avignon, France. Catherine told the Pope that she was sharing Christ's wishes, not her own. Eventually, the Holy Father believed her and returned to Rome. The Pope asked her to come to Rome so that she could be nearby when he needed her spiritual counsel.

By 1379, Catherine's health was deteriorating. She ate little and slept just a few hours each night. She died at thirty-three in Rome on April 29, 1380, after suffering a stroke. Saint Catherine was canonized in 1461. In 1970, together with Saint Teresa of Avila, she was given the title of Doctor of the Church. Saint Catherine's feast is April 29.

Think About It Why did Catherine begin to travel throughout Italy and northern Europe during her 20s? Who were her traveling companions? Why do you think the Church eventually named Saint Catherine as a Doctor of the Church?

Go to the student site at **hs.osvcurriculum.com**

There are two main forms of grace: **sanctifying grace** and actual grace. Sanctifying grace is

QUOTATION TO BE
INCLUDED IN FINAL PRINTING.

(CCC, 2000). Sanctifying grace is God's freely given gift of his love and his constant presence in the soul enabling us to act and live in his love (see CCC, 2000). It identifies God's friendship that heals us and enables us to respond to his love. **Actual grace** is the help God gives us for a particular need, such as an important decision, a period of painful loss and grief, or a time of crisis. Actual grace gives us the strength and power to conform our lives to God's will during these times of need.

The *Catechism* helps us see that God's grace changes our relationship with him. Grace is

QUOTATION TO BE
INCLUDED IN FINAL PRINTING.

DISCUSS

- What are the implications for our lives when we realize that when we live in sanctifying grace, we share in the very life of God within us?

(CCC, 1999). This free gift from God demands a response from us because God created us in his image, gave us freedom, and the ability to know and love him in a communion of love.

QUOTATION TO BE
INCLUDED IN FINAL PRINTING.

—CCC, 2002

Amazing Grace **is a 2006 film about the campaign against the slave trade** in the British Empire led by William Wilberforce and inspired by the experiences of John Newton. Newton was a crewman on a slave ship whose conversion led to the writing of the poem "Amazing Grace," which we know as a hymn. Newton wrote the poem as part of a sermon delivered on New Year's Day in 1773. He describes himself on a spiritual journey as a "wretch" who was saved by God's grace. The final stanza most commonly used with modern renditions of the song was added sometime later. It is a powerful addition that references eternal life. That stanza reads: "When we've been here ten thousands years; bright, shining as the sun; we've no less days to sing God's praise; than when we first begun."

A choir sings, "Amazing Grace," which was written by John Newton in 1773.

- What has been your experience with this hymn?

- Why is it so beloved?

- What would you say is the principle message of the song?

- How much of it can you sing? Try memorizing the whole song.

Faith & Culture

➚ Go to the student site at **hs.osvcurriculum.com**

ADVANCE REVIEW COPY

Grace is the gift from the Holy Spirit who justifies and sanctifies us. Through grace we can:

- cooperate with the work of the Holy Spirit

- associate his the Holy Spirit

- collaborate with the Holy Spirit in the salvation of others

- participate in the Holy Spirit's work to keep growing the Body of Christ, the Church

Sacramental graces are gifts from the Holy Spirit that we receive from the Seven Sacraments. We may also receive certain special graces that we call charisms. Charism comes from the Greek term meaning favor, gratuitous gift, or benefit.

QUOTATION TO BE
INCLUDED IN FINAL PRINTING.

(CCC, 2003).

GO TO THE SOURCE

Saint Paul's fourth chapter in his Letter to the Ephesians begs the faithful to live a moral life using the grace Christ gives each of us.

Read Ephesians 4.

- List seven specific behaviors that Saint Paul encourages us to practice as part of the moral life.

- List five behaviors he asks us to turn away from.

- What does he say is the effect of God's grace on all this?

- What does he ultimately encourage us to do?

The *Catechism* points out that among the special graces are the *graces of state* that come with the responsibilities of living the Christian life and of the ministries within the Church:

QUOTATION TO BE
INCLUDED IN FINAL PRINTING.

—CCC, 2004

Graces are supernatural, meaning they depend entirely on God's initiative to bestow them and reveal them. We cannot gain them by our own power. This is an important point:

QUOTATION TO BE
INCLUDED IN FINAL PRINTING.

—CCC, 2005

Here is how Saint Joan of Arc answered her judges when asked if she was in God's grace:

QUOTATION TO BE
INCLUDED IN FINAL PRINTING.

(CCC, 2005).

All of us need the transformation that the gift of grace brings. All of us could use greater freedom, wisdom, courage, and compassion—qualities that come only with God's help.

Describe How does grace connect us with the Holy Trinity?

Apply Why does the gift of God's grace demand a response from us?

QUICK REVIEW

1a. **List** What are some of the effects of sanctifying grace?

  b. **Compare** How are sanctifying grace and actual grace alike and different?

2a. **Recall** How do we know that grace is working in our lives?

  b. **Explain** Why are sacramental graces and charisms important?

ACT

Think of a way to represent actual or sanctifying grace in a piece of art or in a musical composition.

• You could research how others have represented it in the past.

• Share your representation with a group of classmates.

SELF-ASSESS

Which statement best reflects where you are now?

☐ I'm confident enough about the material in this section to be able to explain it to someone else.

☐ I have a good grasp of the material in this section, but I could use more review.

☐ I'm lost. I need help catching up before moving on.

ADVANCE REVIEW COPY

Habits of the Heart

KEY TERMS IN THIS SECTION

vices bad qualities, habits, or patterns of behavior that incline us to actions that are sinful and harmful to ourselves and others

theological virtues faith, hope, and charity; they are supernatural gifts infused by God into the soul of faithful people that enable them to live and act as God's sons and daughters to merit eternal life

cardinal virtues prudence, justice, fortitude, and temperance; they are stable dispositions of the intellect and will that govern our moral activities; they direct us toward Christ-like behavior and discipline our passions and emotions.

prudence the virtue that helps us make a correct judgment about what to do and to choose the right way to do it

fortitude courage; strength when confronted with difficulties and perseverance in pursuing that which is good

temperance

(CCC, 1809)

(CCC, 1803). It's important to keep in mind that our unique power to do good is a gift of God's grace. With his grace helping us, virtues can build our character and help in doing good. Jesus' free gift of salvation offers us the grace necessary to persevere in virtuous living. Because of our wounded nature, we cannot do this alone. We need God's grace to live in holiness.

QUOTATION TO BE INCLUDED IN FINAL PRINTING.

—CCC, 1811

Virtues are habitual and firm dispositions to do good and avoid evil. They are acquired by cooperating with God's grace. They urge us to make good moral decisions. Conversely, **vices** are habits (CCC, Glossary, p. 903). They incline us to actions that are sinful and harmful to ourselves and others.

QUOTATION TO BE INCLUDED IN FINAL PRINTING.

—CCC, 1803

Virtues allow people to perform good acts and to give the best of themselves.

- What virtues and vices are common to high school students today?
- What can you do to do more good with virtues and steer away from vices?

Theological Virtues

There are three foundational virtues—faith, hope, and love. The term charity is often used for love. These three are known as **theological virtues**. They prepare us to participate in the divine life, and they

(CCC, 1812). In Greek, *theos* means God. They are gifts from God that call for a response on our part.

QUOTATION TO BE
INCLUDED IN FINAL PRINTING.

—CCC, 1813

Faith is a theological virtue, a gift from God, by which we believe in God and all he has revealed

GO TO THE SOURCE

Saint Paul tells the Philippians to use their virtues and recognize what is good.

Read Philippians 4:4-8.

- What does Saint Paul say God will guard in our hearts and minds and what must we do to ensure that we are prepared for that to happen?
- Give an example for each of the characteristics that the passage mentions: something honorable, just, pure, pleasing, commendable, excellent, and worthy of praise.

to us and that the Holy Spirit proposes for our belief.

QUOTATION TO BE
INCLUDED IN FINAL PRINTING.

(CCC, 229).

Faith, then, is a grace given to us by God, and it is a human act, a conscious and free act on our part to respond to God's grace. It is an act of the Church which precedes and makes possible individual faith, supporting and nourishing the faith of all believers. The gift of faith remains with the person who has not sinned against it, but without good works it is dead (see James 2:26).

QUOTATION TO BE
INCLUDED IN FINAL PRINTING.

(CCC, 1815).

QUOTATION TO BE
INCLUDED IN FINAL PRINTING.

—CCC, 1816

Only by faith can we come to know and experience God as the Holy Trinity—the Father, the Son and the Holy Spirit. Without faith we cannot believe in the Trinity and thus without faith we cannot be saved.

Jesus models faithfulness when he prays in the Garden of Gethsemane the night before his Death: "'Abba, Father, for you all things are possible; remove this cup from me; yet, not what I want, but what you want'" (Mark 14:36). Jesus is alone in the garden. His disciples are off sleeping. He has one last chance to abandon the message to which he had committed himself. Instead, no doubt knowing that dire consequences would result, he prays to his Father and pledges obedience.

Faith leads to a faith-filled life. The Blessed Virgin Mary models faith in action when she freely says yes to God's invitation to be the mother of the savior (see Luke 1:26-38). By her faith and obedience Mary becomes the Mother of God and of us all.

My Faith

Morality of Our Speech

"So also the tongue is a small member, yet it boasts of great exploits. How great a forest is set ablaze by a small fire! And the tongue is a fire. The tongue is placed among our members as a world of iniquity; it stains the whole body, sets on fire the cycle of nature. ... With it we bless the Lord and Father, and with it we curse those who are made in the likeness of God.

"Do not speak evil against one another, brothers and sisters."

—James 3:5-6, 9-10, 4:11

Throughout this course we have looked at the key elements of Christian morality. And yet it is easy to overlook the morality of our speech. Sacred Scripture often reminds us to curb our tongues and watch our language.

Our conversations are moral acts. Through our conversations we either convey the virtues we have been discussing in this course or the things that are hurtful or profane. Our conversations reveal our character and the commitment we have made to live as God intended.

- How much effort do you put into controlling what you say?

- How much attention do you pay to the moral nature of your conversations?

- How much time do you spend in the immoral conversations generated by others?

- What can you do to improve?

- Take this time to make some notes to yourself:

You may choose to include any of this in the final report you give at the end of this course.

Discipleship ... within the Body of Christ ... for the glory of God and the good of the world.

Hope is the theological virtue

QUOTATION TO BE
INCLUDED IN FINAL PRINTING.

(CCC, 1817). Hope is the virtue that makes us long for the happiness that God placed in our hearts. It allows us to remain encouraged and sustains us when we're lonely or feeling abandoned. Hope preserves us from selfishness and leads us to the happiness that results from charity (see CCC, 1818).

QUOTATION TO BE
INCLUDED IN FINAL PRINTING.

—CCC, 1820

Hope is expressed and nurtured by prayer and by the Lord's Prayer in particular. The Our Father summarizes everything that hope leads us to want. We can hope for the glory of Heaven because God promised that for those who love him and live in him.

QUOTATION TO BE
INCLUDED IN FINAL PRINTING.

Jesus accepted his Death on the Cross to save us from our sins.

QUOTATION TO BE
INCLUDED IN FINAL PRINTING.

(CCC, 1821).

Charity is the New Commandment to love that Jesus gives us. Charity, or love, is superior to all the virtues. "And if I have prophetic powers, and understand all mysteries and all knowledge, and if I have all faith, so as to remove mountains, but do not have love, I am nothing" (1 Corinthians 13:2).

QUOTATION TO BE
INCLUDED IN FINAL PRINTING.

—CCC, 1828

The virtues are cultivated in us by the Holy Spirit. We will never be adequately filled with them. "True virtue has no limits but goes on and on," Saint Francis de Sales wrote. Charity, he said, "is the virtue of virtues, and which having a definite object, would become infinite if it could meet with a heart capable of infinity." There's no end to how much this virtue could grow in us, he said, if only our hearts were big enough.

Explain Why do we need grace to live a virtuous life?

Elaborate How are the theological virtues the foundation of Christian moral activity?

ADVANCE REVIEW COPY

The cardinal virtues are prudence, justice, fortitude, and temperance.

- Write down specific times when you've demonstrated, experienced, or witnessed each of the cardinal virtues.

- What have you learned about these four virtues through your experience and this chapter?

Cardinal Virtues

Four pivotal virtues in the Catholic tradition are prudence, justice, fortitude, and temperance. They are called the **cardinal virtues** based on the Latin root of the word—*cardo*, which means hinge. The Christian moral life hinges on these four virtues working together. The cardinal virtues are practical, common sense virtues. They are human virtues. Used consistently, they support all our endeavors to live a good life.

Like all virtues, the cardinal virtues are gifts from God, which grow in us through prayer, the Sacraments, good works, education, practice, and perseverance.

QUOTATION TO BE INCLUDED IN FINAL PRINTING.

(CCC, 1810).

The word virtue comes from a Latin root meaning strength or power.

QUOTATION TO BE INCLUDED IN FINAL PRINTING.

(CCC, 1804).

Sometimes we think of habits as actions that we do automatically, without thinking, as if we had no control over them. In fact, good habits do not take away our freedom but instead channel our freedom toward positive ends. We cultivate virtues through acting justly and correctly over a period of time. We are practicing virtues when we act in a morally good way.

(CCC, 1804).

In the face of daily decisions, a virtuous person tends to make wholesome choices. The reason is virtues are influenced by freely practicing the good. Virtuous persons cultivate deep spiritual values, convictions, spiritual discipline, and behavior patterns that become almost second nature. Virtues serve as the basis for consistent responses to the many moral decisions we must make.

(CCC, 1804).

> And if anyone loves righteousness, her labors are virtues; for she teaches self-control and prudence, justice and courage; nothing in life is more profitable for mortals than these.
>
> —Wisdom 8:7

Prudence—Practical Judgment

Prudence is the virtue that

QUOTATION TO BE INCLUDED IN FINAL PRINTING.

(CCC, 1835). It is the virtue of making right judgments. It asks the question: What is the right thing to do in this particular situation? The Book of Proverbs describes prudence concisely in these words:

(CCC, 1806).

Justice—Rights and Responsibilities

Justice is

(CCC, 1836). The virtue of justice reminds us that the people with whom we share our world have rights and that, as much as possible, all people deserve to have basic needs met (see CCC, 1807). Justice is emphasized throughout Scripture and remains as relevant today. A just person recognizes the dignity of everyone and strives to treat rich and poor, friends and strangers—those like us and those unlike us—with equal dignity.

Living according to the virtue of justice is particularly challenging in a world where there is drastically unequal distribution of basic goods, social amenities, opportunities, and justice itself. In justice, all people possess equal rights. Therefore, our own good is never separate from the common good, an important concept in Catholic Social Teaching.

PRIMARY SOURCES

In the 1980s, the United States Conference of Catholic Bishops was very concerned about the economic welfare of a growing number of Americans. They developed and wrote a landmark pastoral letter in 1986, *Economic Justice for All.*

The major goal of the ninety-page document was to emphasize that every society is judged by its treatment of the poor and the marginalized. Jesus introduced his mission to the world by identifying himself as the promised Messiah, the one who would "bring good news to the poor" (Luke 4:18). and the one who would offer "release to the captives and recovery of sight to the blind, to let the oppressed go free" (Luke 4:18). Jesus wanted a just and compassionate world, and he also wanted his disciples to work for that kind of world. In their pastoral letter, the U.S. bishops presented principles of Catholic Social Teaching and how they can be applied to the economy.

The following are three of the principle themes of the United States Conference of Catholic Bishop's Pastoral Letter on Catholic Social Teaching and the Economy titled: *Economic Justice for All*:

13. *Every economic decision and institution must be judged in light of whether it protects or undermines the dignity of the human person.* The pastoral letter begins with the human person. We believe the person is sacred— the clearest reflection of God among us. Human dignity comes from God, not from nationality, race, sex, economic status, or any human accomplishment. We judge any economic system by what it does for and to people and by how it permits all to participate in it. The economy should serve people, not the other way around.

14. *Human dignity can be realized and protected only in community.* In our teaching, the human person is not only sacred but also social. How we organize our society—in economics and politics, in law and policy—directly affects human dignity and the capacity of individuals to grow in community. The obligation to "love our neighbor" has an individual dimension, but it also requires a broader social commitment to the common good. We have many partial ways to measure and debate the health of our economy: Gross National Product, per capita income, stock market prices, and so forth. The Christian vision of economic life looks beyond them all and asks, Does economic life enhance or threaten our life together as a community?

15. *All people have a right to participate in the economic life of society.* Basic justice demands that people be assured at least a minimum level of participation in the economy. It is wrong for a person or group to be excluded unfairly or to be unable to participate in or contribute to the economy. For example, people who are both able and willing, but cannot get a job are deprived of the participation that is so vital to human development. For it is through employment that most individuals and families meet their material needs, exercise their talents, and have an opportunity to contribute to the larger community. Such participation has special significance in our tradition because we believe that it is a means by which we join in carrying forward God's creative activity.

Go to the student site at
hs.osvcurriculum.com

What did the bishops mean by the "dignity of the human person"?

Why did the bishops mean when they said that all people have the right to "participate in the economic life of the society?"

Cardinal Sean P. O'Malley, OFMCap., right, serves people during an event in his Archdiocese of Boston.

ADVANCE REVIEW COPY

Fortitude—The Courage to Act

Fortitude QUOTATION TO BE INCLUDED IN FINAL PRINTING. (CCC, 1837). "Being good" is easy when everyone else is. The challenge is to stand up for what is right in the face of peer pressure or in circumstances when we are being called upon to step out of our usual patterns of behavior. It is fortitude that can give us the resolve to be courageous or firm in our beliefs and actions when others act differently. In extraordinary circumstances, this may even mean being willing to give up our own lives in defense of a just cause.

Fortitude enables us to resist temptations and overcome challenges to the moral life.

QUOTATION TO BE INCLUDED IN FINAL PRINTING.

(CCC, 1808). Here are two quotations that emphasize the meaning of fortitude:

> The Lord is my strength and my might;
> he has become my salvation.

—Psalm 118:14

> 'In the world you face persecution. But take courage;
> I have conquered the world!'

—John 16:33

Temperance—The Virtue of Self-Control

North Americans know the word temperance from the movement to ban alcohol that resulted in Prohibition in the United States. The temperance movement was made up mostly of women. The image they promoted was that of a male factory worker receiving his pay on Friday and heading straight for the nearest bar where he spent a large chunk of his paycheck on whiskey and beer. Meanwhile, his wife was home trying to figure out how to feed the children.

As the temperance movement called for control over the consumption of alcohol, so the virtue of temperance disposes us to self-control and helps us to a balanced use of God's created gifts.

Self-control is a term that is looked down upon by some people in our modern society, as if self-control somehow keeps us from being free. In fact, freedom requires self-control. If we are incapable of regulating the amount of food we eat or the amount of alcohol we consume, we're not very free. Being addicted is not freedom. Being consumed with possessing the latest clothes styles or the latest gadget is not freedom. **Temperance** is the virtue of personal harmony and balance and advocates a wholesome lifestyle. QUOTATION TO BE INCLUDED IN FINAL PRINTING. (CCC, 1809).

A life of harmony and wholeness is not a life devoid of pleasure. It is one that aims to keep things in balance. Saint Augustine noted how these four virtues work in the virtuous person.

REFLECT

Of the following behaviors, select one that might be a virtue that you choose to cultivate in yourself. Explain your choice.

- making more time for God through prayer
- Studying the ways and teaching of Christ
- Respecting my parents
- saying no when I really do not want to do something of questionable moral value
- developing enthusiasm for the spiritual life
- showing patience with my friends
- speaking positively about my friends and not putting them down
- taking better care of my body
- demonstrating concern for others and the environment

The Church reminds us that it's not easy to live a balanced moral life because we are wounded by sin. Catholics know, however, that in Christ and the virtues there is hope.

(CCC, 1811).

Identify Which virtue asks what is the right thing to do in any particular situation?

Connect What is another name for the virtue of temperance?

QUOTATION TO BE
INCLUDED IN FINAL PRINTING.

—CCC, 1809

SECTION 4 REVIEW

QUICK REVIEW

1. Link How do virtues help us do good?

2a. Explain Why are faith, hope, and love known as the theological virtues?

b. Relate How did Jesus model faith, hope, and love?

c. Apply How does hope shape our view toward life?

3. Clarify What are some of the main themes of the pastoral letter, *Economic Justice for All?*

Pray Compose a prayer that will help you with one of the theological virtues and one of the cardinal virtues.

SELF-ASSESS

Which statement best reflects where you are now?

☐ I'm confident enough about the material in this section to be able to explain it to someone else.

☐ I have a good grasp of the material in this section, but I could use more review.

☐ I'm lost. I need help catching up before moving on.

ADVANCE REVIEW COPY

PRAYER

Opening Prayer

We begin in the name of the Father and the Son and Holy Spirit,

Lord God, infuse us with an attitude of hope.

Teach us that our future is a hopeful one—full of the expectation of what is possible.

In your divine providence, help us to know ourselves more deeply and the plan you have for us. Align our thoughts with your will.

Help us to live the Paschal Mystery in our lives. Through your Son's Death and Resurrection, let us be ever mindful of the hope and joy of the Resurrection in our own lives.

Through Christ our Lord,

Amen.

Closing Prayer

Lord, thank you so much for all the blessings you have provided in my life. I ask you today, through your divine providence, to continue to offer me with these blessings.

Lord, I thank you also for providing me with the opportunities to continue to do your work in your vineyard.

Lord, make me aware of your love, blessings, and guidance. In the midst of suffering, give me hope. Help me to internalize that there is no death without resurrection and no resurrection without death.

Lord, you know what my hopes are. Hear my prayers of hope in joy and in suffering. Align my will with yours—today and forever.

Through Christ our Lord,

Amen.

ADVANCE REVIEW COPY

TERMS

Use each of the following terms in a sentence that shows you know what the term means in the context of the chapter. You may include more than one term in a sentence.

grace

justice

vocation

laity

evangelical counsels

consecrated life

sanctifying grace

actual grace

vices

theological virtues

cardinal virtues

prudence

fortitude

temperance

PEOPLE AND IDEAS

Identify the person who best fits each description. Define each person or idea in the context of the chapter.

1. Saint Thérèse of Lisieux

2. Saint Paul

3. Saint Justin

4. Saint Josephine Bakhita

5. *Lumen Gentium*

6. Old Law

7. New Law

8. eremitic life

9. consecrated virgins and widows

10. religious life

11. secular institutes

12. societies of apostolic life

13. Focolare Movement

14. Communion and Liberation

15. Schönstatt Movement

16. Couples for Christ

17. Cursillo

18. Jesus Youth

19. Catholic Charismatic Renewal

20. Sant'Egidio

21. Saint Catherine of Siena

22. sacramental graces

23. graces of state

24. *Economic Justice for All*

UNDERSTANDING

Answer each question and complete each exercise

SECTION 1

1. **Recall** What is the basis for morally good actions?

2. **Link** What is the relationship between talents and vocations?

3. **Explain** How do lay people live out a vocation?

4. **Reflect** Why is marriage a covenant?

SECTION 2

5. **Explain** Why might Jesus have been considered to be in conflict with the law?

6. **Link** How do the evangelical counsels inspire charity in the lives of people who practice them?

7. **Tell** How do the members of a Third Order share in the mission of a religious order?

SECTION 3

8. **Define** What do we mean when we say that God justifies us?

9. **Explain** How do sanctifying grace and actual grace work together?

10. **Connect** What does it mean when we say grace is supernatural?

ADVANCE REVIEW COPY

11. **Describe** What can you do to cultivate good character?
12. **Connect** Why is a consistent response to moral decisions important?
13. **Consider** Why are the cardinal virtues practical tools?
14. **Distinguish** How are the Gifts of the Holy Spirit related to the Fruits of the Holy Spirit?

CONNECTING

Visual This painting shows Jesus speaking with the learned men of his time.

What contrasts do you notice between Jesus and the others in the painting? Do the men seem open to what Jesus is teaching? What can you learn from this image about being a disciple?

Challenge You and a friend see Middle East protesters on the news facing armed soldiers. Your friend wonders how the protesters have the courage to face the military crackdown. After reading this chapter, what do you tell your friend about the virtue of fortitude.

Question After working through this chapter, what would you tell someone who thinks they have no vocation in life?

Imagine You are at a Catholic youth event and a friend at the event asks:

- How does the grace of God work in your life? How do you answer?
- Then the reporter wants to know how aware people are about grace in their lives. How do you explain that?
- How can you help make people aware of how grace works in their lives?

SELF-ASSESS

On Your Own Make a list of the most important things you learned from this chapter.

Select three things that represent your growth in understanding as you worked through this chapter. Write a paragraph explaining your choices.

With a Partner List what you found most helpful or interesting in this chapter as well as any other questions that have surfaced.

CHAPTER 8

- What kind of life did these people choose to live?
- Where are you in living a Christian moral life?

Living a Moral Life

Go to the student site at
hs.osvcurriculum.com

ADVANCE REVIEW COPY

YOU WILL

- Discover how the Gifts of the Holy Spirit help us live a moral life.

- Explore the link between faith and the life we live.

- Realize the role of the Holy Spirit in our lives.

- Discuss the life of Saint Maximilian Kolbe.

- Define conscience and study how to form one throughout a lifetime.

- Study how a conscience can be erroneous.

- See sin as a decision to act contrary to one's conscience.

- Examine the grace of the Sacraments as they impact the moral life.

- Connect prayer, the example of Mary, and the teaching of the Magisterium to growing in spiritual maturity.

A Way of Living

KEY TERMS IN THIS SECTION

Gifts of the Holy Spirit

(CCC, Glossary, p. 880). These spiritual gifts given by the Holy Spirit help us follow his guidance and live the Christian life: wisdom, understanding, counsel (right

judgment), fortitude (courage), knowledge, piety (reverence), and fear of the Lord (awe and wonder)

docile as it pertains to the Gifts of the Holy Spirit, it means being compliant and following the promptings of the Holy Spirit

Fruits of the Holy Spirit twelve "perfections" that the Holy Spirit forms in us all as a glimpse of possible eternal glory

The *Catechism of the Catholic Church* speaks of two ways we can choose to live. The way of Christ leads us to life everlasting. The other way only leads to destruction. We have mentioned the parable of the narrow gate that Jesus gave the Apostles. He wants us to enter the narrow gate. "'For the gate is narrow and the road is hard that leads to life, and there are few who find it'" (Matthew 7:14). A few passages later in the same chapter of Matthew, Jesus also says:

A young woman receives Communion during the 2009 National Catholic Youth Conference in Kansas City.

'Not everyone who says to me, "Lord, Lord" will enter the kingdom of heaven, but only those who do the will of my Father in heaven.'

—Matthew 7:21

This teaching is important for the Church because "it shows the importance of moral decisions for our salvation.

QUOTATION TO BE INCLUDED IN FINAL PRINTING. (CCC, 1696).

This is why Catholic religious education is filled with teaching on the Holy Spirit, grace, the Beatitudes, sin and forgiveness, the virtues, and the two Great Commandments of love. The first and last teaching in Catholic religious education is always Jesus Christ, who we call the way, the truth, and the life.

Blessed Pope John Paul II told us in his encyclical, *Veritatis Splendor*, the "Splendor of Truth," that "it is precisely on the path of the moral life that the way of salvation is open to all." In this course, we have discussed the aspects of the moral life, and now we turn to why the moral life is such a key component of human life.

Christian moral life begins with a loving relationship with God made possible through Christ's sacrifice. Love is the essential foundation of the Christian moral life, which also requires grace. Someone living the Christian moral life seeks to practice and develop his or her conscience, the virtues, and the Gifts of the Holy Spirit. "The most basic principle of

ADVANCE REVIEW COPY

the Christian moral life is the awareness that every person bears the dignity of being made in the image of God" (*U.S. Catholic Catechism for Adults,* p. 310).

Saint John Eudes asked us to recognize Jesus Christ as our true head, and that we are his Body. He belongs to us just as our own head belongs to our body. All that is Christ's is ours, including his spirit; his heart; his body and soul; his mental and physical abilities. We use these things to serve, praise, love, and glorify God.

A Catholic's faith must be alive and active in the world. We need divine guidance in living the Christian moral life. God gives us qualities to assist us and we know them as the Gifts of the Holy Spirit—wisdom, understanding, counsel, fortitude, knowledge, piety, and fear of the Lord. They are freely given to make us more willing to follow the guidance of the Holy Spirit on our journey through the Christian life.

Popular culture has embraced the catch phrase "What Would Jesus Do?" For Catholics, that is the question we try to answer with our whole lives. For that purpose, we are given the Gifts of the Holy Spirit to truly discern what Jesus is telling us to do through the Holy Spirit. Jesus was clear on how to live the moral life. "'I am the way, and the truth, and the life'" (John 14:6).

GO TO THE SOURCE

Jesus denounced the example of the Scribes and Pharisees.

Read Matthew 23:4-36.

- What is the problem with the example of the Scribes and Pharisees?

- What can you learn from the example of the Scribes and Pharisees?

- What happens when we no longer consider ourselves students in the sense that Jesus taught?

- Why was Jesus so strong in his condemnation of hypocritical people?

Jesus also pointed out misguided ways. "'Do whatever they teach you and follow it; but do not do as they do, for they do not practice what they teach'" (Matthew 23:3).

The saints of the Church have also reminded us that there is a strong connection between what we believe and the way we live. Living a moral life must begin with the truth.

> If you believe what you like in the gospels, and reject what you don't like, it is not the gospel you believe, but yourself.
>
> —Saint Augustine of Hippo

To know the truth means a choice on our part to respond to God's love by cooperating with the graces and gifts that the Holy Spirit gives us. We use these gifts to grow closer to the truth and develop our moral life.

Blessed Pier Giorgio Frassati knew this. He lived in the early twentieth century in Turin, Italy. Blessed Pope John Paul II noted at Blessed Pier Giorgio's beatification in 1990, that the young Catholic had set a great example because it is "through prayerful abandonment to God's will that life's great decisions mature." Blessed Pier Giorgio was filled with the Gifts and Fruits of the Holy Spirit. The Pope said, "Indeed, his entire life seems to sum up Christ's words which we find in John's Gospel: 'Those who love me will keep my word and my Father will love them, and we will come to them and make our home with them' (*Jn* 14:23)". Speaking to university students, Blessed Pier Giorgio said as Catholics we know that love is the foundation of our religion. We are truly Catholic when we observe the two Great Commandments of Christ to love God and love our neighbors. Blessed Pier Giorgio said they are proof that our faith is based on real love rather than violence that has marred the history of humankind.

> With violence hatred is sown and then its evil fruits are gathered. With charity Peace is sown among men, but not the peace of the world, True Peace, which only faith in Jesus Christ can give, binding us together in brotherly love.
>
> —Blessed Pier Giorgio Frassati

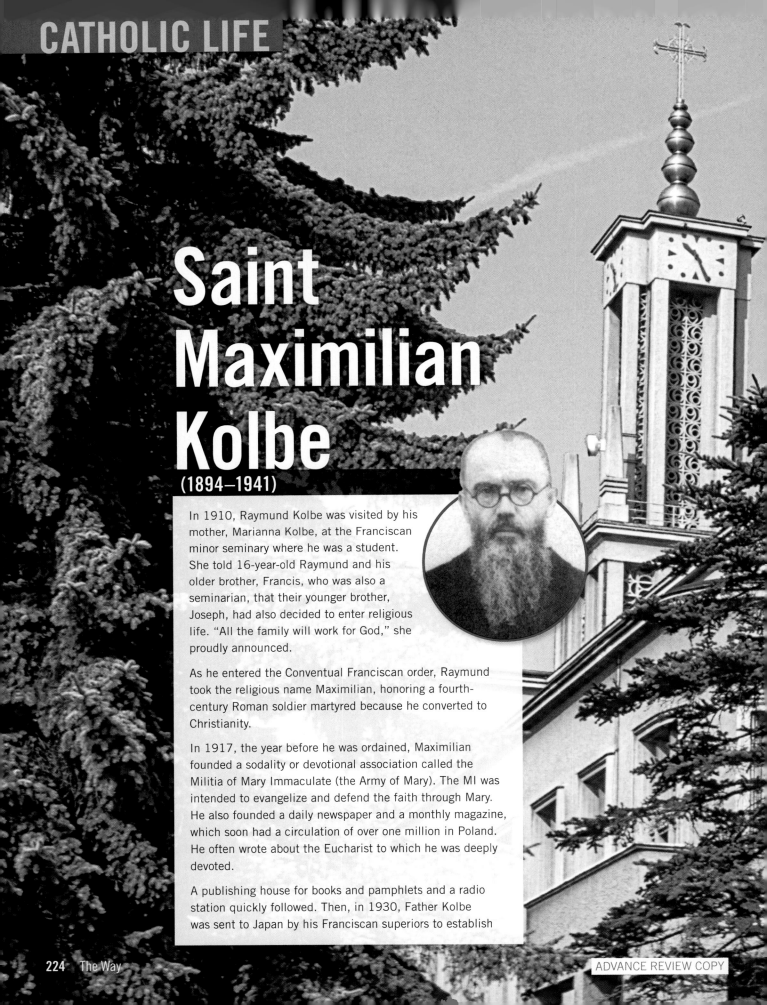

Saint Maximilian Kolbe

(1894–1941)

In 1910, Raymund Kolbe was visited by his mother, Marianna Kolbe, at the Franciscan minor seminary where he was a student. She told 16-year-old Raymund and his older brother, Francis, who was also a seminarian, that their younger brother, Joseph, had also decided to enter religious life. "All the family will work for God," she proudly announced.

As he entered the Conventual Franciscan order, Raymund took the religious name Maximilian, honoring a fourth-century Roman soldier martyred because he converted to Christianity.

In 1917, the year before he was ordained, Maximilian founded a sodality or devotional association called the Militia of Mary Immaculate (the Army of Mary). The MI was intended to evangelize and defend the faith through Mary. He also founded a daily newspaper and a monthly magazine, which soon had a circulation of over one million in Poland. He often wrote about the Eucharist to which he was deeply devoted.

A publishing house for books and pamphlets and a radio station quickly followed. Then, in 1930, Father Kolbe was sent to Japan by his Franciscan superiors to establish

ADVANCE REVIEW COPY

The Basilica of St. Mary Immaculate at Niepokalanow, the religious community near Warsaw, Poland, founded by Saint Maximilian Kolbe in 1927.

and lead a monastery near Nagasaki. When he returned to Europe six years later, Nazi persecution of the Jews had become openly aggressive and violent. The Immaculates used the Catholic media to protest Nazi policies and defend Jewish rights. The Franciscans at Niepokalanow Monastery, which Father Kolbe had established, also sheltered thousands of refugees and more than 2,000 Jews near Warsaw.

It was only a matter of time before the Nazi police, known as the Gestapo, closed down the publishing center. In their last issue, Saint Maximilian wrote: "No one in the world can change Truth. What we can do and should do is to seek truth and to serve it when we have found it."

On February 17, 1941, the Gestapo arrested Father Kolbe and four other friars from Niepokalanow Monastery. The friars were taken first to a prison in Warsaw and later transferred to Auschwitz Concentration Camp.

At Auschwitz, he ministered as best as he could to the prisoners of the camp. He celebrated daily Mass whenever he obtained a tiny bit of bread.

In late July, when two prisoners escaped from the camp, ten men were randomly selected to die in the starvation bunker to discourage other prisoners from escaping. When one of the selected prisoners, Franciszek Gajowniczek began to weep because he would leave behind a wife and children, Father Kolbe approached the officer in charge and offered to take his place.

The men were locked in the starvation bunkers and given no food and water. Father Kolbe's voice could be heard calming the dying men and leading them in prayer and hymns. By August 14, 1941, he was the last man alive. To speed his death so that the bunker could be cleared out, a guard administered a lethal injection of carbolic acid.

Blessed Pope John Paul II, a fellow Pole, canonized Saint Maximilian Kolbe in 1982. The Pope called the new saint a "Martyr of Charity" and a "patron saint for our difficult century." The evangelization ministry that Saint Maximilian founded later continued in a new religious order called the Franciscan Friars of Mary Immaculate whose rule is influenced by Saint Maximilian's spirituality.

Think About It How did Saint Maximilian show the love of Christ to others? How does the name Martyr of Charity fit Saint Maximilian? How can you live your life more like Saint Maximilian and Christ?

Go to the student site at
hs.osvcurriculum.com

ADVANCE REVIEW COPY

Blessed Pier Giorgio modeled a life based on love for Christ.

- When have you recently allowed the question "What Would Jesus Do?" to guide your moral choice?
- Did you wrestle with it or was it an easy choice? Explain your answer.

Blessed Pier Giorgio was loved and beatified because he loved others so much and his life showed that. Blessed Pope John Paul II concluded with this question about the theological virtue of love: "Is it perhaps not true that the only thing that lasts, without ever losing its validity, is the fact that a person 'has loved'?"

Cardinal Donald W. Wuerl of the Archdiocese of Washington, D.C., speaking at Georgetown University in 2012, emphasized how much another theological virtue, the virtue of faith, contributes to the moral life because it forms our understanding of how we relate to one another. "With religious faith comes a way of living, a set of standards for moral and civil behavior," he explained. These expectations, he said, are "woven into the very fabric of our societal life."

'You shall not kill' is not simply a legal convention of any particular political persuasion, but rather a moral imperative rooted in our human nature, proclaimed by our religious heritage and intrinsic to the identity of all of us as a people.

—Cardinal Wuerl

Explain What happens when we look to Christ in faith and love him with the same love he gave us?

Recall In what way did Blessed Pier Giorgio Frassati set a great example for us, according to Blessed Pope John Paul II?

Gifts and Fruits of the Spirit

The seven **Gifts of the Holy Spirit** (see chart, p. 227) strengthen and support the Christian moral life. They belong to Christ and perfect the virtues of those of us who receive them. They are permanent dispositions that

in obeying the promptings of the Holy Spirit (CCC, 1831). Seeking guidance from the Holy Spirit has always been vital for the faith-ful. When we are called by God, we have at our disposal these gifts to help us respond.

Save me, O LORD, from my enemies;
  I have fled to you for refuge.
Teach me to do your will,
  for you are my God.
Let your good spirit lead me on a level path.

—Psalm 143:9-10

In the New Testament, all who are led by the Holy Spirit are sons and daughters of God. The Spirit of God dwells in those who believe and follow Christ. If we are children of God, then we are "heirs of God and joint heirs with Christ—if, in fact, we suffer with him so that we may also be glorified with him" (Romans 8:17).

We see the importance of the Sacraments in living the moral life as the Sacrament of Confirmation seals the Gifts of the Holy Spirit first given to us at Baptism (see accompanying chart). In Confirmation, the baptized are more perfectly bound to the Church and more obligated to act morally.

QUOTATION TO BE INCLUDED IN FINAL PRINTING.

(CCC, 1285). We learn that God anticipates our needs because he knows them.

The **Fruits of the Holy Spirit** give us a glimpse of eternal glory and also equip us to live as faithful, moral Catholics. They are qualities that can be seen in us when we allow the Holy Spirit to work in our hearts. The *Catechism* calls these twelve fruits

(CCC, 1832). "If we live by the Spirit, let us also be guided by the Spirit" (Galatians 5:25).

Fruits of the Holy Spirit	
Charity	Patience
Joy	Kindness
Peace	Goodness
Generosity	Modesty
Gentleness	Self-control
Faithfulness	Chastity

When we see the list of Fruits of the Holy Spirit, we can clearly see the contrast (see Galatians 5:22).

Saint Paul, in the Letter to the Galatians, makes that point that those who belong to Christ have "crucified the flesh with its passions and desires" (Galatians 5:24).

> Let us not become conceited, competing against one another, envying one another.
>
> —Galatians 5:26

The twelve Fruits of the Holy Spirit are observable attributes given by the Holy Spirit that grow in people who have allowed God's grace to be effective in them. These spiritual gifts mature and, and as they do, others can know God through them.

The image of fruit is a familiar one for Catholics. "'In the same way, every good tree bears good fruit, but the bad tree bears bad fruit. A good tree cannot bear bad fruit, nor can a bad tree bear good fruit'" (Matthew 7:17-18).

The Gifts of the Spirit	
Wisdom	Wisdom helps us see and evaluate all things from the viewpoint of God, to see as he sees. This gift helps us make practical judgments that are wise, in accord with God's will. Many saints not educated in a formal way were renowned for their wisdom because they were so close to God and thus could more easily discern his path in many complex situations. The Holy Spirit helps us possess this sort of "simple wisdom."
Understanding	Understanding allows us to see through the eyes and walk in the footsteps of Jesus so that our heart is like the heart of God, filled with compassion and mercy. The Holy Spirit gives us greater vision and perspective in making decisions that are not self-centered, but instead seeks justice and peace for all.
Counsel (Right Judgment)	Counsel helps us make correct judgments about actions that will lead us closer to God. It helps us listen to the prompting of the Holy Spirit within our consciences. It helps us recognize the better course of action in difficult and unclear situations. It also guides us to give better counsel (such as advice) to others who are seeking to discern God's will for their own lives.
Fortitude (Courage)	Fortitude gives us God's special help to courageously face difficulties and sufferings. By reassuring us that we can, with God's assistance, overcome all evil and win his blessing in heaven, this gift strengthens us to resist evil and stay on the right path, no matter what obstacles we face.
Knowledge	Knowledge helps us recognize when and how earthly things can lead us toward or away from God. To put it another way, we are helped by this gift to make correct judgments regarding what can be beneficial or what can harm our spiritual well being so that we can grow in virtue and not be led astray by temptations. This gift is the basis for the Church's teaching about the "sense of the faithful," that is, the innate sense that faithful believers have for what fits with authentic faith and what does not.
Piety (Reverence)	The gift of piety helps us reverence God the Father in prayer and worship, to respect him, and to stand in thankfulness for his loving goodness and for the work of his Son, Jesus and his gift of the Holy Spirit. This gift makes it more natural for us to be prayerful and to call on the Holy Spirit for guidance and strength. If we respond to this gift, we will have an increased respect for all things in God's creation. This gift also helps us see others as God's children and to respect every human because each person is made in the image and likeness of God.
Fear of the Lord (Wonder and Awe)	The fear of the Lord helps us deepen our resolve and desire to do good and never to offend or be separated from God. *Fear* here is not a cowering before a punishing or threatening God. Rather, it is the awe and reverence we have in God's presence, the wonder we have when we see how amazing he is. It is also the fear one has of hurting or betraying one who loves us, and whom we love, above all things. It is our awareness that God is loving and just and that we are accountable for our actions. This gift allows us to deepen our awareness that we are God's children and depend on him for everything, and thus to abhor the thought of breaking our friendship with him.

The Catholic Church uses these symbols in connection with the Holy Spirit.

Water: new birth experienced in Baptism and the ongoing nourishment for the soul.

Oil: used throughout the Bible to anoint anyone who was called or as a sign of blessing.

Fire: symbolizes determination, energy, and passion in those inspired by the Holy Spirit.

Cloud: represents the light, guidance, direction, and insights from the Holy Spirit.

Seal: a permanent mark or sign of identification for one's decision to live with the Spirit.

Hand: a sign of the Holy Spirit's healing touch and protection.

Finger: reflects the Spirit's power to create, for example, "written with the finger of God" (Exodus 31:18).

Dove: a reminder that the Holy Spirit brings comfort, peace, confidence. (see CCC 691-701, 730)

- Which of these reflect the way you most often experience the Holy Spirit?
- Which symbol best reflects the impact of the Holy Spirit on you personally?

To prepare for World Youth Day 2008, Pope Benedict XVI told the world's young people that the Fruits of the Holy Spirit are abundant in the amount that we are prepared to open up to the Spirit's guidance. The Holy Spirit's power makes all things new, he said. "For this reason it is important that each one of us know the Spirit, establish a relationship with Him and allow ourselves to be guided by Him."

Jesus promises to send an Advocate of truth. This is part of what scholars call Jesus' farewell discourse to the Apostles.

Read John 15: 26–16:15.

- What exactly does Jesus say about the Holy Spirit?
- What does he say the Holy Spirit will do?
- What does this tell you about the Holy Spirit's role in your living the moral life?

Pope Benedict XVI made the point that too many Christians do not know the Holy Spirit well. He invited the young people to know the Spirit deeply on a personal level because the Holy Spirit is the source that makes us holy. The Pope added, however, that it's not enough just to know the Holy Spirit.

We must welcome Him as the guide of our souls, as the 'Teacher of the interior life' who introduces us to the Mystery of the Trinity, because He alone can open us up to faith and allow us to live it each day to the full.

—Pope Benedict XVI

The Gifts of the Holy Spirit and the Fruits of the Holy Spirit help Christians to sustain the moral life, which they want to live in the light of the Gospel.

Explain How do the seven Gifts of the Holy Spirit strengthen and support the Christian moral life?

Connect The Fruits of the Holy Spirit give us a glimpse of eternal glory. What might Heaven be like?

Saint Paul contrasts the Fruits of the Holy Spirit with what he calls the desires of the flesh.

Read Galatians 5:16-26.

- How many desires of the flesh does Saint Paul identify?
- What do these desires of the flesh all have in common?
- What words would you use to describe the character of someone who lives with the Fruits of the Holy Spirit?

REFLECT

Pope Benedict XVI urged welcoming the Holy Spirit to guide our lives.

- How would you rate your ability to recognize the Holy Spirit's presence in your life? Explain.
- How would you describe your relationship with Holy Spirit?
- How has that relationship changed since you were a child?

My Faith

The Spirit of Truth

"If you love me, you will keep my command-ments. And I will ask the Father, and he will give you another Advocate, to be with you forever. This is the Spirit of truth, whom the world cannot receive, because it neither sees him nor knows him. You know him, because he abides with you, and he will be in you."

—John 14:15-17

Jesus is saying five things:

- If we love him, we need to keep his commands.
- The Holy Spirit is the Advocate, the one who comes to our aid.
- The Holy Spirit always shows truth.
- The world has different interests and doesn't recognize the ways of the Holy Spirit very well.
- We can recognize the Holy Spirit because he lives within us.

Meditate on the five things Jesus said and answer the following:

Which of these five are you allowing to shape the way you live and to shape your conscience?

Take some time now and make yourself some notes.

You may choose to include any of this as part of the report you give at the end of this course.

Discipleship ... within the Body of Christ ... for the glory of God and the good of the world.

QUICK REVIEW

1a. **Apply** Why would a Catholic want to have a faith that is alive and active in the world?

b. **Explain** How did Jesus use the Scribes and Pharisees as an example?

c. **Expand** If "the foundation of our religion is charity," then what is our primary job as Catholics?

2a. **Link** What did Saint Maximilian Kolbe do to earn the name "Martyr of Charity" and "patron saint for our difficult century by Blessed Pope John Paul II?

b. **Show** How did Saint Maximilian Kolbe's work affect the world?

3a. **Explain** Why is it important for the members of the Church to be docile regarding guidance from the Holy Spirit?

b. **Compare** How are the Gifts and the Fruits of the Holy Spirit alike and different?

c. **Link** Select a Gift of the Holy Spirit and explain how it supports a moral life.

d. **Discuss** What is the effect of the Fruits of the Holy Spirit on our lives?

ACT

Think of one of the virtues or Gifts of the Holy Spirit that you would like to cultivate in yourself.

• Make a plan of action for building the practice of that virtue or gift.

• Implement the plan and assess your progress regularly.

Listen and Discuss Talk about the life of Saint Maximilian Kolbe with a group of classmates.

• What Gifts and Fruits of the Holy Spirit do you recognize in this saint?

• How is his life a model for Catholics today?

Pray Compose a short prayer asking for courage to use the Gifts that you receive from the Holy Spirit.

SELF-ASSESS

Which statement best reflects where you are now?

☐ I'm confident enough about the material in this section to be able to explain it to someone else.

☐ I have a good grasp of the material in this section, but I could use more review.

☐ I'm lost. I need help catching up before moving on.

ADVANCE REVIEW COPY

The Voice of God

KEY TERMS IN THIS SECTION

informed conscience a conscience that is educated and developed through constant use and examination and learning about the teachings of the Church;

(CCC, 1788)

erroneous judgment of conscience when a person follows a process of conscientious decision making but unwittingly makes a wrong decision

disordered affections the emotions and passions of the heart which are not directed toward their proper objects

autonomy of conscience a person relies on one's own self-judgment rather than God's inner voice in our hearts

Conscience is a deep inner voice calling us to love and make good decisions echoing the law written by God on our hearts. It is

QUOTATION TO BE INCLUDED IN FINAL PRINTING.

(CCC, 1778). Conscience is a gift from God to lead us to happiness, that is, to himself. Through our conscience, God the Holy Spirit continually works within, reminding us to follow the way of Jesus Christ.

To live the moral life, we must strive to constantly develop and practice using our conscience. It is at the core of who we are (see CCC, 1783). Nonetheless, we don't decide what conscience dictates; we discover it. Many factors, such as our instincts and desires, can muddy our conscience. Our conscience must be formed through learning the teachings of the Church from Scripture and Sacred Tradition. We possess the freedom to accept or reject what our conscience directs us to do. We are required to follow our conscience because our dignity as persons created by God requires it. Ignoring conscience diminishes our dignity.

The moral conscience present in our hearts urges us at the right moment to do good rather than evil. Our conscience judges the many choices we face by approving the good ones and weeding out the bad ones.

QUOTATION TO BE INCLUDED IN FINAL PRINTING.

—CCC, 1777

The Christian moral life involves developing and practicing our conscience, depicted here in *Contemplation VI* by Bharati Chaudhuri.

ADVANCE REVIEW COPY

- Describe a television show, movie, or novel that depicts a person facing a crisis of conscience. In response to the crisis, what choices does the person make?

- Was conscience in the show, film, or book you described similar too or different from our definition and discussion on conscience? Explain your answer.

An Inner Voice

Conscience is not merely an inner voice. Conscience draws us toward goodness and truth. It should not be viewed as an inner voice that we leave untouched, unexamined, and undeveloped.

The *Catechism* tells us that it's important to know ourselves sufficiently well enough to hear and follow our conscience. This is called the requirement of interiority, which is needed because life distracts us from proper self-reflection and introspection. Saint Augustine reminds us to always turn to our conscience.

QUOTATION TO BE
INCLUDED IN FINAL PRINTING.

—CCC, 1779

Our dignity as humans requires us to be honest with and to respect our moral conscience. The *Catechism* calls it
(CCC, 1780). Our conscience can perceive the principles of morality, such as avoid evil and do good or do unto others as you would want them to do to you. It also applies these principles when we reason that they are needed, and conscience can judge specific actions before and after they are done (see CCC, 1780).

QUOTATION TO BE
INCLUDED IN FINAL PRINTING.

—CCC, 1780

All of us were told many things as we were growing up about what is right or proper and about what is wrong or inappropriate. We carry within us the messages from our early years. Violation of those messages can cause internal conflict.

Conscience is formed and molded—cultivated—by our culture and our community. Significant people in our lives, especially in our early lives, shape our sense of right and wrong.

Our conscience can judge these messages and senses from earlier in our lives. In terms of conscience, we have received valuable lessons from the authority figures of our past, but there are more lessons to learn. We have to educate our consciences.

Explain What role do Sacred Scripture and Sacred Tradition play in forming our conscience?

Elaborate Why can't we simply call our conscience our inner voice?

To Choose the Good

Our basic awareness of and orientation toward goodness is not all that there is to conscience. We must build on and develop this orientation. Therefore, when we speak about following our conscience, we are referring to an **informed conscience:** a conscience that is educated and developed through constant use and examination and learning about the teachings of the Church.

Beloved, do not believe every spirit, but test the spirits to see whether they are from God.

—1 John 4:1a

REFLECT

Significant persons from our childhood might include characters in books, television shows, or movies.

- Name some of these characters who have helped shape your conscience.

- What positive messages did you receive from each?

- What factors influence a person's perception of what is right and good?

Conscience seeks more knowledge, greater refinement, and deeper sensitivity. Therefore, this aspect of conscience refers to all those steps that we take to form and develop our moral capacity.

The *Catechism* expresses concisely what this dimension of conscience requires:

QUOTATION TO BE
INCLUDED IN FINAL PRINTING.

—CCC, 1785

We use the guidance of the Holy Spirit when we actively learn about Jesus, his teachings, and his deeds. It is the Holy Spirit's guidance that develops our habit of prayer and leads us to study Church teaching on morality and to seek advice from others. This is how the Holy Spirit guides the formation of our conscience and helps us grow into informed moral decision makers.

DISCUSS

When college seniors have a morality course, they often say, "This course should be taken in freshman year. By senior year my morality and values are already set." When college freshmen have a morality course, they often say, "This course should be taken in high school. By college my morality and values are already set." High school juniors and seniors sometimes remark that a morality course should be taken in ninth grade.

State your opinion on the following questions. Give reasons to support your opinions.

• Are a person's values ever completely set? Is moral development ever finished?

• Is junior or senior year of high school too late for a morality course to have an impact on the values and moral decision making of students?

APPLY

• Of the six sources that can lead to errors in judgment, which would you say are most common right now? Explain.

• In light of your answer, what would you say is the most important task involved in forming a moral conscience?

An important question related to conscience is: Even though we seek to be as conscientious as possible, can we judge wrongly? The answer to that question is yes. We are imperfect creatures subject to mistakes and misguided judgments. A conscience that judges wrongly, even after a period of conscientious decision-making, is an **erroneous judgment of conscience**—a conscience in error.

The *Catechism* lists six sources that can lead to errors in judgment:

• ignorance of Christ and his Gospel

• bad examples from other people

• enslavement to our passions; **disordered affections**

• assertion of a mistaken notion of **autonomy of conscience**, meaning relying on our own judgment separate from God

• rejecting Church authority and teaching

• lack of conversion and of charity (see CCC, 1792)

Educating our conscience is a lifelong responsibility. Other people may know better than we do that we are wrong. Likewise, hindsight—looking back after we have acted—can show us that we were wrong. Being conscientious means that we make judgments based on our present awareness of the good or evil of an action. We are responsible for seeking truth—especially the truths found in Church teaching—and for acting accordingly.

QUOTATION TO BE
INCLUDED IN FINAL PRINTING.

—CCC, 1801

We are responsible when we make little or no effort to discover what is true and good or when a conscience is blinded by repeatedly committing sin. In those cases, we are culpable for our evil actions (see CCC, 1791). When people do not follow their conscience on moral matters, then they may be committing a sin. We are obliged to follow the certain judgment of our rightly formed and correct conscience.

In making a moral decision, we sometimes make an error in judgment about moral conduct that is not our responsibility. Our ignorance, for example, can be at such a level that we make an error even though we think we're acting in good conscience. In these instances, we are not responsible for our erroneous judgment, and the sin committed cannot be attributed to us. The judgment, however, is still evil, and we have a responsibility to recognize that and correct such errors of moral conscience (see CCC, 1793).

Admittedly, since development of conscience differs somewhat with each individual, one person might conscientiously decide upon a course of action that another would find evil. When we follow our conscience, we remain subject to the limitations of our human condition. While we must keep this caution in mind, a person striving for the good, seeking truth, and acting conscientiously represents the glory and the grandeur of being created in God's image and likeness.

Describe What is an informed conscience?

Identify What three things assist us in forming our conscience?

A Christian Conscience

Conscience begins to develop in children from their earliest years. As they reach the age of reason—about the age of 7, they begin to be morally responsible for their actions. Through the conscience, a person

(CCC, 1778).

The proper formation of a Christian conscience is absolutely crucial to the moral life. Making good judgments is something that has to be learned—and practiced. There are many obstacles. As the *Catechism* states, QUOTATION TO BE INCLUDED IN FINAL PRINTING.

(CCC, 1783). Sin is the choice to act contrary to one's conscience and purposely do wrong. As the *Catechism* points out, sin is also QUOTATION TO BE INCLUDED IN FINAL PRINTING. (CCC, 1440).

Some people may develop a lax conscience and never develop a process of conscientious decision-making that has them face or think about the morality of their actions. Saint Bernard of Clairvaux (1090–1153), a French Cistercian monk, is said to be the author of the famous saying, "The road to hell is paved with good intentions." The saying means that more is required than intending to do something good. We must actually do good and avoid evil.

Unfortunately, even when Christians honestly want a conscience that is well-formed, they can make mistakes in moral judgment. A person may follow a process of conscientious decision-making but can unwittingly makes a wrong decision. A prudent judgment, by contrast, is a rational judgment made after careful consideration of moral principles and the circumstances of the situation.

Since conscience and judgments made with the conscience are usually private, we often take the invisible process of decision-making for granted. It's good to remember that even in everyday life, making good decisions and using your skills selflessly can have *huge* consequences.

GO TO THE SOURCE

First John reminds us to love not in word or speech, but in truth and action.

Read 1 John 3:18-23.

- What is the passage talking about by saying our hearts may condemn or not condemn us?

- If our hearts do not condemn us, why would God give us whatever we ask for?

- How do we know that Jesus abides in us?

ADVANCE REVIEW COPY

PRIMARY SOURCES

In a Catholic Worker newspaper article, social justice activist and Catholic Worker founder Dorothy Day (1897–1980) explained to fellow Catholics that Christ still asks his followers to love their neighbors as themselves. It must be done every single day. Day understood that many Catholics simply didn't understand what poor people dealt with. With Peter Maurin, a French Catholic intellectual, she founded the Catholic Worker movement in 1933.

During the Great Depression, millions of people were losing jobs, houses, and hope. Catholic Worker houses were founded all over the country to offer hospitality, meals, and sometimes lodging for the poor. Catholic Worker farms were established so that the hungry could grow their own food. The Catholic Worker newspaper, selling for a penny a copy, promoted Catholic Social Teaching and told the nation what the movement was doing across the country.

"We must talk about poverty, because people insulated by their own comfort lose sight of it," Day said. She spent her long life speaking, writing, and demonstrating on behalf of justice for the poor and for Christian nonviolence. She attended daily Mass and was devoted to the Rosary and the Sacraments. Day was a devoted witness for the Gospel until her death in New York City in 1980. Her cause for sainthood was opened in the Archdiocese of New York in 2000.

"What we would like to do is change the world—make it a little simpler for people to feed, clothe, and shelter themselves as God intended them to do. And, by fighting for better conditions, by crying out unceasingly for the rights of the workers, the poor, of the destitute—the rights of the worthy and the unworthy poor, in other words—we can, to a certain extent, change the world; we can work for the oasis, the little cell of joy and peace in a harried world. We can throw our pebble in the pond and be confident that its ever-widening circle will reach around the world. We repeat, there is nothing we can do but love, and, dear God, please enlarge our hearts to love each other, to love our neighbor, to love our enemy as our friend."

➚ Go to the student site at
hs.osvcurriculum.com

How did Dorothy Day think that "we" can change the world?

What did the Catholic Worker movement do to help Americans in need during the Great Depression?

Why did Dorothy Day think that social activists needed to talk about poverty all the time?

Dorothy Day founded the Catholic Worker Movement in 1933. Members today still fight poverty and help feed, clothe, and shelter people.

A well-informed conscience is properly educated. It has developed through use and the examination of one's action against Christian principles and Church teaching. The Christian can act morally with the Holy Spirit's help.

Our conscience allows us to assume responsibility for our actions. If someone commits evil, the right judgment of the person's conscience stays with that person as a universal truth of the good, even as the person knows the wrong he or she chose to do. When we figure out or confirm the sinful act that was done, we can then realize the forgiveness that must be asked for and the good that must be done in the future.

QUOTATION TO BE
INCLUDED IN FINAL PRINTING.

—CCC, 1781

Explain How does sin block our efforts to properly form our conscience?

Recall What is a prudent judgment?

SECTION 2 REVIEW

QUICK REVIEW

1a. Explain Tell why this statement is true: Conscience is the core of what we are.

b. Recall Name six sources of error in judgment?

c. Link Why is following your conscience a matter of freedom?

2a. Explain Why is it important for us to actively develop a well-formed conscience?

b. Determine Is this statement true or false: "A responsible person has a well-formed conscience"?

3a. Specify What actions should we take to develop a well-formed conscience?

b. Trace How might individual circumstances affect the development of a person's conscience?

4. Recall What was the goal of Dorothy Day and Peter Maurin in founding the Catholic Worker movement?

ACT

Work with a group of classmates to develop a story about the difference between a person with a well-formed conscience and another person with a faulty one.

- Decide on a plot and write the story. Consider ways to depict the two types of consciences.

- Present your work to classmates.

SELF-ASSESS

Which statement best reflects where you are now?

☐ I'm confident enough about the material in this section to be able to explain it to someone else.

☐ I have a good grasp of the material in this section, but I could use more review.

☐ I'm lost. I need help catching up before moving on.

ADVANCE REVIEW COPY

Sources of Grace

KEY TERMS IN THIS SECTION

justification

QUOTATION TO BE INCLUDED IN FINAL PRINTING.

(CCC, Glossary, p. 885).

reconciliation mercy and forgiveness as one is reconciled with the other. In the

Sacrament of Reconciliation,

QUOTATION TO BE INCLUDED IN FINAL PRINTING.

(CCC, Glossary, p. 896).

alienation an experience of isolation and separateness from God and others

eternal punishment the consequences of unforgiven grave or mortal sin that cuts communication with God making us incapable of eternal life

temperoral punishment the consequences of venial sin and forgiven mortal sins that have not been atoned for on Earth

The Sacraments provide the grace and strength we need to live a moral life. Through his Church, Christ instituted the Seven Sacraments to celebrate and sanctify the important moments of the Christian life.

The Seven Sacraments are celebrated at milestone moments in our lives as Catholics. There is

QUOTATION TO BE INCLUDED IN FINAL PRINTING.

The Sacraments

(CCC, 1210).

The Sacraments of Initiation

The three Sacraments of Initiation—Baptism, Confirmation, and the Eucharist—initiate us into the loving Catholic family, the Body of Christ. These Sacraments

QUOTATION TO BE INCLUDED IN FINAL PRINTING.

(CCC, 1533).

The Sacraments of Healing

Two of the Sacraments are known as the Sacraments of Healing—the Sacraments of Reconciliation and Anointing of the Sick. We need these Sacraments because sin or suffering can separate us from God and our brothers and sisters in the Body of Christ. Eventually, we all become physically sick, weak, or elderly. When

this happens, we need sacramental grace and anointing given by the Church. The Sacrament of Anointing of the Sick can bring physical healing as well as spiritual strength and peace. Healing the sick was a major part of the ministry of Jesus who then entrusted this work to the Church.

Sacraments at the Service of Communion

The two Sacraments at the Service of Communion are Holy Orders and Marriage. As the *Catechism* states, these two Sacraments

QUOTATION TO BE INCLUDED IN FINAL PRINTING.

(CCC, 1534).

A priest listens during the Sacrament of Reconciliation, one of the Sacraments of Healing.

Baptism and Confirmation

Effects of the Sacrament of Baptism include purification from sins, new life in the Holy Spirit, a share in the priesthood of Christ, and incorporation into the Church, the Body of Christ (see CCC, 1267-1268). All sins are forgiven through the Sacrament of Baptism, including Original Sin and personal sins as well as all punishment for sin.

QUOTATION TO BE
INCLUDED IN FINAL PRINTING.

—CCC, 1263

At the same time, certain temporal consequences of sin stay with the baptized, namely suffering, illness, death, weakness of character, and an inclination to sin among others (see CCC, 1964). Baptism not only forgives all our sin, but we become what the *Catechism* calls

(CCC,
1265).

When we are baptized in the name of the Holy Trinity, we receive sanctifying grace, also called the grace of **justification**, which:

- enables us to believe in God, to hope in him, and to love him through the theological virtues of faith, hope, and love

- gives us the power to live and to act through the prompting of the Holy Spirit who provides us gifts to prepare us for his guidance

- allows us to grow in righteousness through the moral virtues (see CCC, 1266).

Our entire spiritual life is rooted in the Sacrament of Baptism. The baptized person now belongs to Christ, who died and rose for all. Therefore, we now serve others and obey the Church's authority. In return, we have rights in the Church, such as receiving the Sacraments, hearing the Word of God, and receiving spiritual help from the Church. We are united through the Church (see CCC, 1269).

APPLY

Saint Ambrose reminds everyone who has been confirmed to:

"Recall then that you have received the spiritual seal, the spirit of wisdom and understanding, the spirit of right judgment and courage, the spirit of knowledge and reverence, the spirit of holy fear in God's presence.

"Guard what you have received.

"God the Father has marked you with his sign; Christ the Lord has confirmed you and has placed his pledge, the Spirit, in your hearts."

- Why would Saint Ambrose tell the confirmed to "guard what you have received"?

- What does this say to you now?

The Sacrament of Confirmation completes the grace of Baptism. As we mentioned, in the Sacrament of Confirmation, baptized people are more perfectly bound to the Church. They are also

(CCC, 1285). Both Baptism and Confirmation are given only once because they seal the soul with an
from Christ, who marks us with the seal of the Holy Spirit (CCC, 1304).

(CCC, 1272).

Recall Which three Sacraments ground the common vocations for all of Christ's disciples?

Tell What does sanctifying grace, or the grace of justification, do for those who baptized?

Sacrament of the Eucharist

The Sacrament of the Eucharist completes our Christian initiation. It is the source and summit of our life of faith. Holy Communion that we receive at Mass keeps us in intimate union with Christ and the Catholic Church (see CCC, 1396 and 1398). A moral life in Christ has the Eucharist as its foundation. Life and resurrection are given to all who share in the Eucharistic liturgy and receive Christ (see CCC, 1391). To

ADVANCE REVIEW COPY

grow in the Christian life, we need the nourishment of the Eucharist, the
(CCC, 1392).

The Eucharist separates us from sin. With Holy Communion, we receive the Body of Christ—given up for us—and the Blood of Christ—"'this is my blood of the covenant, which is poured out for many for the forgiveness of sins'" (Matthew 26:28). The *Catechism* explains:

QUOTATION TO BE
INCLUDED IN FINAL PRINTING.

—CCC, 1393

Saint Ambrose pointed out that as often as we proclaim the Death of Jesus and his blood is poured, we proclaim the forgiveness of sins. We should always participate in the Eucharistic liturgy and receive Holy Communion, especially because we constantly sin. "Because I always sin, I should always have a remedy," Saint Ambrose reasoned.

Daily life tends to weaken our charity toward others, but the Eucharist strengthens it.
(CCC, 1394). The situation is different with mortal, or grave sins. The more we share in the life of Christ, the more difficult it is to separate ourselves from him through mortal sin. So the Eucharist preserves us from mortal sin in the future. The Eucharist, though,

QUOTATION TO BE
INCLUDED IN FINAL PRINTING.

(CCC, 1395).

The Eucharist also commits Catholics to caring for the poor. If we receive the Body and Blood of Christ, which was given up for us, then we must recognize Christ in the poorest among us. As God frees us from sin and invites us to the Eucharistic table, we must become more merciful (see CCC, 1397).

The Eucharist is the anticipation of our glory in Heaven, which is the goal of living a moral life.

QUOTATION TO BE
INCLUDED IN FINAL PRINTING.

—CCC, 1404

Sacrament of Reconciliation

When Peter asks Jesus about forgiving others, Jesus' response shows how we are constantly in need of forgiveness. Jesus tells us that we should forgive one another. Forgiveness is an important aspect of our moral life because it repairs relationships and helps right our wrongs. It also follows the example of Christ.

> Then Peter came and said to him, 'Lord, if another member of the church sins against me, how often should I forgive? As many as seven times?' Jesus said to him, 'Not seven times, but, I tell you, seventy-seven times.'

—Matthew 18:21-22

Jesus instituted the Sacrament of Reconciliation—also called Penance or Confession—to reconcile us to God. The faithful who are truly sorry for their sins can receive forgiveness through this Sacrament. Through Penance, if we have sinned mortally, we are restored to God's grace. If we have committed venial sins, we receive an increase of grace. Approached with a contrite heart and a religious frame of mind, the Sacrament brings a   as our dignity and blessings as sons and daughters of God are restored (CCC, 1468).

The Sacrament of Reconciliation unites us once again with the Catholic Church if we have separated ourselves from her. It revitalizes the life of the Church, which suffers from the sin of her individual members (see CCC, 1469). The *Catechism* points out that our reconciliation with God through this Sacrament leads to strengthening the bond with other members of the Church.

QUOTATION TO BE
INCLUDED IN FINAL PRINTING.

—CCC, 1469

Reconciliation has important implications for eternal life. When we participate in the Sacrament, we put ourselves before God in anticipating the judgment at the end of our lives. In our current life, God gives us the freedom to choose eternal life through our decisions. We can only enter Heaven through conversion of our hearts. Grave sin excludes us from eternal life with God.

QUOTATION TO BE
INCLUDED IN FINAL PRINTING.

(CCC, 1470).

All personal sins committed after Baptism can be forgiven by the Sacrament of Reconciliation. Our participation in this Sacrament presumes our willingness to repent of our sins, genuine sorrow for the sins we have committed, and a resolve to sin no more in the future. We partake of the Sacrament of Reconciliation by confessing our sins to a duly authorized priest, having the intention to make reparation for our sins, and receiving the priest's absolution.

As part of the Sacrament, the priest gives a penance in the form of certain prayers or actions. These acts of penance help us to repair the damage caused by our sins and to lead a life worthy of our call to follow Christ.

Without forgiveness we are out of touch with God and with one another. **Alienation**, a sense of distance and separateness from others and of uneasiness around others, is unsettling and saps our energy. To be spiritually renewed and revitalized, we need to experience forgiveness. With forgiveness comes reconciliation—a word that means reuniting and getting back in touch with others. Therefore, reconciliation is the means of overcoming alienation and of achieving a return to a sense of belonging. We can see how alienation might foster immorality while a spirit of reconciliation supports moral behavior.

There are two types of punishment for sins, eternal and temporal punishment. **Eternal punishment** in Hell deprives the soul of union with God and eternal happiness in Heaven. It results from unforgiven mortal sins that break our union with God and render us incapable of eternal life with him.

Temporal punishment for venial sins and forgiven mortal sins that have not been atoned for on Earth takes place in Purgatory. Venial sin results from what the *Catechism* describes as an _____ (CCC, 1472). This must be purified either in our earthly life, or in Purgatory after we have died. These punishments do not come from God's vengeance; rather they result from the nature of sin. They are the reason that conversion from sin is vital (see CCC, 1472).

QUOTATION TO BE
INCLUDED IN FINAL PRINTING.

—CCC, 1472

Mathilda gives the poet Dante a drink in Purgatory in this oil painting by Jean Delville (1876–1953) depicting Dante Alighieri's *The Divine Comedy*.

GO TO THE SOURCE

Jesus shows scribes the authority given to him.

Read Mark 2:1-12.

- What did describing how the paralyzed man entered the building show?
- What did the scribes find blasphemous?
- What has amazed you about the mercy of God?

ADVANCE REVIEW COPY

Holy Orders and Marriage

The Sacraments of Holy Orders and Marriage focus on the salvation of others and give us grace to live a moral life. While they concentrate on personal salvation, this is accomplished through service of others in union with the Church.

QUOTATION TO BE
INCLUDED IN FINAL PRINTING.

(CCC, 1534).

QUOTATION TO BE
INCLUDED IN FINAL PRINTING.

—CCC, 1535

CONNECT

- How are the Sacraments and the moral life linked together?

All through our lives, as we journey in faith, the Sacraments offer us life-giving milestones. We stop at these divinely instituted experiences to be nourished, strengthened, and encouraged as we make our way to God.

Explain How does the Eucharist nourish our moral life?

Identify What important implications does the Sacrament of Reconciliation have for eternal life?

SECTION 3 REVIEW

QUICK REVIEW

1a. Recall What will give us the grace and strength to lead a moral life?

b. Tell Why is forgiveness important?

c. List What are the purposes of the Sacraments of Initiation? the Sacraments of Healing? the Sacraments at the Service of Communion?

2a. Name What are the major effects of the Sacrament of Baptism?

b. Identify What temporal consequences of sin stay with the baptized person?

c. Describe What does the grace of justification do?

3a. Relate How does the Sacrament of Reconciliation continue the mission of Baptism?

b. Recall Who does the forgiven penitent reconcile himself with?

c. Connect What implications does reconciliation have for eternal life?

d. Link How does reconciliation overcome alienation?

4a. Identify What is our foundation of a moral life in Christ?

b. Explain What does the Eucharist do to our sins?

c. Connect What is the connection between the Eucharist and mortal or grave sin?

5. Explain How do the Sacraments of Holy Orders and Marriage relate to the moral life?

Write Compose a journal entry based on your experiences with reconciliation.

- Choose an incident when you forgave someone or received forgiveness.

- Explore how the incident made you feel about the other person.

Pray Compose a short act of faith, hope, or love based on what you learned in this section of the chapter.

SELF-ASSESS

Which statement best reflects where you are now?

☐ I'm confident enough about the material in this section to be able to explain it to someone else.

☐ I have a good grasp of the material in this section, but I could use more review.

☐ I'm lost. I need help catching up before moving on.

Living Like Christ

Along with the Sacraments, prayer offers us the grace and strength to lead a moral life. At the first Pentecost, the Apostles devoted themselves to prayer, and the Holy Spirit, who teaches the Church about everything Jesus said, also forms her in the life of prayer (see CCC, 2623). The Holy Spirit unites us through prayer to Christ. Through our devotion to prayer, we are united in the Church with Mary, Jesus' Mother and our Mother, who shows us the way to her Son (see CCC, 2673).

We, who go about our daily lives surrounded by temptations and difficulties, have Mary, our Mother, as our inspiration and guide. She can pray to Jesus, her Son, for us. He is our one mediator and the focus of our prayer, while Mary shows the way to Christ and is in fact the sign of the way to him (see CCC, 2674).

Mary is important to the Christian moral life because her life magnifies the Lord as noted in countless hymns and in the Magnificat. We venerate her as the one who

(CCC, 2675).

'My soul magnifies the Lord,
and my spirit rejoices in God my Savior,
for he has looked with favor on the lowliness of his servant.'

—Luke 1:46-48a

The Hail Mary and all prayer is described as the QUOTATION TO BE INCLUDED IN FINAL PRINTING. (CCC, 2697). We must pray at all times, but we can only do that by first praying at specific times.

(CCC, 2697).

GO TO **THE SOURCE**

Several key concepts in this course can be found in the Acts of the Apostles Chapter 2.

Read Acts 2.

- List two effects of the Holy Spirit.
- List three essential points Saint Peter makes in his speech.
- Describe how the Apostles and the early Church lived at that time.
- How can this apply to living the moral life?

ADVANCE REVIEW COPY

In 2009, when Pope Benedict XVI visited Africa, the growing Catholic population on the continent was estimated at 158 million. By 2025, one-sixth (or 230 million) of the world's Catholics are expected to be African. As the Catholic population in Africa continues to grow, so too does the number of priests. The world's largest seminary is in Nigeria, and over all, Africa produces the largest percentage of priests. From 2007 to 2012, the percentage of seminarians entering African seminaries grew by fourteen percent.

- In general terms, what's happening to Catholic population growth in Africa?

Young people dance near Pope Benedict XVI during his 2009 visit to Benin in western Africa.

↗ Go to the student site at **hs.osvcurriculum.com**

The Holy Spirit forms the Church in her life of prayer. Through living a moral life, our hearts become ordered to Christ.

QUOTATION TO BE
INCLUDED IN FINAL PRINTING.

(CCC, 2700).

Vocal prayer, meaning praying with spoken words, is essential for Catholics because it gives us grace and strength to live the moral life. Jesus taught us the Our Father and gave us many examples of vocal prayer, as when he prayed aloud. "Abba, Father, for you all things are possible; remove this cup from me; yet, not what I want, but what you want" (Mark 14:36). We need to involve the senses in our prayer because we are body and spirit.

QUOTATION TO BE
INCLUDED IN FINAL PRINTING.
(CCC, 2702).

Meditation and contemplative prayer are forms of mental prayer. They are important methods of prayer as well. In meditation, we try to understand QUOTATION TO BE INCLUDED IN FINAL PRINTING. (CCC, 2705). It engages our ideas, our imagination, and our emotions and desires.

QUOTATION TO BE
INCLUDED IN FINAL PRINTING.

(CCC, 2708).

Contemplative prayer is described by Saint Teresa of Avila as a (CCC, 2709). It is taking time to be alone with Jesus, the one who loves us. Contemplative prayer is when we, as sons and daughters of God, welcome the love of God with a desire to respond by sharing our love more. The *Catechism* describes contemplative prayer as a gift, a grace, and an intense time of prayer (see CCC, 2713 and 2714). We fixate on Christ, hear the Word of God, and pray in silence. It is a union with Christ that makes us part of his mystery that the Church celebrates in the Eucharist. And here is where it translates to our moral life.

QUOTATION TO BE
INCLUDED IN FINAL PRINTING.
(CCC, 2718).

Prayer is connected with the theological virtues that help us lead a moral life. A necessary dimension of living the virtues is prayer, our mysterious encounter with God (see CCC, 2591).

Through prayer we reach out to God and discover that he is already reaching out to us. God takes the initiative; prayer is always a response to his presence within us. Each of the theological virtues is ultimately connected with prayer.

Faith is prayerful longing to encounter the mystery of God, confident that he makes such an encounter possible. We always pray in *hope*, trusting that he will answer our prayers even if not in the way we would like. And finally, *love* is the source and goal of all prayer since ultimately prayer is a loving relationship with God (see CCC, 2658).

And all along our journey, we are united in prayer by the Holy Spirit to Jesus, his Church, and to Mary, the Mother of God.

Identify How is Mary important to our Christian moral life?

Connect How are the moral life and prayer connected?

Living Christ's Moral Teaching

We have studied Jesus Christ as the teacher of Christian morality. We find Christ in his Church, and we receive continuing guidance in morality through the Church. Jesus appointed the Apostles to be teachers in his name. Likewise, the successors to the Apostles—the Pope and bishops in union with him—carry on their role as teachers, ensuring that Church teaching remains faithful to Jesus and the Apostles. As the Magisterium, the Pope and the bishops instruct us in the faith, which we apply to our moral lives.

We know that we are nourished and strengthened by the Word of God in living a moral life. Guided by the Holy Spirit, the Church's

GO TO THE **SOURCE**

Saint Paul offers some advice on how we ought to pray.

Read Romans 8:26.

- How can you better respond to the Holy Spirit and let him deepen your prayer life?

Magisterium authentically interprets the Word of God found in Scripture or in the form of Sacred Tradition. The Magisterium ensures that the Church remains faithful to the teaching of the Apostles in matters of faith and morals. The Magisterium studies moral questions involving natural law and reason that arise in our changing world and provides us with guidance for moral decision-making.

Mary, the Mother of God, always leads us to her Son, Jesus, and her life is an important example for growing in the Christian moral life. At the beginning of the public ministry of Jesus, Mary offered advice to those serving the wedding in Cana—and to us. At the wedding feast which she and Jesus and several of his earliest followers were attending, the wine ran out. One of those disciples with Jesus was John. John was an eyewitness to the first miracle of Jesus and the role that the mother of Jesus played in it (see John 2:1-12).

Scripture and Morality

The Church constantly is nourished and strengthened by God's Word. To truly appreciate the moral wisdom found in the Bible, we must keep in mind the following biblical facts:

1. By inspiring its human authors, God is the true author of Scripture.

2. To interpret the words of Scripture, (CCC, 137). Knowing the context of each Bible passage can be helpful in doing this. We must always interpret each part of Scripture in the context of the whole message of Scripture.

3. The Catholic Church defines the Bible as the forty-six books of the Old Testament and the twenty-seven books of the New Testament.

4. Because Jesus is the focus of the four Gospels, they occupy a place of great importance and centrality in the life of the Church.

ADVANCE REVIEW COPY

When Jesus intervened, at the request of his Mother, the servers may have wondered why they should take six empty stone water jars and fill them with water. There was no wine left to serve wedding guests.

"'Do whatever he tells you,'" Mary told the servants (John 2:5).

Doing what Jesus tells us is a first step. "Hearing" Jesus requires us to prayerfully listen. The Church founded by Jesus guides us and strengthens us to follow in his footsteps once we understand his will. The Church invites us to become incorporated into Christ through the Sacraments (see CCC, 1694). This union is called "mystical" because it participates in the mystery of Christ through the Sacraments.

The Church also tutors us in prayer.

Though thousands of books and sermons about prayer have been shared with the Christian community, one of the most useful explanations of prayer is more than a thousand years old. Prayer is the "raising of one's heart and mind to God," wrote the eighth-century Doctor of the Church, Saint John Damascene. Saint John's description of prayer has stood the test of time. The

Catechism uses it at the beginning of its section on Christian prayer. At every age and in every situation, we can raise our hearts and mind to God, seeking an ever more intimate union with Christ (see CCC, 2014).

As the Catholic Church and Gospels also remind us, we will live like Jesus when we can accept his Cross. "'If any want to become my followers, let them deny themselves and take up their cross and follow me,'" Jesus told his disciples (Matthew 16:24). The *Catechism* further explains that:

QUOTATION TO BE INCLUDED IN FINAL PRINTING.   (CCC, 2015).

Spiritual progress and growth in our moral life means practicing strong self-discipline that leads over time to living in the peace and joy of the Beatitudes.

In personal prayer, in regular participation in Mass which is the community's prayer of praise, and in living in accordance with the moral teachings of Christ and his Church, we live like Jesus. We can do so because we have been given the courage, grace, and strength to do whatever he tells us.

Hail Mary

Probably the best-known prayer to Mary is the Ave Maria, or Hail Mary. It expresses a two-fold movement of prayer to the Mother of God. The first part magnifies the Lord for the great things he did for her, the lowliest of his servants. The second part asks Mary to intercede for us to God. The *Catechism* breaks down the prayer this way:

Hail Mary: God speaks through the angel Gabriel, and we dare to invoke the same greeting for this servant of God.

Full of grace, the Lord is with thee: again echoing Gabriel, we recognize the grace Mary has received. She is full of grace because the Lord is with her. He is the source of all grace and fills her with grace.

Blessed art thou among women and blessed is the fruit of they womb, Jesus: this part echoes the greeting of Mary's cousin Elizabeth, who is the first to call her blessed.

Holy Mary, Mother of God: We marvel as Elizabeth did about why the Mother of the Lord would visit us. Because she gives us Jesus, her Son, we can be confident that she will pray for us.

Pray for us sinners, now and the hour of our death: As we acknowledge ourselves as sinners, we ask the all-holy Mother of God to pray for us. We entrust our cares to her in the present and when we die confident that she will be present to us as she was at the Cross to lead us to her Son, Jesus, in Heaven (see CCC, 2676 and 2677).

A balloon Rosary floats above a crowd waiting to hear Pope Benedict XVI in Lebanon.

How often do you call on Mary by praying the Hail Mary?

When have you called on the help of Mary in your life?

Memorize the Magnificat.

ADVANCE REVIEW COPY

QUOTATION TO BE
INCLUDED IN FINAL PRINTING.

—CCC, 2016

REFLECT

Mary played a role in Jesus' first miracle.

- What message about living like Jesus can we learn from Mary in the Gospel story about the wedding feast at Cana?

Incorporated Into Christ

The constant thought behind living a moral life is uniting ourselves with Christ. We are incorporated into Christ through our Baptism and the moral life keeps us connected with him.

QUOTATION TO BE
INCLUDED IN FINAL PRINTING.

(CCC, 1694).

The grace we receive from the Sacraments and through living a moral life does not negatively impact our freedom. In fact, the opposite is true.

QUOTATION TO BE
INCLUDED IN FINAL PRINTING.

—CCC, 1742

We are free from the unhealthy pressures and choices that society makes if we stay united with Christ. Jesus told us so when he said: "'If you continue in my word, you are truly my disciples; and you will know the truth, and truth will make you free'" (John 8:31-32). We want to be united with Christ because it is the love of Christ that is the source of the goodness of our acts and our character. The saints know that our merits are pure grace, as Saint Thérèse of Lisieux says:

> I thank You, O my God! for all the graces You have granted me, especially the grace of making me pass through the crucible of suffering. It is with joy I shall contemplate You on the Last Day carrying the sceptre of Your Cross.

—Saint Thérèse

Explain How does the Church help strengthen our moral life?

Recall What does Jesus say we have to do to become one of his followers and how is that connected with living a moral life?

QUICK REVIEW

1a. Relate How is prayer "the life of the new heart"?

b. Connect How are the theological virtues connected to prayer?

2a. Identify Where does the way of perfection pass?

b. Recall What are three ways we can live like Jesus?

3a. Reflect What lesson are we meant to draw from the story of the wedding at Cana?

b. Consider If we are to make spiritual progress, what does that mean?

c. Recall How does the grace we receive from the Sacraments impact our freedom?

4. Relate What is the source of the goodness of our actions?

Listen and Discuss In a small group, name one thing you have discovered or remembered about the Holy Spirit because of this chapter and listen to the thoughts shared by the others.

SELF-ASSESS

Which statement best reflects where you are now?

☐ I'm confident enough about the material in this section to be able to explain it to someone else.

☐ I have a good grasp of the material in this section, but I could use more review.

☐ I'm lost. I need help catching up before moving on.

ADVANCE REVIEW COPY

PRAYER

Opening Prayer

We begin in the name of the Father and the Son and Holy Spirit.
Lord God, help us to be people of intentional discipleship, committed to Jesus your Son.

Help us to understand the beauty of your joyous Gospel and the transforming power of your grace.

Strengthen us as disciples of Jesus, committed to the mission of the Church and eager to share the Good News of your Son with the Holy Spirit's Gift of fortitude.

Like your disciples, let our own hearts burn within us as we share your message of your loving plan for us.

Through Christ our Lord,

Amen.

Closing Prayer

Lord, help us to be faithful disciples in the small things, realizing that it is where we will learn to be worthy of your trust in the greater things.
Lord, help us to be faithful disciples to the great treasure of the Gospel you have placed in the care of your Church. Keep reminding us that your Gospel is joyful.

Lord, help us to realize that there is work to be done in our journey of discipleship. From the moment we arise until the moment we lie down, make our every thought and action pleasing to you.

For the times we have failed in being your disciple, please forgive us. Forgive us for the times we are half-hearted in our efforts, lazy in our approach, and lacking joy in our convictions.

Finally, send your Holy Spirit to remind us that you are ever faithful to us. Help us to follow the model of your Son who willingly gave his life that we may have life in him.

Through Christ our Lord,

Amen.

ADVANCE REVIEW COPY

TERMS

Use each of the following terms in a sentence that shows you know what the term means in the context of the chapter. You may include more than one term in a sentence.

Gifts of the Holy Spirit

docile

Fruits of the Holy Spirit

informed conscience

erroneous judgment of conscience

disordered affections

autonomy of conscience

justification

reconciliation

alienation

eternal punishment

temporal punishment

PEOPLE AND IDEAS

Define each person or idea in the context of the chapter.

1. Blessed Pier Giorgio Frassati

2. Saint Maximilian Kolbe

3. sodality

4. Saint Teresa of Avila

5. Dorothy Day

6. Peter Maurin

7. Catholic Worker movement

8. Magisterium

9. Wedding at Cana

10. Saint John Damascene

11. Saint Thérèse of Lisieux

UNDERSTANDING

Answer each question and complete each exercise

SECTION 1

1. **Explain** What did Jesus mean when he said, "'I am the way, and the truth, and the life'" (John 14:6)?

2. **Summarize** How was the life of Saint Maximilian Kolbe a series of spiritual battles?

3. **Explain** How does Confirmation more completely connect us to the faith?

4. **Conclude** How do the Gifts of the Holy Spirit and the Fruits of the Holy Spirit help us sustain a moral life?

SECTION 2

5. **Explain** How is a conscience the voice of God?

6. **Reflect** What are cultural and community influences on conscience formation?

7. **Evaluate** Can a conscientious person make an incorrect moral judgment? Explain?

8. **Retell** How did Dorothy Day work to inform consciences?

SECTION 3

9. **Link** How is the Sacrament of Reconciliation connected to the Sacrament of Baptism?

10. **List** What are the benefits of the Sacrament of Penance?

11. **Recall** What is eternal and temporal punishment?

12. **Connect** What is the connection between the Eucharist and mortal or grave sin?

ADVANCE REVIEW COPY

13. **Reflect** What must we do to become followers of Christ?

14. **Consider** Why is the Church's union with God considered mystical?

15. **Explain** How do the Sacraments impact our freedom?

CONNECTING

Visual This photograph from Cuba shows Father Domingo Lorenzo meeting with convicted murderer Jose Cipriano Rodriguez, a short while before Rodriguez was executed.

What does the image convey about reconciliation and justice? What led these men to this situation? What is the Holy Spirit's role?

Challenge You are driving to a game and talking about some unwise choices that some friends have made when another friend asks a question: How can you tell if some decision is bad or good? How do you answer that questions using the information from this chapter.

Question After working through this chapter, what advice would you give someone who wants to know why Catholics pay so much attention to Church teachings and to the Word of God?

Imagine In this chapter, you read about the message we received from the account of the miracle at the wedding in Cana. Think about a specific way that you could share that message.

- What method would you choose?

- How would you use the medium to convey the message?

- How would you circulate your work to the greatest number of people?

SELF-ASSESS

On Your Own Make a list of the most important things you learned from this chapter.

Select three things that represent your growth in understanding as you worked through this chapter. Write a paragraph explaining your choices.

With a Partner List what you found most helpful or interesting in this chapter as well as any other questions that have surfaced.

As Catholics, we travel the journey that Jesus asked his disciples to follow. We do it as a community of believers. Jesus made it clear that discipleship was not something to be lived on one's own in a "me and Jesus" relationship. He established the Church based on the rock of Saint Peter and the Apostles, and entrusted to them the Good News of salvation, his mission, and saving work. In every generation, through their successors, the Pope and bishops in union with him, continue to lead the Church and uphold her in the truth. Inspired by the Holy Spirit, the Pope and bishops hand on the faith of the Apostles until Christ returns in glory.

With Peter as their first universal leader, the Bible says "they devoted themselves to the Apostles' teaching and fellowship, the breaking of the bread and to the prayers." (Acts 2:42). The "Breaking of the bread" and "the prayers" refers to the celebration of the Eucharist. In so doing, the Apostles and disciples followed Jesus' command to "do this in memory of me." Catholicism traces its roots to Peter and the Apostles. It is a historical fact.

The Catholic Church preserves the special gifts, given to Peter, the Apostles, and the disciples. These make us who we are and are at the center of our Catholic identity. However, we know that many expressions of holiness and truth exist outside the Church. Catholics base their faith and beliefs on Jesus' revelation of the Trinity, his founding of the Church, the Sacraments, Scripture and Tradition, and other gifts listed below. We root our Catholic belief in the Paschal Mystery—Jesus' Passion, Death, Resurrection, and Ascension.

The gifts, given by Jesus to the Church, are described here in terms of "special characteristics." Taken together, they form the core of Catholic belief and practice. In a sense, they make us Catholic. These characteristics are consistent in Catholic Tradition from the time of the Apostles. They have not and will not change, no matter what's happening in society and the world. In every generation the Church passes them on to the next and teaches why they are important to understanding ourselves and our calling in life.

Characteristics of Catholicism

1. The Church is Trinitarian.	The great mystery of the Trinity—God the Father, God the Son, and God the Holy Spirit—permeates every aspect of Catholic belief, practice, and worship. The Trinity is a unity of three equal, yet distinct Persons, possessing the same divine nature. The Trinity is a divine community, from which all loving human communities take their origin. The communal nature of the Catholic Church is based in the Trinity.
	The Trinity is the central mystery of our faith. Trinitarian belief roots who Catholics are, what we believe, how we pray, and what we teach. The Church administers the Sacraments using the Trinitarian formula. In the Rite of Baptism, for example, the bishop, priest, or deacon baptizes in the name of the Father, and of the Son, and of the Holy Spirit. The priest invokes the Trinity in the Eucharistic Liturgy, the Sacraments, and the Divine Office. Catholics begin and end their prayers with the Sign of the Cross, a reminder of our Baptism and the Trinity.
	Every time the Church celebrates the Eucharist, we remember the reality of Trinitarian love, witnessed in Jesus' eternal sacrifice, which he offered to the Father through the Holy Spirit. In the Eucharist, we receive Jesus, really present, Body and Blood, soul and divinity. Church members are united to Christ and one another. Together we form the Mystical Body of Christ.

Characteristics of Catholicism

2. The Church is Christ-centered.	The Catholic faith centers on Jesus Christ, *(Catechism of the Catholic Church,* 423). Jesus is the alpha and the omega, the beginning and end of all things. Jesus is the heart and center of the Catholic faith. He is the way, the truth, and the life. He reveals deep mysteries of the Triune God, heads the Church, shows us the moral path to salvation, and gives us the Sacraments as means to salvation. He teaches us about his Father and sends the Holy Spirit to be with us always.
	Because of his great love, Jesus died on the cross for our sins and rose from the dead. He left us a perpetual reminder of his sacrifice in the Mass, when he is present among us, body and blood, soul and divinity. Jesus invites us into an intimate relationship of friendship with him, encourages us to praise the Triune God, and tells us to ask God for help in our needs. He promises eternal life to his faithful followers.
3. The Church is a community.	Jesus gifted us with the love that the three Persons in the Trinity share with each other. He founded his Church on the divine love that the Trinity has for humankind. United in the Holy Spirit, this Pilgrim People lives in the world, as Jesus did, but aspires for a more fulfilling happiness than this world provides. The Church anticipates Jesus' coming again and our eternal reward in Heaven.
	The Trinity, a communion of love, shares divine grace through the Church, which is the Sacrament of the Trinity's unity with the People of God. The Church gives us the age-old teachings and practices that keep us on the right path. These are Jesus' gifts to us. Indeed, Catholicism is a community-based faith, following Jesus' way and inspired by the Holy Spirit that praises and honors the Father in appreciation for what we received.
	Catholics on Earth are united in faith and love with the Saints in Heaven and the souls Purgatory. We call this the "Communion of Saints." Every Sunday at Mass, we pray in the Creed: "I believe in the communion of saints." After Mass, some Catholics remain and pray the Rosary or before a statue of a Saint. Our grandparent, aunt, or uncle may have a prayer table at home with a picture of a deceased loved one and a candle. Because we on Earth are united with the Saints in Heaven and the souls in Purgatory, we ask all our friends to pray for us—those living on Earth, those being purified in Purgatory, and those rejoicing forever in Heaven.
4. The Church is sacramental.	Jesus is the fundamental Sacrament and most fully reveals God to us. The Catholic Church is a sacramental people. She carries on Christ's work on Earth and communicates his message and way of life through her teaching, social ministries, and liturgy. The seven Sacraments of the Catholic Church continue to celebrate Jesus' Paschal Mystery, each one celebrating a special aspect of this Mystery. The Sacraments are holy signs of God's desire to be one with us. For example, Baptism gives us the new life of grace, as we are reborn as sons and daughters of God. Matrimony reflects God's desire to share his love in the love that a husband and wife have for each other. Every Sacrament celebrates God's love and invites us into a special relationship with Jesus through the Sacrament celebrated.
	Sacramental belief is fundamental to who we are and what we do as Catholics. The Sacraments help us fulfill our spiritual needs and draw us into relationships with Christ and one another. Instituted by Christ to give us grace, the seven Sacraments are outward signs of this grace. They use rituals and symbols reflecting the holy presence of the divine.
	As concrete actions rooted in the things that we use daily (water, bread, wine), Sacraments do two things: they point beyond themselves to something else—a sacred reality—and they bring about what they signify by making that reality present—new life, healing, forgiveness, membership, and so on. We know that Sacraments point to something else, but often we forget that they bring about or effect what they signify. For example, the Anointing of the Sick brings about spiritual and sometimes physical healing.
	Catholic sacramentality goes beyond the seven Sacraments. Rooted in them, we celebrate other sacred signs of God's love, called *sacramentals*. They bear a certain resemblance to the Sacraments, but are given to us by the Church, not Christ. Catholics walk into a Catholic Church, dip their hand into "holy water," and make the Sign of the Cross. We genuflect or bow to Jesus, present in the tabernacle, before entering their pew and kneeling down. Some Catholics focus on the life-sized crucifix hanging above the altar. During Advent, we see a wreath with four candles at the front of the church. During Easter, we see a large, white Paschal candle near the altar. If we attend a Baptism, we see oils and water. Catholics use colors, symbols, and actions that speak to us in ways that don't require words.

Characteristics of Catholicism

5. The Church is Eucharistic.	The root meaning of Eucharist in Greek means "thanksgiving." Our thanksgiving rests in the great sacrifice that Jesus offered for us on the cross, which we celebrate in the Eucharist.

As a sacramental community, Catholics root everything in the Eucharist. All the other Sacraments lead to it and flow from it. The Eucharist is the source and summit of our lives. Catholics also call the celebration of the Eucharist "the Mass." The Eucharist is not simply a symbolic reminder of Jesus' sacrifice. Christ is present in this celebration in special ways. He is present in the community gathered together, in the Word proclaimed, in the person of the priest-celebrant, and most especially in the consecrated Eucharistic species, Jesus' Body and Blood.

By "Real Presence" we mean that the Eucharist is the real presence of Christ, whole and entire, under the appearances of bread and wine. While a memorial of Jesus' sacrifice on the cross, the Eucharist is more. It is Christ's real presence.

In a wide sense, Catholics realize that we can be "eucharist" to each other when we share God's love with others. Since God dwells within us, we give thanks for the blessings we received by sharing our gifts with our brothers and sisters. |
| **6. The Church is biblically based.** | The *Catechism* says, QUOTATION TO BE INCLUDED IN FINAL PRINTING. (CCC, 103-104). These words indicate the importance of Scripture for Catholics.

The early Church saw the Old Testament as containing the revelation of God's plan of salvation for humankind. They recognized the unity of this plan in the Old and New Testaments, studied the prophecies of a coming Messiah, and showed how Jesus fulfilled them. New Testament writers wrote down faithfully the teachings of Jesus and interpreted the Old Testament in light of his death and Resurrection (see CCC, 129).

New Testament writers, under the inspiration of the Holy Spirit, testified to the faith of the early Christian community. The New Testament must be interpreted in light of this faith, passed down to us in the Church's Tradition. Scripture and Sacred Tradition are bound closely together, as two distinct modes of transmitting God's Revelation.

Catholics cherish the Scripture, read it, and use it in their prayers. The Church's Liturgy of the Hours and the Sacraments, and especially the Mass, contain readings from both New and Old Testaments. The Church encourages Catholics to read and study the Scriptures as key sources of spiritual nourishment and growth. |
| **7. The Church is one.** | There are four marks of the Catholic Church, that is, essential identifying characteristics by which she is known—one, holy, catholic, and apostolic. The descriptions that follow, as all the summaries in this section, are overviews to give the general sense of each.

QUOTATION TO BE INCLUDED IN FINAL PRINTING. (CCC, 813).

(CCC, 813).

The Church is one Body in Christ, in faith, in the Sacraments, and in hope (see CCC, 866). The Church is formed and united through the work of the Holy Spirit and under the leadership of the bishops united with the bishop of Rome, the Pope. |
| **8. The Church is holy.** |) (CCC, 823)

The Church is made holy because of her union with Christ; in turn, she makes others holy. She disseminates through her ministries the graces won by Jesus on the cross that make us holy. The Church, then, is holy in her members. |
| **9. The Church is catholic (universal).** | Church is catholic in two ways. (CCC, 830-831).

Jesus dwells in the Catholic Church. Through his Holy Spirit he energized the Church to live and act in his name. The Church is for all people, everywhere. We are called to share the Good News by what we say and how we act. The Church's missionary work continues today, as the Holy Spirit guides her to go "to the ends of the earth" (Acts 1:8) to preach, baptize, and minister in Jesus' name. |

Characteristics of Catholicism

9. The Church is catholic (universal). *continued*	Wherever we go, Catholics profess the same beliefs and celebrate the same Sacraments, under the leadership of the Pope and bishops. When at Mass, no matter where we are, we can recognize it as the same Mass as the one in our parish. Its style, language, or music may differ, but it is the same Mass, because Jesus himself again offers his eternal sacrifice to the Father, through the ministry of the priest.
	Catholicism accepts people from every place and walk of life. If we want to attend Mass every day, welcome to the Catholic Church. If we want to pray the Rosary, this is a great Catholic blessing. If we want to study the Bible, the Church encourages it on all levels. If we want to serve the poor, this is a prime commitment of the Catholic Church. The Church unites diverse spiritual traditions, interests, devotions, and practices under the essential teachings of our faith.
10. The Church is apostolic.	The Church is founded and built on Peter and the twelve Apostles. After his Ascension, Jesus led the Church through Peter and the other Apostles. When they died, his leadership continued through their successors, namely the Pope and the bishops acting in union with him. Pope Francis succeeded Pope Benedict XVI, who succeeded Pope John Paul II, who succeeded Pope John Paul I, who succeeded Pope Paul VI, who succeeded Pope John XXIII. This line of Popes can be traced historically all the way back to Saint Peter, the first Pope.
	The Catholic community is apostolic because we can trace our roots back to Peter and the Apostles and those who came after them. We are the sole Church led and united by the Pope and bishops, and ministered to by the ordained ministry of bishops, priests, and deacons. We profess in the Creed that the Church is one, holy, catholic, and apostolic.
	Consecrated brothers and sisters and the laity exercise other important kinds of leadership. Lay ministry today has a big impact on the Catholic Church in the United States. There are lay and consecrated religious diocesan chancellors, canon lawyers, pastoral administrators, pastoral team members, liturgists, musicians, catechists, servers, readers, and others.
	National Catholic organizations, social agencies, hospitals, diocesan staffs, pastoral councils, finance councils, youth organizations, and more help to bring the Jesus' message to all people. Catholicism has a clear leadership and organizational structure to which many different Church ministries contribute and share in the Church mission.
11. The Church advocates justice for all.	Many Catholic organizations serve those in need. Catholic Charities provides direct aid to people in need because of various circumstances or natural disasters. Catholic Relief Services works around the world as an advocate for change, empowering people to overcome such things as poverty and armed conflict. Bishops lead national discussions about stopping the nuclear arms race and opposing abortion and euthanasia. They speak out on matters of social justice. The Church encourages her members to perform works of mercy by reaching out to the needy in our midst. She also advocates acts of social justice that challenge unjust social structures that keep people impoverished.
	The Catholic Church emphasizes seven principles of social justice. They are: 1) the life and dignity of the human person; 2) the rights and responsibilities of humans; 3) participation in family and community; 4) preference for the poor and vulnerable; 5) the dignity of work and the rights of workers; 6) the solidarity of the human family; and 7) care for all of God's creation.
12. The Church has a positive view of creation, the world, and human nature.	The Original Sin of Adam and Eve wounded creation. We are born into a flawed and imperfect world. Catholics believe that this world is not totally corrupt. God is very much present, and we recognize his presence in creation's beauty, truth, and love. We are made in the image of God and enter life with both goodness and imperfection.
	To be saved, we need God's grace won by Jesus' death on the cross. As we reflect on our true meaning on Earth, we rely on our faith and reason to know more about God and our eternal destiny. Through faith and reason we probe more deeply into the world and human nature. In so doing, we discover how the Spirit is leading us.
	For Catholics, faith and reason are partners. Catholicism fully accepts the Bible as God's word and welcomes ongoing biblical study and discussion. Often new insights come by using our reason to probe into the mysteries revealed in Scripture.
	Catholics have always affirmed the importance of both faith and reason. Both are central to us and interconnected. Although we can come to certain knowledge of God's existence through reason alone, knowledge of the divine mysteries require both faith and reason.

CATHOLIC SOCIAL TEACHING

(From Primary Sources, page 20)

The Catholic Church's Social Teaching helps build a just society and shows how to live lives of holiness amidst the challenges of modern society. The wisdom of this tradition can be understood best through a direct reading of Church documents, but here is a synopsis of the seven key themes that are part of our Catholic social tradition.

Life and Dignity of the Human Person

"The Catholic Church proclaims that human life is sacred and that the dignity of the human person is the foundation of a moral vision for society. This belief is the foundation of all the principles of our social teaching. In our society, human life is under direct attack from abortion and euthanasia. The value of human life is being threatened by cloning, embryonic stem cell research, and the use of the death penalty. The intentional targeting of civilians in war or terrorist attacks is always wrong. Catholic teaching also calls on us to work to avoid war. Nations must protect the right to life by finding increasingly effective ways to prevent conflicts and resolve them by peaceful means. We believe that every person is precious, that people are more important than things, and that the measure of every institution is whether it threatens or enhances the life and dignity of the human person."

Call to Family, Community, and Participation

"The person is not only sacred but also social. How we organize our society—in economics and politics, in law and policy—directly affects human dignity and the capacity of individuals to grow in community. Marriage and the family are the central social institutions that must be supported and strengthened, not undermined. We believe people have a right and a duty to participate in society, seeking together the common good and well-being of all, especially the poor and vulnerable."

Rights and Responsibilities

"The Catholic tradition teaches that human dignity can be protected and a healthy community can be achieved only if human rights are protected and responsibilities are met. Therefore, every person has a fundamental right to life and a right to those things required for human decency. Corresponding to these rights are duties and responsibilities— to one another, to our families, and to the larger society."

Option for the Poor and Vulnerable

"A basic moral test is how our most vulnerable members are faring. In a society marred by deepening divisions between rich and poor, our tradition recalls the story of the Last Judgment (*Mt* 25:31-46) and instructs us to put the needs of the poor and vulnerable first."

The Dignity of Work and the Rights of Workers

"The economy must serve people, not the other way around. Work is more than a way to make a living; it is a form of continuing participation in Gods creation. If the dignity of work is to be protected, then the basic rights of workers must be respected--the right to productive work, to decent and fair wages, to the organization and joining of unions, to private property, and to economic initiative."

Solidarity

"We are one human family whatever our national, racial, ethnic, economic, and ideological differences. We are our brothers and sisters keepers, wherever they may be. Loving our neighbor has global dimensions in a shrinking world. At the core of the virtue of solidarity is the pursuit of justice and peace. Pope Paul VI taught that if you want peace, work for justice.[22] The Gospel calls us to be peacemakers. Our love for all our sisters and brothers demands that we promote peace in a world surrounded by violence and conflict."

Care for God's Creation

"We show our respect for the Creator by our stewardship of creation. Care for the earth is not just an Earth Day slogan, it is a requirement of our faith. We are called to protect people and the planet, living our faith in relationship with all of Gods creation. This environmental challenge has fundamental moral and ethical dimensions that cannot be ignored."

QUOTATION TO BE
INCLUDED IN FINAL PRINTING.

—*Catechism of the Catholic Church, 2745*

The following prayers and practices are based in Sacred Scripture and have evolved through Church Tradition. Some wording in these creeds changed when the Third Edition of the *Roman Missal* was introduced in November 2011.

Apostles' Creed

The Apostles' Creed contains a summary of the faith of the Apostles. It was developed from an early baptismal creed, and has existed since the second century. It was modified by early Church councils.

I believe in God,
　the Father almighty,
　Creator of heaven and earth,
　and in Jesus Christ, his only Son, our Lord,

*At the words that follow, up to and including
the Virgin Mary, all bow.*

　　who was conceived by the Holy Spirit,
　　born of the Virgin Mary,
　　suffered under Pontius Pilate,
　　was crucified, died and was buried;
　　he descended into hell;
　　on the third day he rose again from the dead;
　　he ascended into heaven,
　　and is seated at the right hand of God the Father almighty;
　　from there he will come to judge the living and the dead.
I believe in the Holy Spirit,
　the holy catholic Church,
　the communion of saints,
　the forgiveness of sins,
　the resurrection of the body,
　and life everlasting. Amen.

Nicene Creed

The Nicene Creed was formed as a response to the Arian heresy, which denied the divinity of Christ. It takes its name from the city of Nicea, site of the First Council of Nicea in A.D. 325. The original creed underwent modifications at ecumenical councils in Constantinople in A.D. 381 and Chalcedon in A.D. 451.

I believe in one God,
　the Father almighty,
　maker of heaven and earth,
　of all things visible and invisible.
I believe in one Lord Jesus Christ,
　the Only Begotten Son of God,
　born of the Father before all ages.
　God from God, Light from Light,
　true God from true God,
　begotten, not made, consubstantial with the Father;
　through him all things were made.
For us men and for our salvation
　he came down from heaven,

*At the words that follow up to and including
and became man, all bow.*

　　and by the Holy Spirit was incarnate of the Virgin Mary,
　　and became man.
For our sake he was crucified under Pontius Pilate,
　he suffered death and was buried,
　and rose again on the third day
　in accordance with the Scriptures.
He ascended into heaven
　and is seated at the right hand of the Father.
He will come again in glory
　to judge the living and the dead
　and his kingdom will have no end.
I believe in the Holy Spirit, the Lord, the giver of life,
　who proceeds from the Father and the Son,
　who with the Father and the Son is adored and glorified,
　who has spoken through the prophets.
I believe in one, holy, catholic and apostolic Church.
I confess one Baptism for the forgiveness of sins
　and I look forward to the resurrection of the dead
　and the life of the world to come. Amen.

The Lord's Prayer

QUOTATION TO BE
INCLUDED IN FINAL PRINTING.

(CCC, 2759).

Our Father, who art in heaven,
hallowed be thy name;
thy kingdom come,
thy will be done on earth as it is in heaven.
Give us this day our daily bread;
and forgive us our trespasses
as we forgive those who trespass against us;
and lead us not into temptation,
but deliver us from evil.
Amen.

Pater Noster

Pater noster, qui es in caelis:
sanctificetur nomen tuum;
adveniat regnum tuum;
fiat voluntas tua, sicut in caelo, et in terra.
Panem nostrum quotidianum da nobis hodie;
et dimitte nobis debita nostra,
sicut et nos dimittimus debitoribus nostris;
et ne nos inducas in tentationem;
sed libera nos a malo.
Amen.

Glory to the Father

Glory to the Father,
and to the Son,
and to the Holy Spirit,
as it was in the beginning
is now, and ever shall be
world without end.
Amen.

Gloria Patri

Glória Patri,
et Fílio
et Spíritui Sancto,
Sicut erat in princípio,
et nunc et semper
et in sáecula saeculórum.
Amen.

Prayer to the Holy Spirit

Come, Holy Spirit, fill the hearts of your faithful.
And kindle in them the fire of your love.
Send forth your Spirit and they shall be created.
And you shall renew the face of the earth.
Let us pray:
Lord, by the light of the Holy Spirit
you have taught the hearts of your faithful.
In the same Spirit, help us to choose what is right
and always rejoice in your consolation.
We ask this through Christ our Lord.
Amen.

Veni, Sancte Spiritus, reple tuorum corda fidelium,
et tui amoris in eis ignem accende.
Emitte Spiritum tuum et creabuntur;
Et renovabis faciem terrae.
Oremus:
Deus, qui corda fidelium Sancti Spiritus illustratione
docuisti.
Da nobis in eodem Spiritu recta sapere,
et de eius semper consolatione gaudere.
Per Christum Dominum nostrum.
Amen.

The Hail Mary

QUOTATION TO BE
INCLUDED IN FINAL PRINTING.

(CCC, 2675–2676).

Hail, Mary, full of grace,
The Lord is with thee.
Blessed art thou among women
and blessed is the fruit of thy womb, Jesus.
Holy Mary, Mother of God,
pray for us sinners,
now and at the hour of our death.
Amen.

Ave Maria

Ave María, grátia plena,
Dóminus tecum.
Benedícta tu in muliéribus,
et benedíctus fructus ventris tui, Jesus.
Sancta María, Mater Dei,
ora pro nobis peccatóribus,
nunc et in hora mortis nostrae.
Amen.

The Magnificat

The Magnificat (also called the Canticle of Mary) is recorded in the Gospel according to Luke (1:46-55) and is Mary's joyous prayer in response to her cousin Elizabeth's greeting (Luke 1:41-45). This prayer forms part of the Church's prayer in the Liturgy of the Hours.

My soul proclaims the greatness of the Lord,
and my spirit rejoices in God my Savior,
for he has looked with favor on his lowly servant.
From this day all generations will call me blessed:
the Almighty has done great things for me,
and holy is his Name.
He has mercy on those who fear him in every generation.
He has shown the strength of his arm;
he has scattered the proud in their conceit.
He has cast down the mighty from their thrones,
and has lifted up the lowly.
He has filled the hungry with good things,
and the rich he has sent away empty.
He has come to the help of his servant Israel
for he has remembered his promise of mercy,
the promise he made to our fathers,
to Abraham and his children forever.
Glory to the Father and to the Son
     and to the Holy Spirit,
as it was in the beginning, is now,
     and will be forever.
Amen.

Magníficat ánima mea Dóminum,
et exsultávit spíritus meus in Deo
     salvatóre meo,
quia respéxit humilitátem
     ancíllæ suæ.
Ecce enim ex hoc beátam me dicent
     omnes generatiónes,
quia fecit mihi magna, qui potens est,
et sanctum nomen eius,
et misericórdia eius in progénies et
     progénies timéntibus eum.

Fecit poténtiam in bráchio suo,
dispérsit supérbos mente cordis sui;
depósuit poténtes de sede
et exaltávit húmiles.
Esuriéntes implévit bonis
et dívites dimísit inánes.
Suscépit Ísrael púerum suum,
recordátus misericórdiæ,
sicut locútus est ad patres nostros,
Ábraham et sémini eius in sæcula.
Glória Patri et Fílio
et Spirítui Sancto.
Sicut erat in princípio, et nunc
et semper,
et in sæcula sæculórum.
Amen.

Act of Contrition (traditional)

O my God, I am heartily sorry for having offended you, and I detest all my sins, because of your just punishments, but most of all because they offend you, my God, who are all good and deserving of all my love. I firmly resolve, with the help of your grace, to sin no more and to avoid the near occasion of sin.

Act of Contrition (contemporary)

My God, I am sorry for my sins with all my heart. In choosing to do wrong and failing to do good, I have sinned against you whom I should love above all things. I firmly intend, with your help, to do penance, to sin no more, and to avoid whatever leads me to sin. Our Savior Jesus Christ suffered and died for us. In his name, my God, have mercy.

Prayer for Justice

Father, you have given all peoples one common origin.
It is your will that they be gathered together
as one family in yourself.
Fill the hearts of mankind with the fire of your love
and with the desire to ensure justice for all.
By sharing the good things you give us,
may we secure an equality for all
our brothers and sisters throughout the world.
May there be an end to division, strife, and war.
May there be a dawning of a truly human society
built on love and peace.
We ask this in the name of Jesus, our Lord.
Amen.

The Rosary

The Rosary is called the Psalter of Mary because all fifteen of its mysteries, with their 150 Aves, correspond to the number of Psalms. Saint Dominic popularized the fifteen-decade Rosary. He is so connected with this form of the Rosary that often it is referred to as the Dominican Rosary. Blessed Pope John Paul II added five luminous mysteries to the previous fifteen glorious, joyful, and sorrowful mysteries.

The Rosary is the most well-known and used form of chaplet (a devotion using beads; from a French word meaning "crown" or "wreath"). There are other chaplets, including Saint Bridget's Chaplet and the Chaplet of the Immaculate Conception.

1. Sign of the Cross and Apostles' Creed
2. Lord's Prayer
3. Three Hail Marys
4. Glory to the Father
5. Announce mystery
6. Lord's Prayer
7. Ten Hail Marys
8. Glory to the Father

Repeat last four steps, meditating on the other mysteries of the Rosary.

The Mysteries of the Rosary and Recommended Scriptural Meditations

Joyful Mysteries
(Mondays and Saturdays)

1. The Annunciation (humility)
   Isaiah 7:10-14; Luke 1:26-38
2. Visitation (charity)
   Isaiah 40:1-11; Luke 1:39-45; John 1:19-23
3. The Nativity (poverty)
   Micah 5:1-4; Matthew 2:1-12; Luke 2:1-20; Galatians 4:4
4. The Presentation (obedience)
   Luke 2:22-35; Hebrews 9:6-14
5. The Finding of Jesus in the Temple (piety)
   Luke 2:41-52; John 12:44-50; 1 Corinthians 2:6-16

Sorrowful Mysteries
(Tuesdays and Fridays)

1. The Agony in the Garden (repentance)
   Matthew 26:36-46; Mark 14:26-42; Luke 22:39-53; John 18:1-12
2. The Scourging at the Pillar (purity)
   Isaiah 50:5-9; Matthew 27:15-26; Mark 15:1-15
3. The Crowning with Thorns (courage)
   Isaiah 52:13–53:10; Matthew 16:24-28, 27:27-31; Mark 15:16-19; Luke 23:6-11; John 19:1-7
4. The Carrying of the Cross (patience)
   Mark 8:31-38; Matthew 16:20-25; Luke 23:26-32; John 19:17-22; Philippians 2:6-11
5. The Crucifixion (self-renunciation)
   Mark 15:33-39; Luke 23:33-46; John 19:23-37; Acts 22:22-24; Hebrews 9:11-14

Glorious Mysteries
(Sundays and Wednesdays)

1. The Resurrection (faith)
   Matthew 28:1-10; Mark 16:1-18; Luke 24:1-12; John 20:1-10; Romans 6:1-14; 1 Corinthians 15:1-11
2. The Ascension (hope)
   Matthew 28:16-20; Luke 24:44-53; Acts 1:1-11; Ephesians 2:4-7
3. The Descent of the Holy Spirit Upon the Apostles (love)
   John 14:15-21; Acts 2:1-11; 4:23-31; 11:15-18
4. The Assumption (eternal happiness)
   John 11:17-27; 1 Corinthians 15:20-28, 42-57; Revelation 21:1-6
5. The Coronation of Mary (Marian devotion)
   Matthew 5:1-12; 2 Peter 3:10; Revelation 7:1-4, 9-12; 21:1-6

Luminous Mysteries

(Thursdays)

1. Baptism in the Jordan (commitment)
   Matthew 3:13-17; Mark 1:9-11; Luke 3:21-22;
   John 1:29-34
2. The Wedding at Cana (fidelity)
   John 2:3-5, 7-10; John 13:14-15; Luke 6:27-28, 37;
   Luke 9:23; John 15:12
3. Proclamation of the Kingdom of God (conversion)
   Mark 1:14-15; Luke 4:18-19, 21; Matthew 5:38-39, 43-
   44; Matthew 6:19-21; Matthew 7:12; Matthew 10:8
4. The Transfiguration (promise)
   Matthew 5:14, 16; Matthew 17:1-2, 5, 7-8; Luke 9:30-
   33; John 1:4-5, 18; 2 Corinthians 3:18
5. Institution of the Eucharist (grace)
   John 13:1; Matthew 26:18; Luke 22:15-16, 19-20;
   Matthew 5:14, 19-20; 1 Corinthians 11:26; John 17:20-
   21; 1 Corinthians 12:13, 26-27

The Ten Commandments

The Catechism of the Catholic Church *follows the order
established by Saint Augustine which has become the Catholic
(and Lutheran) tradition. The first three Commandments concern
love of God and the other seven command concern for love of
neighbor (see Exodus 20:1-17, Deuteronomy 5:1-21).*

1. I am the Lord your God: you shall
   not have strange gods before me.
2. You shall not take the name of the
   Lord your God in vain.
3. Remember to keep holy the Lord's day.
4. Honor your father and your mother.
5. You shall not kill.
6. You shall not commit adultery.
7. You shall not steal.
8. You shall not bear false witness against your neighbor.
9. You shall not covet your neighbor's wife.
10. You shall not covet your neighbor's goods.

The Eight Beatitudes

*The Gospels according to Luke and Matthew contain the
Beatitudes. They are statements of praise, stressing the joy of
those who participate in the Kingdom of God. The Beatitudes
also tell us about what it means to be a member of the Church.
(see Matthew 5:3-11; Luke 6:20-26).*

1. Blessed are the poor in spirit, for theirs is the kingdom of
   heaven.
2. Blessed are those who mourn, for they will be comforted.
3. Blessed are the meek, for they will inherit the earth.
4. Blessed are those who hunger and thirst for righteousness,
   for they will be filled.
5. Blessed are the merciful, for they will receive mercy.
6. Blessed are the pure in heart, for they will see God.
7. Blessed are the peacemakers, for they will be called
   children of God.
8. Blessed are those who are persecuted for righteousness'
   sake, for theirs is the kingdom of heaven.

The Seven Corporal Works of Mercy

*"Just as you did it to one of the least of these who are members
of my family, you did it to me"
(Matthew 25:40).*

1. Feed the hungry.
2. Give drink to the thirsty.
3. Clothe the naked.
4. Shelter the homeless.
5. Visit the sick.
6. Visit the imprisoned.
7. Bury the dead.

The Seven Spiritual Works of Mercy

*Based on Christ's teachings and Christian practice since the
Apostles.*

1. Counsel the doubtful.
2. Instruct the ignorant.
3. Admonish sinners.
4. Comfort the afflicted.
5. Forgive offenses.
6. Bear wrongs patiently.
7. Pray for the living and the dead.

Saint Thomas Aquinas (1126–1274)

Saint Thomas Aquinas was born to a noble Italian family and was sent to Benedictines of Monte Casino at the age 5 to begin his studies. He joined the Dominicans of Naples at the age 17, despite his family's objections. He became a priest and in 1261, and was called to Rome by Pope Urban IV to teach. He refused any promotions within the Church and focused on his theological writings, including *Summa Theologiae*. He is a Doctor of the Church and is the Patron Saint of schools and students. His feast day is January 28.

Saint Leo the Great (unknown–461)

Saint Leo the Great was born in Italy and served the Church as Pope from 440 until his death in 461. He was known for his great eloquence and persuasive abilities, even using those skills to stop Attila the Hun at the gates of Rome. His letter to the Patriarch of Constantinople on the Doctrine of the Incarnation serves as an accurate expression of our faith concerning the Person of Christ. During his lifetime, Saint Leo the Great wrote many significant letters and documents on our faith and Church history. His feast day is November 10.

Saint Damien of Molokai (1840–1889)

Saint Damien of Molokai is known as the leper priest and the hero of Molokai. He was born in Belgium and joined the Sacred Hearts Fathers at the age 20. He was sent to Honolulu, Hawaii, four years later and was ordained there. After spending nine years working in missions on the big island of Hawaii, he volunteered to work at the colony of people sticken with Hansen's disease (leprosy) on the island of Molokai. Saint Damien contracted the disease himself, but continued to work tirelessly, constructing hospitals, clinics, and churches. He also made more than 600 coffins before succumbing to his illness in 1889. He became a Saint in 2009. His feast day is October 11.

Saint Basil the Great (330–379)

Saint Basil the Great was the son of two Saints, Saint Basil the Elder and Saint Emmelia, and several of his ten siblings are also Saints. After opening a school of oratory and practicing law, he decided to become a monk and founded several monasteries. He was made Bishop of Caesaria in 370. Saint Basil was known for his intelligence, knowledge, personal holiness, and charity, and played a key role in the victory of the Nicene orthodoxy over Arianism. He is the Patron Saint of hospital administrators, and his feast day is January 2.

Saint Augustine (354–430)

Saint Augustine of Hippo, the son of Saint Monica, led a wild life as a young man. Thanks to the prayers of his mother and the advice of Saint Ambrose, Saint Augustine eventually gave up his sinful ways and was baptized. He became a priest, and later a bishop, and one of the Church's most important leaders. After his conversion, Saint Augustine spent his years living in poverty, supporting the poor, and writing about the faith. He was known for his inspiring preaching and fervent prayers. He regretted his wasted youth, once crying out to God, "Too late have I loved you!" He is the Patron Saint of theologians and printers, and his feast day is August 28.

Saint Francis of Assisi (1181–1226)

Saint Francis was born in Assisi, Italy, to a wealthy family. He enjoyed a privileged, spoiled life, and dreamed of becoming a knight. But on his way to fulfill that dream he had another, a dream in which God told him go home. Saint Francis obeyed, and began his journey towards holiness. He founded the Franciscan Order, giving up all of his possessions and preaching in pairs with his companions. Saint Francis eventually became blind, which was when he wrote the *Canticle of the Sun*, beautifully expressing his brotherhood with Creation and praise of God. He is the Patron Saint of animals, ecology, and merchants, and his feast day is October 4.

Saint John Chrysostom (344–407)

Because of his eloquence, Saint John was called Chrysostom, which means "golden-mouthed." Starting at age 30, he lived as religious hermit for more than a decade, but declining health compelled him to return to civilization, where he became a priest. In 398, he was promoted to the See of Constantinople, but enemies conspired to have him exiled. Although he suffered, Saint John found peace and happiness knowing that he had the support of the Pope. But that friendship wasn't enough to save him from his banishment, and he died when he was further banished to the farthest reaches of the empire. He is the Patron Saint of speakers and preachers and his feast day is September 13.

Saint Gregory of Nyssa (335–394)

Saint Gregory of Nyssa was the son of Saints and the brother of several Saints, including Saint Basil the Great. After working as a rhetorician for a time, he entered his brother's monastery and became the Bishop of Nyssa sometime around 371. He was deposed by the Arians in 376, but was restored to the position when the Arian Valens died two years later. Saint Gregory was a true defender of the faith, and remains revered for works, including ones on Trinitarian theology. His best-known works are the *Catechetical Oration, The Life of Moses,* and a biography on his sister, *The Life of Saint Macrina*. Also known as Saint Gregory the Great, he is the Patron Saint of teachers, students, and musicians, and his feast day is March 9.

Blessed Mother Teresa (1910–1997)

Blessed Mother Teresa was born in Albania and left home at 18 to join the Institute of the Blessed Virgin Mary, also known as the Sisters of Loreto, in Ireland. After making her First Profession of Vows, Sister Teresa was assigned to serve in Calcutta. In 1937, she made her Final Profession of Vows, and was then called Mother Teresa. Then 1946, Mother Teresa was called by Jesus to found a religious community to serve the poor. In 1950, the new congregation of the Missionaries of Charity was officially established in the Archdiocese of Calcutta, and her ministry expanded dramatically over the years. Six years after her death, she was beatified by Blessed Pope John Paul II. She is the Patron of World Youth Day and her feast day is September 5.

Saint Thérèse of Lisieux (1873–1897)

Known as the "Little Flower," Saint Thérèse of Lisieux was just 24 when she died. She had spent a pampered childhood until she followed her sisters into the Carmelite Order at the age of 15. Although she had been a spoiled and emotional child, Saint Thérèse always had a strong prayer life, and even witnessed a Marian apparition and miraculous cure when she was eleven years old. In the convent, she sought holiness in small sacrifices she called "little flowers." When she died, her journal was published as the "Story of a Soul." Demand for her canonization was so great after her death that she was made a saint twenty-eight years later. She is the Patron Saint of florists, missionaries, and pilots, and her feast day is October 1.

Saint Josephine Bakhita (1869–1947)

Born in Sudan and kidnapped into slavery, Saint Josephine Bakhita eventually settled in Italy, where she is still known as "Mother Moretta," or "Our Black Mother." She learned about God and the Catholic faith from the Canossian Sisters of the Institute of Catechumens in Venice and received the Sacraments of Christian Initiation in 1890. She decided to stay with the Sisters and was consecrated as a religious six years later. Saint Josephine was known for her kindness and constant smile, and she lived the rest of her life as a devoted witness to the faith. She is the Patron Saint of Sudan, and her feast day is February 8.

Saint Maximilian Kolbe (1894–1941)

Saint Maximilian was devoted to the Blessed Mother his entire life and founded Immaculata Movement dedicated to her before he was ordained as a priest. He earned a doctorate in theology and published a magazine in order to promote the Immaculata Movement, eventually forming a community of eight hundred men and expanding the movement to Japan and India. His health declining, Saint Maximilian returned to his Polish homeland in 1936. After the Nazi invasion, he was imprisoned by the Nazis and sent to Auschwitz. When ten men were sentenced to death for the escape of one prisoner, Saint Maximilian offered to take the place of a young father. He is the Patron Saint of addicts, and his feast day is August 14.

Saint Teresa of Avila (1515–1582)

Saint Teresa of Avila was a typical child and an even more typical teenager, more interested in clothes and boys than a life of faith. When she was 16, her rebelliousness led her father to send her to a Carmelite convent. Miserable at first, Teresa began to embrace the religious life, but struggled with prayer for many years. After surviving malaria, she gave up prayer completely, using a variety of excuses. Finally, at age 41, she returned to prayer and decided to found a new convent devoted to prayer two years later. She was denounced for her efforts but was undeterred, eventually establishing a number of convents for her order, the Discalced Carmelites. She wrote extensively about prayer, and was named a Doctor of the Church in 1970 for her writings and teachings. She is the Patron Saint of headache sufferers, and her feast day is October 15.

Saint John Damascene (645–749)

Saint John Damascene was a great poet and one of the fathers of the Eastern Church. He wrote three important treatises on the veneration of icons, during a critical time when such veneration was controversial. His efforts earned him the title "The Doctor of Christian Art." He lived during a time of much persecution against Christians, and was even treated poorly by his own abbot until the abbot had a vision instructing him to stop. Saint John Damascene helped to establish the Eastern Church's heritage of religious poetry, and wrote many great hymns that are still sung today. He is the Patron Saint of computers, and his feast day is December 4.

Saint Stephen (first century)

Saint Stephen was one of the Church's first deacons and the first Christian martyr. He is first one mentioned of the seven deacons appointed to help poor members of the Church in Acts 6:5. Not much is known of Saint Stephen's life prior to the mention in Acts. From Acts, we know that he was a man "full of grace and power, [who] did great wonders and signs among the people" (Acts 6:8). Unjustly accused of blasphemy, he was arrested and brought before the Sanhedrin. As he was being stoned to death, he asked Jesus to receive his spirit. He is the Patron Saint of deacons, bricklayers, and stonemasons, and his feast day is December 26.

GLOSSARY

A

abortion the
(CCC, Glossary, p. 864) (p. 96)

acedia spiritual laziness, an uncaring attitude, apathy, boredom, and the absence of joy (p. 73)

actual grace the help God gives us for a particular need to help us conform our lives to his will (p. 206)

alienation an experience of isolation and separateness from God and others (p. 240)

apathy an attitude of not getting involved, not caring, not acting when action is called for (p. 50)

atheism the denial that God exists in theory or practice (p. 74)

autonomy of conscience a person relies on one's own self-judgment rather than God's inner voice in our hearts (p. 233)

avarice (CCC, 2552) (p. 122)

B

Beatitudes eight teachings from Jesus that guide our moral attitudes and actions, and which lead to

(CCC, Glossary, p. 868) (p. 18)

blasphemy speech or action that shows disrespect or contempt for God or persons or things dedicated to God (p. 76)

C

calumny telling lies that injure someone's character (p. 132)

Canon Law
QUOTATION TO BE
INCLUDED IN FINAL PRINTING.

(CCC, Glossary, p. 869) (p. 171)

capital punishment the death penalty; state-sanctioned execution of people convicted of murder or other serious crime (p. 102)

cardinal virtues prudence, justice, fortitude, and temperance; they are stable dispositions of the intellect and will that govern our moral activities; they direct us toward Christ-like behavior and discipline our passions and emotions. (p. 212)

charity (also called love) the theological virtue representing the core of the Christian life

(CCC, 1822) (p. 71)

chastity
QUOTATION TO BE
INCLUDED IN FINAL PRINTING.

one of the Fruits of the Holy Spirit (CCC, Glossary, p. 870) (p. 109)

commutative justice an exchange between persons and institutions in accordance with a strict respect for their rights (p. 119)

conscience
QUOTATION TO BE
INCLUDED IN FINAL PRINTING.

p. 872) (p. 5)

consecrated life refers to
(CCC, Glossary, p. 872) in which a person is set aside and totally devoted to God's work and the pursuit of Christian perfection. For example, religious order brothers and sisters, consecrated virgins, and hermits (p. 197)

covenant
QUOTATION TO BE
INCLUDED IN FINAL PRINTING.

(CCC, Glossary, p. 873) (p. 11)

D

Decalogue name for the "ten words," or the Ten Commandments, that God gave to Moses and the Israelites (p. 62)

detraction revealing derogatory information about a person's faults or weaknesses without just cause (p. 132)

dignity worthy of honor or respect; our dignity is based on being created in the image and likeness of God (p. 6)

discrimination a situation in which people suffer disadvantages simply because they are members of a particular group (p. 138)

disordered affections the emotions and passions of the heart which are not directed toward their proper objects (p. 233)

distributive justice
QUOTATION TO BE
INCLUDED IN FINAL PRINTING.

(CCC, 2411) (p. 119)

divine filiation through our union with Christ, we become the adopted children of God the Father (p. 13)

docile as it pertains to the Gifts of the Holy Spirit, it means being compliant and following the promptings of the Holy Spirit (p. 226)

E

envy (CCC, 2553)
(p. 122)

erroneous judgment of conscience when a person follows a process of conscientious decision making but unwittingly makes a wrong decision (p. 233)

eternal punishment the consequences of unforgiven grave or mortal sin that cuts communication with God making us incapable of eternal life (p. 240)

euthanasia
QUOTATION TO BE
INCLUDED IN FINAL PRINTING.

(CCC, Glossary, p. 877) (p. 96)

evangelical counsels teachings of the New Law that have as their aim QUOTATION TO BE INCLUDED IN FINAL PRINTING.
(CCC, 1973). These are embodied especially in the vows of poverty, chastity, and obedience. They lead to the perfection of Christian life (p. 197)

F

faith a gift from God and a human act by which we believe in him and all that he has revealed; the theological virtue of seeking to know and to do God's will (p. 21)

fecundity fruitfulness and the ability to bear children that is a gift of the Sacrament of Marriage; (CCC, 2366). (p. 111)

fortitude courage; strength when confronted with difficulties and perseverance in pursuing that which is good (p. 213)

free will the power or ability to act on our own discretion and thereby shape our own life (see CCC, 1731) (p. 7)

freedom QUOTATION TO BE INCLUDED IN FINAL PRINTING. (CCC, 1731) (p. 14)

Fruits of the Holy Spirit twelve "perfections" that the Holy Spirit forms in us all as a glimpse of possible eternal glory (p. 226)

G

Gifts of the Holy Spirit (CCC, Glossary, p. 880). These spiritual gifts given by the Holy Spirit help us follow his guidance and live the Christian life: wisdom, understanding, counsel (right judgment), fortitude (courage), knowledge, piety (reverence), and fear of the Lord (awe and wonder) (p. 226)

grace the gift of the Holy Spirit; it is (CCC, Glossary, p. 881) (p. 188)

greed the desire to amass limitless earthly goods (p. 122)

H

Hell QUOTATION TO BE INCLUDED IN FINAL PRINTING. (CCC, Glossary, p. 881) (p. 38)

hope QUOTATION TO BE INCLUDED IN FINAL PRINTING. (CCC, Glossary, p. 882) (p. 69)

I

Incarnation QUOTATION TO BE INCLUDED IN FINAL PRINTING. (CCC, Glossary, p. 883) (p. 7)

informed conscience a conscience that is educated and developed through constant use and examination and learning about the teachings of the Church; (CCC, 1788) (p. 232)

J

justice the virtue stating that we are to give God his due and that all people have rights and should have their basic needs met; (CCC, 1836) (p. 189)

justification QUOTATION TO BE INCLUDED IN FINAL PRINTING. (CCC, Glossary, p. 885) (p. 238)

L

laity all the faithful who are members of the Catholic Church through Baptism except ordained men and those in consecrated life. The laity share in the priestly, prophetic, and kingly office of Christ and have their own role in the mission of the whole Christian people in the Church and in the world (see CCC, 897) (p. 191)

lying (CCC, 2508) (p. 132)

M

Magisterium the living, official teaching office of the Church, consisting of the Pope and the bishops acting in union with him. The office interprets Scripture and Tradition and ensures faithfulness to the teachings of the Apostles. (p. 164)

morality QUOTATION TO BE INCLUDED IN FINAL PRINTING. (CCC, Glossary, p. 888) (p. 4)

mortal sin an action so destructive that it mortally wounds our relationship with God; complete rejection of God; (CCC, 1855) It turns us away from God by preferring an inferior good to God (p. 38)

N

natural law the law inscribed in our hearts by God as a moral sense that allows us to discern by reason what is good and what is evil (p. 5)

New Law the Law of the Gospels or the New Testament presented by Jesus (p. 167)

nonviolence conflict-resolving techniques that do not rely on physical or psychological injury of an opponent (p. 151)

O

Old Law the Law of Moses and the Ten Commandments; the law of the Old Testament (p. 167)

Original Holiness the initial state of our first parents in which they had a share in the divine life (p. 32)

original innocence the state after creation but before the Fall when mankind lived in harmony with God and participated in his interior life (p. 32)

Original Justice the harmony between God, our first parents, and all creation (p. 32)

Original Sin disobedience against God by our first parents, Adam and Eve. This sin marks all human beings as needing the salvation brought about through Christ. (p. 16)

P

perjury making a promise under oath with no intention of keeping the promise; lying under oath (p. 77)

precepts general rules, directions, or commandments intended to regulate behavior or thought (p. 173)

prudence the virtue that helps us make a correct judgment about what to do and to choose the right way to do it (p. 213)

R

rash judgment presuming as true the worst about a person without sufficient information (p. 132)

reconciliation mercy and forgiveness as one is reconciled with the other. In the Sacrament of Reconciliation,

(CCC, Glossary, p. 896). (p. 240)

reparation making amends for harming another; returning stolen property (p. 119)

S

sacrilege the act of profaning or disrespecting the Sacraments, the liturgy, or persons, things, or places consecrated to God (p. 73)

sanctifying grace a share in God's life; a gift from God that enables the soul to live with him and respond to his friendship. It is a habitual, stable, and supernatural disposition (p. 206)

scandal wrongdoing that serves to disillusion or harm more vulnerable people; QUOTATION TO BE INCLUDED IN FINAL PRINTING. (CCC, 2284) (p. 104)

self-assertion the promotion of ourselves, our views, and our ideas contrary to the dictates of reason (p. 33)

Sermon on the Mount a part of the Gospel according to Matthew in which Jesus preaches important moral teachings, including the Beatitudes (p. 18)

simony the buying and selling of spiritual things, such as demanding payment to receive God's forgiveness in the Sacrament of Reconciliation. This is prohibited by the Catholic Church. (p. 73)

sin an offense against God and an action contrary to his eternal law; purposely doing wrong (p. 4)

sin of commission purposely doing an action that is harmful to oneself or another thereby violating charity and offending God (p. 38)

sin of omission not doing an action that is called for. This violates charity and offends God and neighbor (p. 38)

superstition attributing magical power to certain practices (i.e., rubbing a rabbit's foot, carrying a lucky coin) or things (i.e., crystals, tarot cards, statues).

(CCC, Glossary, p. 900) (p. 74)

T

temperance "the moral virtue that moderates the attraction of pleasures of the senses and provides balance in the use of created goods" (CCC, 1809) (p. 215)

temperoral punishment the consequences of of venial sin and forgiven mortal sins that have not been atoned for on Earth (p. 240)

theological virtues faith, hope, and charity; they are supernatural gifts infused by God into the soul of faithful people that enable them to live and act as God's sons and daughters to merit eternal life (p. 210)

V

venial sin an action that weakens our relationship with God;

(CCC, 1855) (p. 38)

virtues habitual and firm dispositions to do what is good and right. Through repeated practice, they make it easier to practice the good (p. 19)

vocation calling or destiny to love and serve God and our neighbor in this life which prepares us for eternal happiness in Heaven (p. 190)

vices bad qualities, habits, or patterns of behavior that incline us to actions that are sinful and harmful to ourselves and others (p. 209)

Chapter 1

1. Leo XIII, *Libertas præstantissimum*, 597.

2. Vatican Council I, *Dei Filius 1*: DS 3003; cf. *Wis* 8:1; *Heb* 4:13.

3. Cf. 1 *Jn* 4:19.

4. *1 Cor* 3:9; *1 Thess* 3:2; *Col* 4:11.

5. *Mt* 6:6.

6. *Phil* 1:27.

7. St. Irenaeus, *Adv. haeres.* 3, 19, 1: PG 7/1, 939.

8. St. Thomas Aquinas, *Opusc.* 57: 1–4.

9. St. Gregory of Nyssa, *Orat. catech.* 15: PG 45, 48B.

10. *GS* 17.

11. St. Basil, *Reg. fus. tract., prol.* 3: PG 31, 896 B.

12. St. Irenaeus, *Adv. haeres.* 4, 20, 5: PG 7/1, 1034-1035.

13. John Henry Cardinal Newman, "Saintliness the Standard of Christian Principle," in Discourses to Mixed Congregations (London: Longmans, Green and Co., 1906) V, 89-90.

14. Cf. the parable of the sower: *Mt* 13:3-23.

15. St. John Eudes, Tract. *de admirabili corde Jesu*, 1, 5.

16. *Phil* 1:21.

17. St. Athanasius, *Ep. Serap.* 1, 24: PG 26, 585 and 588.

Chapter 6

18. Psalm 110:4.

19. Luke 22:19; I Corinthians 11:24-26.

20. Matthew 26:26 f.

21. John 6: 58

Catholic Social Teaching

22. Day of Peace, 1 January 1972.

PHOTO CREDITS

Cover Image Copyright ollyy, 2012 Used under license from Shutterstock.com; **i** Image Copyright ollyy, 2012 Used under license from Shutterstock.com; **iv** dieKleinert/SuperStock; **v** Photo by Jeff J Mitchell/Getty Images; **viii** Ocean/Corbis; **x** Jim West/age fotostock; **xi** Mr. Richard Clark; **xii** iStockphoto.com/fotoVoyager; **2-3** Vstock LLC/Tetra Images/Corbis; **5** Steve Raymer/Corbis; **6** Even in the darkness of out sufferings Jesus is close to us, **1994** (oil on panel), Wang, Elizabeth (Contemporary Artist)/Private Collection/© Radiant Light/The Bridgeman Art Library; **8-9** (bg) Courtesy: Everett Col/age fotostock; **8** (inset) John Elk III/Alamy; **11** Fred de Noyelle/Godong/Corbis; **12** Blend Images/SuperStock; **14** Melanie Stetson Freeman/The Christian Science Monitor via Getty Images; **15** iStockphoto.com/fotoVoyager; **18** Juanmonino/E+/Getty Images; **19** Nathan Benn/Alamy; **20** Photo by Spencer Platt/Getty Images; **23** Fotosearch Illustration/Corbis; **24** Richard T. Nowitz/CORBIS; **25** Mike Skirvin/Demotix/Corbis; **27** iStockphoto.com/jcarillet; **29** Bill & Peggy Wittman; **30-31** Paul Souders/Corbis; **33** dieKleinert/SuperStock; **34** imagebroker.net/SuperStock; **36** Richard Levine/age fotostock/SuperStock; **37** AP Photo/Osservatore Romano, pool; **40** AP Photo/Rogelio V. Solis; **42** Mitchell Funk/Photographer's Choice/Getty Images; **48** Photo by Joe Raedle/Getty Images; **48** Our Sunday Visitor; **52** Christ of St. John of the Cross, 1951 (oil on canvas), Dali, Salvador (1904-89)/Art Gallery and Museum, Kelvingrove, Glasgow, Scotland/© Culture and Sport Glasgow (Museums)/The Bridgeman Art Library; **53** Jim Stipe/CRS; **54** iStockphoto.com/fotoVoyager; **57** iStockphoto.com/jcarillet; **59** SuperStock/SuperStock; **60-61** Radius Images/Corbis; **62** God gives the Ten Commandments to Moses on Mount Sinai, 2004 (w/c on paper), Wang, Elizabeth (Contemporary Artist)/Private Collection/© Radiant Light/The Bridgeman Art Library; **64-65** Stockbroker/SuperStock; **68** Tony Savino/Corbis; **71** Photononstop/SuperStock; **72** iStockphoto.com/fotoVoyager; **75** DINODIA/age fotostock; **76** Ocean/Corbis; **78** Bjarki Reyr/age fotostock; **79** Jeff Schmaltz/Kinetikon Pictures/Corbis; **80-81** (bg) Tips Images/SuperStock; **80** (inset) Head of the Madonna (oil on canvas), Sassoferrato, Il (Giovanni Battista Salvi) (1609-85)/His Grace The Duke of Norfolk, Arundel Castle/The Bridgeman Art Library; **83** Matt Bird/Corbis; **84** Kablonk/SuperStock; **87** Hill Street Studios/Blend Images/Corbis; **89** iStockphoto.com/jcarillet; **91** FRANCISCO LEONG/AFP/Getty Images; **92-93** Steve Sucsy/E+/Getty Images; **94** Photo by Alex Wong/Getty Images; **98-99** culliganphoto/Alamy; **100** JGI/Tom Grill/age fotostock; **102** Courtesy of Benedictine Sisters of Perpetual Adoration; **105** Kumar Sriskandan/Alamy; **107** Jim Craigmyle/Corbis; **109** Odilon Dimier/PhotoAlto/Corbis; **110** iStockphoto.com/fotoVoyager; **112** ZUMA Press, Inc./Alamy; **115** Our Sunday Visitor; **118** Steven Puetzer/Photographer's Choice/Getty Images; **120** Richard Levine/age fotostock; **123** Design Pics/SuperStock; **125** iStockphoto.com/jcarillet; **127** Bill & Peggy Wittman; **128-129** Don Bayley/E+/Getty images; **130** Radius Images/Corbis; **132** CARE International/Handout/Reuters/Corbis; **133** Yellow Dog Productions/The Image Bank/Getty Images; **136** Spencer Grant/PhotoEdit; **138** John Springer Collection/CORBIS; **140** Christ Teaching, English School, (20th century)/Private Collection/© Look and Learn/The Bridgeman Art Library; **144** Heiner Heine/age fotostock; **146** Walter Bibikow/age fotostock/SuperStock; **148** Enigma/Alamy; **149** Humberto Olarte Cupas/Alamy; **152-153** (bg) Atlantide Phototravel/Corbis; **152** (inset) Courtesy of Pittsburgh History & Landmarks Foundation; **155** iStockphoto.com/fotoVoyager; **157** iStockphoto.com/jcarillet; **159** RAVEENDRAN/AFP/Getty Images; **160-161** Photo by Jeff J Mitchell/Getty Images; **162** ALBERTO PIZZOLI/AFP/Getty Images; **165** André Gonçalves/age fotostock; **167** Philippe Caron/Corbis; **169** Pentecost (w/c on paper), Canziani, Estella (1887-1964)/Private Collection/Photo © Peter Nahum at The Leicester Galleries, London/The Bridgeman Art Library; **171** Neil McAllister/Alamy; **172** Kevin Gunn; **173** Our Sunday Visitor; **174-175** (bg) Franz-Marc Frei/Corbis; **174** (inset) Bettmann/CORBIS; **176** (b) DEA PICTURE LIBRARY/age fotostock; **178** Our Sunday Visitor; **179** AP Photo/Alessandra Tarantino; **181** iStockphoto.com/fotoVoyager; **183** iStockphoto.com/jcarillet; **185** Images.com/Corbis; **186-187** Our Sunday Visitor; **188** AP Photo/Tony Dejak; **192** Our Sunday Visitor; **193** Hoberman Collection/SuperStock; **197** Jesus Washing the Disciples' Feet, 2000 (acrylic on canvas), James, Laura (Contemporary Artist)/Private Collection/The Bridgeman Art Library; **198** iStockphoto.com; **201** Ed Kashi/Corbis; **203** Our Sunday Visitor; **204-205** (bg) Evgeny Shmulev/Alamy; **204** (inset) Photo by DeAgostini/Getty Images; **206** Jim West/age fotostock; **209** Bob Daemmrich/Alamy; **211** iStockphoto.com/fotoVoyager; **212** Design Pics/SuperStock; **214** Rick Friedman/Corbis; **217** iStockphoto.com/jcarillet; **219** SuperStock/SuperStock; **220-221** Harald von Radebrecht/imagebroker.net/SuperStock; **222** Mr. Richard Clark; **224-225** (bg) Pegaz/Alamy; **224** (inset) INTERFOTO/Alamy; **229** iStockphoto.com/fotoVoyager; **231** Bharati Chaudhuri/SuperStock; **235** MEYER LIEBOWITZ/The New York Times; **237** Mr. Richard Clark; **240** Dante, illustration to Canto XXVIII of 'Purgatory', Mathilda makes the poet drink from the river Lethe to purge himself of past sins and prepare for passage to Paradise, 1919 (oil on canvas), Delville, Jean (1867-1953)/Private Collection/Photo © Christie's Images/The Bridgeman Art Library; **242** SuperStock/SuperStock; **243** ISSOUF SANOGO/AFP/Getty Images; **245** Flirt/SuperStock; **246** CNS/Reuters; **249** iStockphoto.com/jcarillet; **251** Bettmann/CORBIS